THE SURVIVAL OF THE SMALL FI

The Economics of Survival and Entrepreneurship

Lincolnshire College of Agriculture
and Horticulture

Riseholme

THE SURVIVAL OF THE SMALL FIRM 1

The Economics of Survival and Entrepreneurship

**Edited by
JAMES CURRAN
JOHN STANWORTH
DAVID WATKINS**

Gower

Published by
Gower Publishing Company Limited,
Gower House,
Croft Road,
Aldershot,
Hants GU11 3HR
England

Gower Publishing Company,
Old Post Road
Brookfield
Vermont 05036
U.S.A.

British Library Cataloguing in Publication Data

The survival of the small firm.
  1. Small business
  I. Curran, J.   II. Stanworth, John
  III. Watkins, D.S.
  338.6'42   HD2341

Library of Congress Cataloging in Publication Data

The survival of the small firm.
  Contents: V. 1. The economics of survival and entrepreneurship –
  V. 2. Employment, growth, technology, and politics.
  1. Small business – addresses, essays, lectures.
  1. Self-employed – addresses, essays, lectures.
  3. Small business – employees – addresses, essays, lectures.
  I. Curran, James. II. Stanworth, John. III. Watkins, David, 1947-.
  HD2341.S87   1986   338.6'42   85-27035

ISBN 0-566-00725-8 (Hbk)   0-566-05222-9 (Pbk) (V. 1)

Typeset in Great Britain by Graphic Studios (Southern) Ltd, Godalming, Surrey.
Printed in Great Britain at the University Press, Cambridge

Contents

Part II THE SURVIVAL OF ENTREPRENEURSHIP

Part III CONTEMPORARY VARIETIES OF SMALL ENTERPRISE

List of Figures

List of Tables

Notes on Contributors

Graham Bannock was Director of Research for the UK Committee of Inquiry on Small Firms which published its highly influential Report in 1971. He has held executive positions in several firms and industries and now runs his own consultancy. He has written or contributed to nine books and written extensively on the small firm.

Frank Bechhofer is Director of the Research Centre for Social Sciences at Edinburgh University and was formerly at the Department of Applied Economics at Cambridge University. He has had a long involvement in research on small business owners — especially small shopkeepers — and has published extensively on the situation of the petite bourgeoisie in modern industrial society.

Martin Binks is Lecturer in Economics at the University of Nottingham. He was Research Officer for the Committee to Review the Functioning of Financial Institutions (the Wilson Committee) responsible for research into the small firms sector. Since 1981 he has also been a director of the University of Nottingham's Small Firms Unit.

Elizabeth Chell is Lecturer in Organisational Behaviour at the University of Salford. She received her PhD from the University of Nottingham and has an MPhil from the University of Edinburgh. She has published widely on participation, most recently, *Participation and Organisation: A Social Psychological Approach* (Macmillan, 1985). Her research on small firms has recently focussed on the factors influencing the sales performance of retail newsagents.

Chris Cornforth is Research Fellow in the Co-operatives Research Unit at the Open University. Over the past five years he has conducted research on the organisation and development of co-operatives and is currently co-directing a project concerned with the factors and critical processes affecting the social and economic performance of worker co-operatives.

James Curran is Reader in Industrial Sociology and Director of the Small Business Research Unit at Kingston Polytechnic. He has been involved in research on the small enterprise for well over a decade and has published widely on the subject. He is currently researching the impact of environmental influences, such as government policies and local labour markets, on small firms in the electronics and printing industries.

Brian Elliott is Senior Lecturer in Sociology at Edinburgh University and has also taught at Glasgow University and the University of British Columbia. He has published widely on urban sociology, social stratification and social mobility and has maintained a long term interest in the small business owner, the small shopkeeper in particular, in relation to these areas of interest.

Robert Goffee is Lecturer in Organisational Behaviour at the London Business School and he has previously held posts at the Universities of Bath, Kent and Surrey. He has co-authored two previous books on the small enterprise and most recently, *Women in Charge: the Experience of Female Entrepreneurs* (Allen & Unwin, 1985), co-written with Richard Scase.

Jensine Hough was until recently a researcher in the Small Business Unit at the Polytechnic of Central London where she was involved in a major research project on franchising in Britain. She is currently completing her PhD also on franchising.

Patrick Hutchinson is Lecturer in the Department of Accounting and Financial Management at the University of New England, New South Wales, Australia. Previously he was at the University of Bath in England. He has written several articles and case studies on the financing of the small enterprise.

Andrew Jennings is Lecturer in Economics and Econometrics at the University of Nottingham. His particular field of interest is the analysis of multivariant time series data with application in small firms research and agricultural economics.

Trevor Jones is Senior Lecturer in Geography and Race Relations in the Department of Social Studies at Liverpool Polytechnic. He has co-written several papers on minority business development and racial residential segregation and is currently collaborating on two books.

David Kirby is Senior Lecturer in Geography and Director of the Small Shops Research Unit at Saint David's University College, University of Wales at Lampeter. He has written and researched extensively on the situation of the small retail outlet in Britain and other industrial societies.

David McEvoy is Principal Lecturer in Geography in the Department of Social Studies at Liverpool Polytechnic. He has researched on a wide range of topics including retail geography, the proposed abolition of the metropolitan county councils, teaching political geography as well as on ethnic minorities' residential patterns and their role in retailing. He has published widely, especially on the latter topic.

Graham Ray is Senior Lecturer in the School of Management at the University of Bath. He has a long established interest in both the theory and practice of small enterprise development and has published numerous articles and case studies on the topic.

Richard Scase is Professor of Sociology at the University of Kent, England. He is the author of several books including two on the small firm (co-authored with Robert Goffee) and *Women in Charge: the Experience of Female Entrepreneurs* (Allen & Unwin, 1985). He also lectures frequently on business start-up programmes and advises small business owners.

John Stanworth is Professor and Director of the Small Business Unit at the Polytechnic of Central London. He was a pioneer of research on the small business in Britain and has recently completed a major study of the franchised small enterprise. He has written several books and a large number of articles on various aspects and varieties of the small firm.

David Storey is Senior Research Associate at the Centre for Urban and Regional Development Studies at the University of Newcastle upon Tyne. He has authored and edited books on the small firm including *Entrepreneurship and the New Firm* (Croom Helm, 1982) and *The Small Firm: An International Survey* (Croom Helm, 1983) as well as several articles.

David Watkins is Director of the New Enterprise Centre at the Manchester Business School where he has taught entrepreneurship and small business courses for the past eight years. He was principal author of the *Small Business Kit* which accompanied a major television series for entrepreneurs in Britain, and co-edited three major research-based books on the small enterprise, and more recently, the female entrepreneur.

Jean M. Watkins was formerly an educational administrator who was involved in the creation of one of Britain's earliest adult literacy programmes and co-founder of the UK National Association of Adult Literacy. Most recently she has been evaluating the effectiveness of entrepreneurial training programmes and is leading a research and education programme aimed at stimulating female entrepreneurship in Britain.

Clive Woodcock is Small Business Editor of the *Guardian* and publisher of the *International Small Business Journal*. He has written a number of books both on the running of a small business and on finance and the small enterprise.

Preface

The expanding body of literature which has accompanied the re-discovery of the small enterprise in recent years is now vast — one recent bibliography, for example, lists over 4000 items on the small business, a quarter of which have been published since 1980. Two principal characteristics distinguish this literature. The most important is its sheer diversity — the range of sources is now wider than for almost any other equivalent subject area. Many areas of the behavioural sciences claim to be multidisciplinary but the study of the small business has achieved this to an extent that most other areas can only envy. The cost of this richly varied range of input is that it has become extremely difficult for interested parties to keep up to date and remain aware of current thinking and research outside their immediate areas of disciplinary expertise. For newcomers to the small business field, acquainting themselves with what has been written has become a daunting task.

The second characteristic of writings on the small business is their variability in quality. Of the large number of publications much is 'dross' which can, at times, act to bury the 'gold'. Those constructing the increasing number of small business courses on MBA and other postgraduate level courses, as well as courses run for undergraduates, find it relatively easy to locate 'nuts and bolts' material on running the small firm (although even here the quality varies substantially). Much more difficult, however, is the location and identification of sources which provide the conceptual and theoretical rigour demanded by abler students and colleagues sitting on validating bodies. Yet, if small business studies are to achieve academic respectability and attract first-rate researchers, the existence of high-quality work needs to be highlighted.

Policy-makers and their advisers have become heavily involved in discussions on the role of the small business in contemporary industrial society. Their preparation for this involvement, however, has usually been minimal, often combining simple enthusiasm, or even blind optimism, with a modicum of ill-understood research. Frequently reiterated statements by policy-makers on the employment-generating potential of small firms are one example of this phenomenon and confident assertions about conflict-free industrial relations in small establishments are another. To be fair, the diversity and variable quality of writing on the small enterprise is a particularly difficult problem for policy-makers and their advisers given that the small firm is often only one of a number of concerns for which policies have to be developed.

We have brought together in two volumes a large selection of contributions — 24 in all — analysing and discussing various kinds of small enterprise and facets of their operations. About half the contributions consist of materials abstracted from books and articles selected because they offer an authoritative summary statement, often with the support of research materials. In some instances, authors have also taken the opportunity to update figures and information contained in the original publication. In about half of the areas we wished to cover we were unable to find a previously printed source which met our criteria of authority and relevance and so we invited an established specialist to write a paper specially. We are happy to be able to say that not one of those invited declined to contribute.

The resulting collection covers most of the important aspects of the contemporary small enterprise. Each contribution offers a thoughtful and stimulating analysis and, having two volumes at our disposal meant that, fortunately, we did not need to sacrifice depth for breadth of coverage. The reader — academic, researcher, policy-maker and, hopefully, the small business owner himself who wants to stand back a little from his day-to-day involvement — will find the collection both provocative and demanding.

Inevitably, it will be asked what the practical use is of a publication like this: how does it help the ordinary small business owner solve the problems of running his or her own enterprise? The answer to this question is that sound, effective help to the aspiring and established small business owner depends enormously on the quality of the original thinking and research underpinning that help. For instance, teaching small business owners about investment decision-making requires a real understanding of how small business owners define investment and of the investment environment faced by small firms in particular areas of the economy. Too often small business studies have been undermined by an anti-intellectual and atheoretical bias which sees practice as invariably superior to theory or research: in fact, good practice invariably rests on a sound, carefully developed and research-based understanding.

Finally, we should like to acknowledge the authors and publishers who have generously allowed us to edit and reproduce their work (full acknowledgements are given on the title page for each contribution). Thanks are also due in equal measure to the authors of the commissioned contributions which appear in print here for the first time. Our publisher, in the guise of editorial director, John Irwin, also deserves our thanks for agreeing to publish a two-volume reader committed to showing what small business thinkers and researchers have achieved in advancing our understanding of this most important expression of economic endeavour.

James Curran
John Stanworth
David Watkins

PART I
THE ECONOMICS OF
SURVIVAL

Introduction

All four papers in this section are concerned with the economics of the small enterprise. Economists have rather neglected contemporary small-scale economic activities despite the pivotal importance of the idealised small firm in classical economic theory. In this they merely demonstrate, albeit in a clearer way, the pronounced bias in favour of the analysis of large-scale economic activities which has been so distinctive of the applied behavioural sciences generally.

It should be unnecessary to point to the continuing and even increasing importance of the small enterprise in modern industrial economies, but it seems that this economic fact needs restating as a preface to any serious analysis of the role of small-scale economic activity. Equally, untenable assumptions confining the small business to the most backward or peripheral areas of the economy also need to be questioned explicitly as a beginning to any proper understanding of the necessary and integral function that the small firm performs in the economy.

Of course, the prior question in any such analysis is what is meant by 'small'. Despite a great deal of agonising over the issue of definition by small business theorists and researchers (see, for example, Bolton, 1971: Ch. 1; Binks and Coyne, 1983: 17–30; Curran and Stanworth, 1984) no entirely satisfactory solutions have emerged. But, whichever of the conventional definitions are adopted, there is no doubt that small businesses remain economically important in every free enterprise industrial society. In Britain, for instance, Binks and Coyne (1983: 20) suggest that there are about 1.3 million small enterprises, strongly represented in almost every major sector of the economy. Moreover, they continue to provide substantial employment not only in traditional, well-established industries such as construction but also in the newer, expanding tertiary sectors such as professional and scientific services. Binks and Coyne (1983: 22) estimate, for example, that almost half of those working in the latter area are employed in small enterprises.

Even in manufacturing, where large firms clearly dominate, small firms (those employing up to 200) employed 23.1 per cent of the manufacturing labour force in 1979 according to the *Census of Production* and were responsible for just under one-fifth of net manufacturing output. While these shares indicate a minority role for the small enterprise, it is none the less a substantial one and, contrary to popular assumption, *Census of Production* data indicate a tendency for small manufacturing firms to have increased their share of both employment and output in recent years.

Other industrial societies have even larger small enterprise sectors — Britain, in fact, has the smallest small business sector of any advanced free enterprise industrial society. By way of comparison, Japan, the most dynamic and economically successful free enterprise economy of the last two decades, has one of the largest small business sectors (Anthony, 1983). Putting aside the finer issues of definition, data on other industrial societies show no evidence for the widely held economic assumptions that small enterprise representation in the economy and level of economic development, and still less rates of economic growth, are inversely related.

An outstanding exception to the collective neglect of small-scale activities by economists is Graham Bannock who has spent well over a decade analysing the small firm's economic significance. A contribution from his book, *The Economics of Small Firms* (1981) provides the opening paper of this section. In it he examines in depth the issues introduced above, paying particular attention to international dimensions. One issue he discusses — picked up also in several later papers — is the importance of government for the survival of the small firm. He also introduces two further issues, again much debated by other writers in this collection: the contribution that small firms make to overall levels of employment and the role of the small firm in economic development and change.

Binks and Jennings, authors of the second paper in this section (and the first of the dozen or so papers specially written for the two

4

volumes), take up the issue of the role of the small firm in economic change, focusing specifically on the part it might play in recovery from the 1980s economic recession. One of the more popular theses offered (certainly among politicians and, interestingly, contrary to the conventional economist's view of the role of the small firm in a modern economy) gives to the small firm a pioneering function in developing new products, new technologies and new industries. Economic rejuvenation spearheaded by small enterprises, many of them to become the large firms of tomorrow, is the view which has stimulated much of the recent state interest in the small firm.

Examining in detail data for the United Kingdom for the period 1971–2, Binks and Jennings conclude that new firms are unlikely to constitute a leading source of economic recovery from the current recession. Moreover, the government has not yet developed the most effective ways of helping small firms since much of the help is misdirected because it is based upon untenable assumptions about the role of the small firm in economic change. Indeed, some of the present policies simply help new small firms to displace existing businesses with little or no net gain to the economy as a whole.

The remaining two papers in this section (both specially written for this collection) focus more narrowly on the financial and accounting aspects of the economic performance of the small firm. Clive Woodcock, Britain's leading financial journalist specialising in the small firm, offers a detailed guide to the highly complex financial and capital environment faced by the contemporary small firm. He demonstrates convincingly that only the most dedicated could ever hope fully to understand the jungle of financial sources allegedly available to help the small business owner. Certainly it is very unlikely that most small business owners will have more than the sketchiest understanding but, more seriously, Woodcock suggests that accountants and other financial specialists likely to have regular contact with small firm owners will also have a very incomplete knowledge.

The paper concludes, again contrary to popular belief among politicians and others, that not only have sources of finance expanded substantially in recent years in Britain, but also that the supply now probably outstrips demand. The main problem and the reason the enormous efforts of government and the private sector to expand sources of finance for the smaller enterprise have not produced the results intended, is the lack of financial sophistication among small business owners. Not only do many small business owners lack even a basic knowledge of financial management but as other research has shown (Hankinson, 1984) it is difficult to persuade them that their lack

5

of sophistication is a real problem in the running of their enterprise.

Ray and Hutchinson in the final paper in this section examine the financial problems of the growing small firm. Based on research on the financial experiences of small, rapidly growing firms up to the point of flotation, the authors question the traditional view of the financial life-cycle of the rapidly expanding small firm. The latter suggests several stages in financing, beginning with owner's resources and retained profits plus outside sources such as trade credit and bank loans. Later comes longer-term finance from specialist financial institutions, the new-issue market and the normal range of sources available to the mature large firm. At each stage the enterprise may exhibit symptoms of 'financial stress' ranging from under-capitalisation to loss of control by the original owners.

Ray and Hutchinson found that the traditional view was correct in that their supergrowth firms did indeed demonstrate low liquidity up to flotation. They also showed high levels of profitability and extensive use was made of long-term debt finance. As Woodcock's analysis also suggests, the firms did not experience a 'finance gap': neither the supergrowth firms nor the control sample of small firms which did not achieve flotation felt starved of funds or advice (though as Woodcock's analysis also suggests many small firm owners may be entirely unaware of a lot of the relevant information).

The authors conclude that the supergrowth small firm poses problems for financial institutions since, in some key accounting aspects, such firms may have many of the appearances of a failing enterprise. (Analysis showed that on one sophisticated measure, nearly half of the supergrowth firms would have been classified as bankrupt at some stage up to flotation.) The owner-managers of the supergrowth firms, on the other hand, appeared to have developed a high sensitivity to financial performance indicators, many of them informal in character, together with the ability in some cases to shape their financial control system to anticipate problems well before they emerge.

Of course, supergrowth small firms are quite untypical of the small-firm population as a whole. Most small firms never grow to any substantial size and their role in the economy will be minor in any absolute sense. The papers in this opening section, however, join together in making two key points in relation to the economic survival of the small enterprise in any modern economy: firstly, that, however the small business is analysed, the collective importance of small-scale economic activities is fundamental to the operation of a modern economy; and secondly, that misconceptions about small firms and their role in the economy abound.

References

Anthony, D. (1983). 'Japan' in Storey, D.J., (ed.) *The Small Firm an International Survey,* Croom Helm, London.

Binks, M. and Coyne, J. (1983). *The Birth of Enterprise,* Hobart Paper 98, Institute of Economic Affairs, London.

Bolton, J.E. (1971). *Report of the Committee of Enquiry on Small Firms* (Bolton Report), Cmnd. 4811, HMSO, London.

Curran J. and Stanworth J. (1984). 'Small Business Research in Britain' in Levicki, C. (ed.) *Small Business, Theory and Policy,* Croom Helm, London.

Hankinson, A. (1984). 'Small Firms' Investment: a Search for the Motivations', *International Small Business Journal,* vol. 2, Winter.

1 The Economic Role of the Small Firm in Contemporary Industrial Society

GRAHAM BANNOCK*

The small firm: international comparisons

Perhaps the thing which struck readers the most in the research findings of the Bolton Report was not that small firms were declining in Britain and other countries (the conventional wisdom was that this was inevitable with modern technology), but that the decline had gone further and faster in Britain than elsewhere.

If small firms in industry were outmoded and a sign of technological and economic immaturity, why were they more numerous and important in all other advanced countries, including the United States and Germany which were more advanced than the UK? If competing abroad and faster growth required the concentration of industry into bigger units, how was it that Japan and Italy could sustain exceptionally rapid growth in exports and output with a much bigger proportion of output in small firms than most other countries? How could a tiny country like Switzerland meet foreign competition and sustain high standards of living with twice the proportion of employment in small firms as the UK?

It was not that UK firms were heavily concentrated in the middle range, had fewer small firms and fewer large firms. Among the world's

---

* Edited extracts from Chapters 4 and 5 of: *The Economics of Small Firms: Return from the Wilderness* (Basil Blackwell, Oxford, 1981).

500 largest companies in the mid-1960s only the United States had more firms than the United Kingdom. Britain had nearly as many multinationals in that list as the six countries of the EEC put together and considerably more than Japan. Britain's industry was, and probably still is, the most concentrated in the world.

Table 1.1 presents data on the importance of small establishments in manufacturing in OECD countries. The relative importance of small firms has not changed very much between countries since the figures published by Bolton (which related mainly to the early 1960s). These figures show that the decline in the share of small establishments in employment has continued in about half the countries listed, though it

Table 1.1
The proportion of manufacturing employment in small establishments, GDP per head and rate of growth in GDP, selected OECD countries

	Proportion of manufacturing employment in small firms		Real per capita GDP (1970, US dollars)	Annual compound rate of growth in real GDP per capita 1950–78
	per cent			per cent
Japan	65 (1966)	66 (1975)	3578	7.3
Italy	66 (1961)	59 (1971)	2880	4.1
Switzerland	61 (1965)	64 (1975)	4292	2.5
Australia	60 (1963)		4209	2.3
Norway	64 (1967)	58 (1975)	4327	3.5
France	51 (1963)		4383	3.8
Belgium	51 (1962)	45 (1975)	4391	3.4
Netherlands	47 (1960)	42 (1977)	4052	3.3
Canada	47 (1963)	44 (1975)	4806	2.8
Sweden	53 (1965)	41 (1975)	4695	2.6
USA	39 (1963)	38 (1972)	5160	2.2
Federal Republic of Germany	34 (1963)	31 (1976)	4160	4.5
UK	31 (1963)	29 (1975)	3572	2.1

Source: National Statistical Offices. Dutch data relate to enterprises. German data exclude *Handwerk*. GDP data from Angus Maddison, *Per Capita Output in the Long Run* (Kylos, 1979 Fasc.1/2). Small establishments are those employing 200 persons or fewer.

has actually increased in Japan and Switzerland. However, since large firms have been acquiring small ones in all countries, on an enterprise basis the share of small firms in manufacturing employment probably declined virtually everywhere. There has been considerable growth in employment in small firms in service industries also. Since the mid-1970s, however, the world recession seems to have been accompanied by a slowing down and even a reversal in the decline of small firms.

At first glance Table 1.1 does not suggest any clear relationship between economic performance and the importance of small firms. Contrary to earlier received wisdom, however, it is obvious that a high small-firm ratio is consistent with either high levels of growth or output and that the UK is at the bottom of the table in all respects. Correlations of this kind are difficult to interpret even where the data are strictly comparable (which in this case they are not). Historical factors, natural resource endowment and all sorts of things other than industrial structure must influence economic growth. There are many technical factors which affect the comparability of data. The German definition of establishment is less restrictive than the UK definition, for example, while German statistics, which include 'Handwerk', include 'sausage' makers and other service-related activities, some of which (if they existed) would not be included in manufacturing in the UK. There also seem to be differences in the 'quality' of small firms in different countries though quality in this context is an elusive and possibly misleading concept. Willibrord Sauer of the German Handwerk Association has pointed out that many of the small manufacturing firms in France and Italy are not stable 'modern' enterprises but family-based craft firms whose members earn less than the national minimum wage and which disappear in recession and re-emerge again in boom times. Other commentators suggest that much of Italy's recent export successes are attributable to small businesses operating in an underground economy. Certainly in Japan a large proportion, perhaps 40 per cent, of small manufacturing firms are subcontractors to large firms and have little independence.

In fact when larger numbers of countries (including developing countries) are examined, it seems that there is a clear tendency for both the rate of economic growth and the importance of small firms to decline as levels of income reach those of the richer advanced countries. It is clear that the achievement of high levels of wealth does not depend upon a reduction in the importance of small firms. It is rather that other factors associated with high living standards, notably the increased role of government, act as a brake upon the formation and growth of small firms. At the same time there are other factors which also combine to promote slower growth at high levels of affluence, for instance the emergence of social limits to growth and the more limited scope for productivity gains in the service industries (into which employment shifts from agriculture and manufacturing) (Bannock 1976).

The UK has a much smaller proportion of employment in small firms in manufacturing (and probably in non-manufacturing, too) than would be expected from its level of economic development, while other countries, for example Japan and the United States, have larger small-firm populations than might be expected.

It is a question of some importance as to whether Britain has fewer small firms than other countries because it has a lower birth rate for new enterprises or a higher death rate. The difficulty in answering this question is simply that very little information on entries to and exits from the small firm population is available for any country. The Bolton Committee calculated that new incorporations per thousand of the human population were lower in the UK than in the United States and that the death rate was higher, though there was some evidence in these and later data that the death rate was declining and the birth rate increasing. The Committee also concluded from the available evidence that the average age of small firms was higher in the UK than in the USA, although this could be consistent with either a lower birth rate or a lower death rate. Other data suggest that both birth and death rates of small enterprises are lower in the UK than elsewhere. Birth rates also appear to be higher than average in the more prosperous parts of Britain and other countries and lower in areas where the bulk of employment is concentrated in branch plants of large firms.

One particularly interesting finding of international research on the demography of small firms has been that the initial size of new enterprises seems to be declining in the long term, even though the average size of surviving small (and large) enterprises has been increasing. These findings are important and are consistent with the view that shortages of start-up capital are inhibiting the establishment of new firms.

Public support for small firms

There have been no comprehensive studies of the legal and economic environments of small firms in various countries though the author was commissioned to carry out such a study by Shell UK Ltd. (Bannock 1980). It is obvious, however, that the governments of most European countries as well as those of Japan and the United States have committed more effort and resources into promoting small business than Britain.

The West German government, for example, spent £165 million on programmes to promote small firms in 1980, while the Länder (regional) governments will probably spend almost half as much. UK expenditure is a tiny fraction of these amounts, as is illustrated by the fact that the number of staff employed in the small-firm sponsoring departments in the two countries are 25 in the UK and 200 in Germany. The federal government's grant to the Small Firm Research Institute, which carries out economic research into the subject, is £280,000 per annum. Not included in these figures are interest-rate subsidies from ERP (Economic Recovery Plan) funds for small firms or the value of various tax concessions given to small businesses.

While government attitudes, which reflect more clearly articulated philosophies on the economic and social importance of small business, are more favourable in other countries, the greater size of the small-firm sector outside the UK is also favoured by greater independent initiatives to help small firms. Thus in many European countries, powerful chambers of commerce (membership of which is a legal obligation in several countries) play an important role in providing information and assistance for small firms. In Germany, Switzerland, Japan and other countries there are mutual assistance organisations which provide credit guarantees for small firms which wish to borrow from the banking system, but are unable to do so through lack of suitable collateral. Small-firm representative bodies are also very much stronger in most other countries than they are in Britain.

The small firm problem and measures to promote small businesses are not confined to the developed countries. In the period immediately following World War II the developing world was also caught up in the fever for bigness in industrial organisation. Development aid from the international agencies such as the World Bank was heavily concentrated in favour of large-scale infrastructural projects and resource exploitation involving joint ventures with multinational groups. If the advanced countries had oil refineries, large steel mills and chemical plants, so too must the poorer countries: it was assumed that the general path of development must be the same, but that the new developing countries could skip the stage of small-scale industry and pass directly to the concentrated industry of modern times. Disillusionment with this philosophy was soon to set in, not only because it meant heavy reliance upon foreign enterprise and capital, but because the development of capital intensive industry did nothing to help reduce unemployment, nor did it ease the horrific problems of congestion and poverty in the big cities; in short it was not effective.

Small firms and economic development

A great deal of recent empirical research has buttressed the case against the view that contemporary economic development depends and will continue to depend almost entirely upon large firms. (No one has ever denied that small firms were the crucial engine of change and development during the industrial revolution; the argument under criticism here is that under modern conditions there is no longer an important role for the smaller firm.) Comparative studies of the industrial structure of economies in different countries, as we have seen, do not suggest any correlation between the importance of large firms and the level of output, or the rate of economic growth. At a microeconomic level, careful studies by Newbould, Singh, Meeks and others have shown that mergers and acquisitions, which have contributed substantially to increased concentration, have had disappointing effects upon the financial performance of the participating firms. Other studies show that profitability tends to be higher in concentrated than in fragmented industries, which suggests that concentration is profitable, even if it may not be socially beneficial, although too much should not be made of that, for comparisons of returns on assets are full of pitfalls.

Various attempts have been made to compare the profitability of small with large firms in the belief that this might throw light upon their relative efficiency, but these comparisons are not meaningful. Not only should the degree of competition and other factors such as the inclusion of some return on capital in directors' remuneration among small firms be allowed for, but comparisons of return on capital (profitability) are only valid measures of the efficient use of resources where inputs of capital and labour are similar. Although most studies suggest that small firms are more profitable than large, it is also found that value added per employee is higher in large firms than in small. All such studies show that small firms get a better return on capital and a worse return on labour, which simply reflects the well-known fact that they are more labour intensive than large firms.

Small firms and employment

Recent research on the contribution of firms of different sizes to the growth of employment in different countries has shown that small

13

firms have accounted for a major proportion of long-term gains in jobs, while the largest firms have been shedding labour. Much interest has been aroused by the publication from 1978 onwards of some research by David Birch of MIT into the components of employment change in the United States (Birch 1979). His frequently quoted result that 'small firms [those with 20 or fewer employees] generated 66 per cent of all new jobs in the US' in the period 1969–76 was clearly, if valid, of tremendous importance. It seemed that here, at last, was irrefutable evidence of the vital role of small firms in the economy that would justify a major shift in public policy towards the promotion of small businesses. (Small firms in this study are defined to include subsidiaries and branches of larger enterprises; independents employing 20 or fewer employees accounted for 51.8 per cent of new jobs.)

However, when the details of Birch's research were studied it became clear that most of the new jobs had been generated in the service sector (in which small firms predominate anyway) and not in manufacturing, which is the sector that most politicians (and most economists) are most concerned with. There is now some confusion about the significance of Birch's results for economic policy.

The first point to make is that *all* statistics on very small firms are suspect, but for what they are worth it is possible to see from ordinary census statistics that the overall reduction of employment which has taken place in Britain (and in the USA) during the last decade has been concentrated entirely among medium and large firms. Table 1.2 shows that employment in UK firms with less than 100 persons increased in the period 1973–76. In the USA, similar statistics show that employment increased in establishments employing under 250. (These figures cover different periods but are the latest available in each case.) A similar pattern is to be found in Japanese census figures.

There are several difficulties in drawing conclusions from figures of this kind, although the simple one that small firms are still creating jobs while big firms are shedding them is broadly correct. It must be understood, however, that within each of the employment size classes indicated, some firms are expanding their employment while others are contracting, and that between the dates shown some firms will have gone out of business while others will have moved up or down into different size classes. A further problem is that you will get different results according to the time period you choose for the comparison. Between 1954 and 1972, for example, figures from the same source show that total employment in firms with less than 20 employees *declined* in the United States even though total employment in manufacturing rose during that period. In the UK in particular, the increase in small-firm employment dates from the early

14

Table 1.2
Net employment change in manufacturing in the United Kingdom (1973–76) and the United States (1967–72) by size of firm

Number of employees in individual firms	Total employed (thousands)		
	United Kingdom 1973	1976	Net change
1–99	1,108.6	1,189.4	+80.8
100–199	396.9	386.9	−10.0
200 and over	5,762.9	5,394.9	−368.0
TOTAL	7,268.4	6,971.2	−297.2
	United States 1967	1972	Net change
under 19	1,042.3	1,114.2	+71.9
20–99	3,276.4	3,355.7	+79.3
100–249	3,069.2	3,233.4	+164.2
250 and over	11,103.8	10,331.1	−772.7
TOTAL	18,492.0	18,034.4	−457.6

Source: UK reports on the *Census of Production* (enterprises); US *Census of Manufactures* (establishments).

1970s, reversing a long period of decline. These are some of the reasons why Birch, following the pioneering work of Graham Gudgin and others, attempted a different approach: that of comparing the contribution of firms of different sizes to net employment change using a data file of employment in individual firms at different dates.

Birch has, in fact, been criticized by Gudgin (who first clearly established the importance of small firms in employment change) for exaggerating the role of the smallest firms in job creation by failing to disaggregate his results between manufacturing and non-manufacturing (Fothergill and Gudgin, 1979). Gudgin thinks job creation in manufacturing is much more important because of its importance in foreign trade and because the creation of wealth in manufacturing is a prior condition for increased employment in services. Gudgin and his co-authors in another study (Gudgin, Brunskill and Fothergill, 1979) seem not to be sympathetic to small firms on other grounds: 'the desirability of encouraging new firms depends a great deal on longer-term political goals. It is worth remembering, for example, that small firms (and most new firms are small) pay lower wages on average, and offer fewer fringe benefits to their employees'. However, even in manufacturing, Birch's data (Table 1.3), Gudgin's own figures for the East Midlands and the crude statistics in Table 1.2 all show that smaller firms as a group are responsible for net increases in employment while larger firms have been responsible for a net *loss* of jobs. These data suggest, incidentally, that small firms in Britain run out of steam at some point below 100 employees while in the USA job losses set in after 250 employees, although it is difficult to draw any clear conclusions.

Table 1.3
Net employment change, United States manufacturing, 1969–76, by size and status of enterprise (figures in thousands)

	Size in numbers of employees					
	0–20	21–50	51–100	101–500	501+	Total
Independent firms (single establishment)	+355	−38	−116	−217	−55	−70
Headquarters and branches of multi-plant firms	+139	+83	+41	−43	−247	−28'
Partnerships and subsidiaries	+49	+48	+34	+6	−190	−52
Total	+543	+93	−41	−254	−492	−150

Source: Birch (1979).

It can be seen from Table 1.2, that firms with less than 100 employees account for only a small part of total employment and the 81 000 employment increase in these firms between 1973 and 1976 was only about 1 per cent of total manufacturing employment. Because of this, Gudgin's argument goes, these firms cannot be relied upon to have much effect upon total employment in the short run. However, it is obvious that the contribution of these firms in this period is in a different direction to that of large firms as a group and quite large in relation to the total employment change. However, Gudgin seems quite justified in emphasising that small firms offer no quick panacea to the economic problem.

In all these studies, it has been shown that firm migration has been of little importance in regional employment growth; the main factor has been the setting up of new firms. Gudgin has shown that the origins of small firms are highly localised and that small businesses breed and interrelate with each other in an organic fashion. This is because people who work in small firms are much more likely to set up a business of their own than employees in large firms. Regions which have no source of employment other than the branch plants of large companies, therefore, will experience few employment gains unless the activities of those plants happen to be in growth industries, few new activities are likely to be generated in them. This is why some of the areas dominated by large firms in the shipbuilding, steel and other declining industries are economic deserts which have remained unaffected by the attempts of successive governments to encourage other large firms to set up branch plants in them. Thus, much of regional policy as well as the broader policies to promote rationalisation and mergers have proved ineffective, based as these policies were on an incomplete understanding of the roots of industrial expansion. It is not even true, as was once thought, that small firms are not significant in export trade. In the service trades small hotels and restaurants serving tourists as well as commodity brokers and others contribute to 'invisible' exports though, of course, many small firms cannot export. In manufacturing it seems that small firms export about the same proportion of their output, on average, as large firms. According to a survey of companies carried out by the Department of Trade in 1973, firms with a turnover of less than £10 million exported 14.5 per cent of turnover while firms with a turnover of over £250 million exported only 10 per cent (quoted in Hannah and Kay, 1977).

The implications of all this research have not yet been fully digested by economists and further changes are probably under way that may leave our understanding trailing behind events. It should not be thought that Schumpeter was necessarily wrong at the time he was writing. In the 1930s, 1940s and 1950s, large monopolistic firms may well have been the engines of economic progress in some sense that is not our concern here. He was certainly right and very far-sighted in focusing upon the dynamic as against the static aspects of the competitive process. But we cannot look to large firms alone now as the engine of development and it was an error to do so in the past.

References

Bannock, G. (1976). *Smaller Business in Britain and Germany,* Wilton House Publications.
Bannock, G. (1980). *The Organisation of Public Sector Promotion of Small Business,* Economists Advisory Group for Shell UK Ltd.

Birch, D.L. (1979). *The Job Generation Process,* Massachusetts Institute of Technology, mimeograph.

Fothergill, S. and Gudgin, G. (1979). *The Job Generation Process in Britain,* Centre for Environmental Studies Research Series no. 32, November.

Gudgin, G., Brunskill, I. and Fothergill, S. (1979). *New Manufacturing Firms in Regional Employment Growth,* Centre for Environmental Studies Research Series, October.

Hannah, L. and Kay, J.A. (1977). *Concentration in Modern Industry,* Macmillan.

Schumpeter, J.A. (1943). *Capitalism, Socialism and Democracy,* Allen and Unwin.

2 Small Firms as a Source of Economic Rejuvenation

MARTIN BINKS AND ANDREW JENNINGS

Introduction

This paper attempts to answer two main questions related to the potential of new firms as a source of recovery in a period of severe economic recession. The first concerns the extent to which new firms are attracted into newer industries and towards innovation. The second considers whether recession causes an increase in the number of newly created firms. While the methodologies involved in addressing each question are very different, it is important to consider them together to assess the validity of one possible and attractive interpretation. If firms which start up in a period of recession are more likely to enter 'new industries' and innovate new products and production techniques while their number tends to rise as a result of recession then there would appear to be a natural process of economic regeneration through changes in the pattern of industrial production. If either or both of these trends fail to occur, then any reliance placed upon new firms to make a significant contribution towards the inception of economic rejuvenation is inappropriate.

The ability of small firms, in the event of economic recovery, to respond in terms of the production required of them to sustain it, is vital. To rely upon them as a cause of that recovery may be misguided.

These points are considered with particular reference to the case of the UK for the period 1971–82.

1. New firms and industrial change

The births and deaths of firms

The recent record levels of firm births and deaths in the UK are often interpreted as the necessary consequences of industrial evolution and long-term regeneration. Schumpeter has described this process as one of 'creative destruction' which 'incessantly revolutionizes the economic structure from within, incessantly destroying the old one, incessantly creating a new one'.[1] The extent to which this view is appropriate is singularly significant as it represents one of the prime underlying sources of debate between political analysts in defence of their respective economic ideologies. Whether high rates of firm formation and cessation reflect a beneficial process of industrial change or one of damaging decay is uncertain, and recourse to both empirical evidence and theoretical argument is necessary in any attempt to resolve the question.

The arguments set out below indicate the possible dangers of assuming that high birth and death rates in a period of severe recession imply a necessary if painful reorganisation of the industrial structure. Rather than contributing to a 'healthier' industrial structure, they may be more likely to further economic decay and increase vulnerability to import penetration.

While it is not possible to present data which refer to the actual numbers of firm births and deaths over the last decade, it is useful to consider new company registrations alongside firm liquidations.[2] Graphs of these for the UK (1971–82) indicate clearly the present pattern of growth in each (Figures 2.1 and 2.2).

The underlying trend of firm births has been upward, if discontinuous, since the early 1950s and the *apparent* tendency for it to rise faster in periods of recession has already been demonstrated in several studies.[3] The main reason given for this rise is the larger number of new entrepreneurs who have been 'pushed' or 'forced' into starting their own business by redundancy or job uncertainty.

The rise in firm deaths is to be expected in periods of recession, and reflects the stagnant or declining level of economic activity in general.

In themselves, therefore, these trends are not surprising; their significance only emerges fully if the interrelationships involved are considered. By ascertaining where births and deaths are more likely to

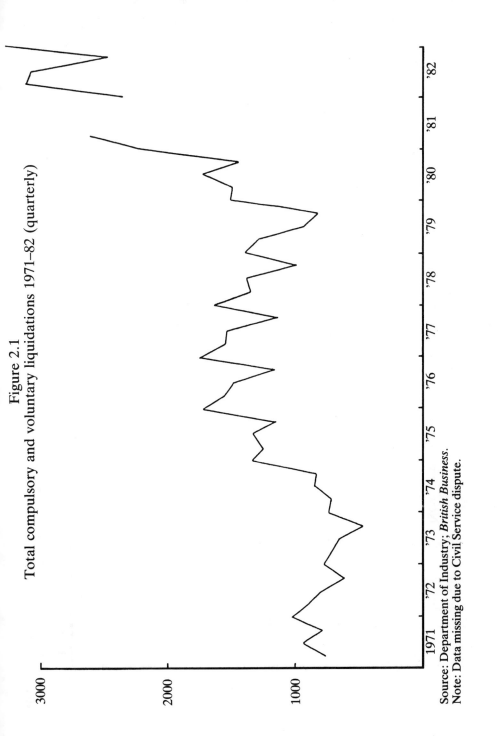

Figure 2.1
Total compulsory and voluntary liquidations 1971–82 (quarterly)

Source: Department of Industry; *British Business.*
Note: Data missing due to Civil Service dispute.

21

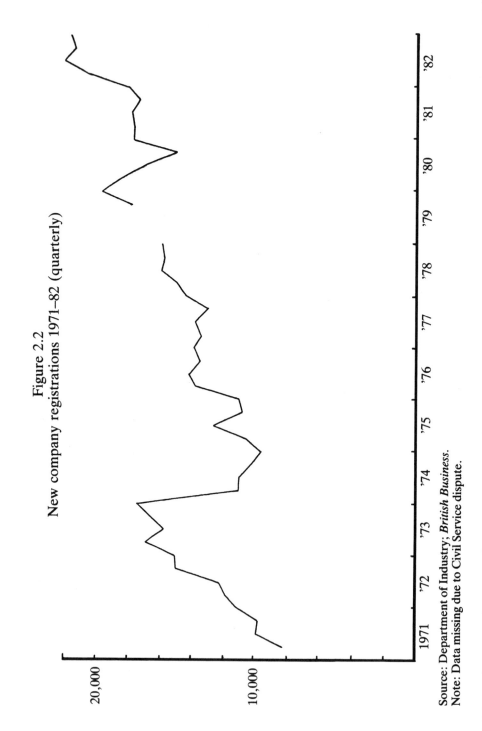

Figure 2.2
New company registrations 1971–82 (quarterly)

Source: Department of Industry; *British Business*.
Note: Data missing due to Civil Service dispute.

22

occur and how each trend affects the other, it is possible to indicate the nature of the economic process which they reflect.

The data presented above simply illustrate the rising trend in starts and failures. It is the causal linkages involved which are important here.

Underpinning the philosophy described earlier by Schumpeter is a belief in the market's ability to reallocate resources of production from less to more efficient usage. The present high rates of start-up and closure could therefore be interpreted as the rapid transfer of factors of production necessary for the creation of a new and more efficient industrial structure. Central to this issue is the way in which market forces actually operate. The way in which factors of production are transferred from one usage to another will vary considerably from one case to another. The important point here is to identify what is more likely to happen to a firm's assets and labour on ceasing trading, and where, if anywhere, those factors of production are likely to be re-employed when the economy is so depressed.

The nature of factor transfers

On closure the assets of most companies are sold. The prices realised from stocks of finished products and the firm's plant and machinery are typically very low. In many cases sale is by auction and creditors' interests are seen as best served by rapid disposal even when such low prices are obtained.[4] These are likely to prevail while rapid sale is seen as an important element in the repayment of outstanding debts to creditors. This attitude is represented quite strongly in Part 1 of the Cork Committee's report:

> We believe that the aims of a good modern insolvency law are these — . . .
> (e) to realise the assets of the insolvent which should properly be taken to satisfy his debts, with the minimum of delay and expense.[5]

The object here is to highlight the implications of this approach in terms of the prices which such assets will tend to command, rather than to question its justification.

(i) Plant and machinery The purchaser of second-hand plant and machinery may wish to re-employ it in a new or existing firm, sell it at a higher price for re-employment or sell it for scrap. The export or scrapping of such capital assets clearly negates their potential role in

any domestic economic recovery. The extent to which this occurs is hard to ascertain. Recent evidence for the UK does indicate, however, the common ability of new and existing entrepreneurs to accumulate capital at prices which frequently fail to reflect their 'realistic' market value.[6] The process may also be witnessed in other countries. In the USA, for example, profiteering on a bankrupt corporation's assets is big business:

> Hundreds of corporations seek relief every year under the provisions of the recently enacted Bankruptcy Code. Underneath their fatal or near fatal financial difficulties most of these debtors possess valuable assets or rights that are up for grabs on bargain terms. Few investors know these assets exist but astute people in business can reap profits from these situations.[7]

As is made clearer below, as far as the UK economy is concerned, the availability of cheap capital from deceased firms has further implications in terms of the nature and industrial distribution of new firms.

(ii) Labour The other factor of production which is usually released by firm cessations is labour. The number of people registered with the Department of Health and Social Security indicates that in most cases this is a transfer from employment to unemployment. While this may be true for the vast majority the point is still important in the context of the present argument, however, as there is also an identifiable transfer from employee status to that of self-employed and potential employer. It is the influences upon these new entrepreneurs which are significant because they determine in which industries the newcomers choose to start up.

In his survey of new firms in Cleveland in the late 1970s, David Storey found that about 20 per cent of new owner managers were 'forced' into starting their own businesses.[8] More recent research into new firm formation in the Nottingham area[9] indicates that an appropriate figure for the early 1980s would appear to be about 50 per cent. The evidence suggests that the disparity in levels reflects the deepening recession between 1978 and 1982. While 'pushed' entrepreneurs are not necessarily less efficient than those who have been attracted into running their own business, the industries which they naturally choose to enter may differ substantially.

In general terms it is necessary to distinguish between those who are attracted by a particular innovation in production technique or market area and those who are pushed into founding their own firm by redundancy or job insecurity. While the former have always been recognised as a prerequisite for dynamic economic progress it is the present proliferation of the latter which requires closer analysis in terms of any reallocation of factors of production.

While some proportion of the factors of production released by firm closures may be re-employed in existing firms, it is natural to regard any redeployment into new firms and industries as an indicator of the changing pattern in industrial structure. In terms of 'creative destruction' it is these firms which must reflect either economic regeneration or self-perpetuating industrial decay and immobility.

(iii) Finished goods Although not a factor of production, the sale of finished products under these conditions has implications for surviving firms in the same and related industries — a point which will be taken up in more detail below.

In summary, the present increase in firm deaths leads to a growing supply of cheap finished products and plant and machinery, while the level of firm births reflects a significant increase in the number of new entrepreneurs who have been 'pushed' rather than 'pulled' into starting their own business.

The interrelationships between firm births and deaths

The nature of the factor transfers described above does not substantiate the conventional wisdom that the present high levels of firm births and deaths imply a rapid evolution towards a new industrial structure. The supply of very cheap capital from established industries along with the growing proportion of new owner-managers who are pushed rather than attracted into business suggests the opposite.

For the purposes of this argument it is sufficient to identify three main causal linkages between births and deaths. These refer to the way in which: (i) firm deaths cause firm births; (ii) firm births cause firm deaths; and (iii) firm deaths cause firm deaths. While each of these is to some extent related to the other two it is helpful to consider them separately to clarify the mechanisms involved. These do not represent general rules but rather relative probabilities in terms of the likely experience of deceased and new firms.

(i) Deaths cause births The closure of firms leads to the birth of new ones, first by the provision of plant and machinery, and secondly by providing new entrepreneurs. The realisation of deceased firms'

capital assets at relatively low prices, as described above, provides an attractive source of start-up capital for many new firms. In the survey of 100 new small manufacturing firms in the Nottingham area it was found that the majority (70 per cent) relied to a significant extent upon cheap second-hand plant and machinery to set up in business.[10]

The price of new plant and machinery which embodies the latest technological developments is much higher as it reflects more realistically the costs of their production. When the assets of a firm are sold the increase in supply involved of the particular type of machinery may be very large as compared with the demand for them. For someone who is considering starting up his own business, this source of cheap capital is naturally very attractive, particularly if start-up finance is quite limited.[11] The result, therefore, is that new entrepreneurs are more likely to enter those industries which are most severely affected by the recesssion, as it is there that the supply of cheap capital is often greater.

The impending or actual closure of firms provides a source of new entrepreneurs. These represent those who are 'pushed' into starting their own business; they are not enticed from their previous employment by a new idea or product innovation. This difference in motivation means that they are less likely to be innovative and more likely to refer to their previous experience in deciding what type of goods or service to produce and how to produce them. The relatively higher probability of plant and machinery with which they are familiar being available at lower prices is a further incentive to re-enter the industry which they have left, or a related product area.

Only a very small proportion of those who are made redundant, or who see the prospect as likely, set up their own business. In periods of recession, the proportion of new owner-managers who are pushed into business by these influences is much higher, however, and it is their typical choice of industry which is salient to the argument presented here.

(ii) Births cause deaths Evidence from the Nottingham survey indicates that most new owner-managers work a large number of hours for relatively little remuneration while their business becomes established. Many of the employees involved do the same because they perceive their own fortunes as being inextricably tied to those of the firm. Such low labour costs are usually regarded as a prerequisite for successful market penetration. The ability to maintain market share through strict quality control is naturally seen as a goal which can only be attained when that share has been established.

This combination of cheap plant and machinery and low labour costs enables this type of new firm to set very low prices. Older surviving firms in the same industry may still be required to service debts incurred by the purchase of plant and machinery at the much higher prices which prevailed prior to that industry's decline. They will also have established a more realistic scale of payment to their employees. Despite the fact that these older firms may be operating at or near their minimum unit costs, they may still be unable to lower their prices sufficiently to meet such competition without incurring losses and possible insolvency.

The extent to which this phenomenon occurs in practice is difficult to ascertain but its direction is clear. There is a potential for the displacement of firms whose previous viability has been undermined by the operation of short-term aberrations in factor markets. It is unlikely that medium-sized and large firms would be much affected in this way by new entrants but it may constitute a significant cause of failure among other established small-firm competitors. The high levels of births and deaths are to some extent explained by this 'turnover' of small firms.

(iii) Deaths cause deaths Firms cessations lead to further insolvencies more directly than in the manner described above. The selling off of the stocks of finished products of deceased firms at relatively low prices also presents problems to surviving firms in the same industry due to the short-term erosion of their market.

Conventionally the effects of a competitor's liquidation upon surviving firms in an industry can be interpreted as primarily beneficial. If market demand is stable or growing the survivors may increase their share; if it is declining their share will tend to decline less rapidly. In most situations this process of adjustment will tend to occur naturally as the previous customers of the deceased firm switch their custom to one or more of the survivors (assuming no new entrants). This will not occur, however, if some surviving firms are unable to cope with any short-term market erosion caused by the realisation of the deceased firm's finished product stocks at abnormally low prices. If more firms are pushed into liquidation in this way then an entirely different process can occur as remaining firms find it increasingly difficult to continue trading for long enough to experience the beneficial effects of longer-term market adjustment. Firm liquidations serve to pull surviving firms towards and maybe across the margin between survival and liquidation as a short-term phenomenon. Long-term adjustments may never arise.

The extent to which firms and industries are susceptible to this alternative experience of increasing market erosion depends upon various factors such as the volume of stocks involved, the prevailing market conditions and the number of firms near or at the margin of receivership and possible subsequent liquidation.[12]

A cumulative collapse of the industry would occur if each successive marginal firm were unable to accommodate the effects of the released stocks of preceding marginal firms. Industries characterised by larger firms with greater product diversification may be less vulnerable to this 'domino effect' than others which are not.

If the domino effect is successfully avoided in the short term then it is probable that the more familiar medium-term experience described earlier will obtain. The more it occurs unabated, the greater the threat of import penetration in the long run. In the event of a recovery in demand in the market concerned, the remaining domestic suppliers may be unable to respond sufficiently. In their attempts to resist the domino effect through price cutting and smaller profit margins they will have been less able to upgrade production techniques. Competition from foreign firms which have innovated such techniques would therefore be felt more severely, further hindering the modernisation of the domestic industry. Profit margins must still be reduced merely to ensure the firm's survival.

The present practice of firm insolvency can lead to the liquidation of others which are viable under more typical market conditions.

Each of the three causal links between firm births and deaths discussed above stems from the natural operation of market forces. Each serves to reduce the prospect of economic recovery based upon the reallocation of factors of production from less to more efficient usage. Existing firms are also confronted by a form of competition with which they are ill-equipped to cope because their own birth and growth occurred under very different economic conditions.

An aggregate analysis of new firm births and the level of economic activity

As indicated above it is commonly believed that there is a causal relationship between the level of economic activity and the number of new business enterprises created. This hypothesis may be stated more formally by asking whether changing levels of economic activity actually 'cause' the creation of new enterprise, and, as a natural extension, whether the creation of new enterprise 'causes' changes in the level of economic activity.

In practice it would be expected that the net change in new firm formations would reflect the balance between two separate reactions to economic recession. Firstly, those potential entrepreneurs with an innovative product or process may be less inclined to implement their ideas in a period of recession when markets are depressed and expectations pessimistic. This negative effect on firm formation will be counteracted by the second group who are pushed into owner-management through redundancy and job insecurity.

In the following empirical investigation no theoretical arguments or justifications are presented for the lag structures used in the final model. They are based purely on statistical relationships. This is not entirely satisfactory but an improvement on many of the past attempts to test this hypothesis which seem deficient on both theoretical and statistical grounds.

(i) The statistical concept of causality The concept of causality is understandably difficult to define in an operational way. For temporal systems there has been much debate between econometricians and statisticians of a suitable working definition. A commonly adopted approach is due to Granger (1969).

Granger's definition hinges on the idea of predictability. In its simplest terms, we may infer that a variable X causes Y, with respect to a given universe or information set that contains both, if using past and present X produces better predictions of Y than by not doing so, all other information in the universe being used in either case.[13] Operationally we cannot consider 'all other information in the universe' and so consider only present and past information on X and Y. X, then, causes Y if we can produce better predictions of Y by incorporating information on past and present X rather than using only information on past and present values of Y.

Even under the above restrictive definition one may be doubtful as to whether X causes Y because of the influence of third variables; for instance a variable Z may cause both Y and X but there be no direct relationship between Y and X. Y and X may now appear to be related in some causal way although it is really the variable Z which is the causal link. Further, basing the causal test on time-based information requires that the causal relationship between X and Y must itself follow an explicit time path. Thus, if X causes Y, the time lag between a movement in X and the induced change in Y must be roughly constant if a useful relationship is to be established.

(ii) Data There is no unique measure of the level of economic activity or of new firm creation. This study uses monthly data on the numbers of registered unemployed (excluding school leavers) and new company

registrations for 1971–82. It is customary in such studies where the forecasting ability of different models is being compared, for example the bivariate causal model with a univariate model, to retain some observations for post-sample model evaluation. Since the primary objective of the current paper is to ascertain whether any relationship exists between the level of economic activity and new company registrations, rather than evaluate the forecasting performance of different econometric and time-series models, all the sample information currently available is used for the purpose of estimation. Thus there are 144 observations available on each of the original series.[14]

The evidence already presented provides a prima facie case for using the level of unemployment as a measure of changing economic activity, and will then reflect the forces which both 'push' and 'pull' new entrepreneurs.

The data for new company registrations is considerably less satisfactory as a measure of new business creation, and the reasons for this are well documented.[15] A further complication in the series is the missing observations for March and April 1979 due to industrial dispute. The effect of this is not only to create a gap in the data but also to inflate artificially the number of firms registered for a number of months after. To overcome these problems it was decided to split the data into two parts using one to forecast forward over the missing and inflated observations and the other to forecast back, or backcast, over the relevant period.[16] The two forecasts so produced were then modified according to a standard maximum likelihood procedure to minimise the forecast error variance of each. The final 'best estimate' of the missing and inflated observation is then achieved by combining the two modified forecasts, weighting each by their respective forecast error variances, and standardising on the sum of the two respective error variances.

(iii) Testing for causality Given our definition of causality, it is appropriate to look for such relationships by cross-correlating the two series over different time lags, looking for significant correlations between the current value of Y and past value of X, and vice versa. However, ascertaining a significant correlation between two variables is not an indication of causality. It is possible for variables to be related in some functional sense but not to be correlated, or to display significant correlation through time but not to be causally related. The former case arises because of non-linearity in the functional relationship, the latter, and probably the more important, because of an association of each with other factors. Economic series have a tendency to move smoothly through time so that apparent but, in fact,

spurious correlations may arise simply because of trending.

Given this possibility it is incorrect to apply Granger's causality test unless one or both of the series are 'de-trended' or 'pre-whitened'. The objective of the pre-whitening process is to remove from each series any systematic elements it may display. This is usually achieved by identifying and estimating a univariate model for each series based solely on the past history of that variable, as developed by Box and Jenkins (1970).[17] When the correct models have been found the estimated residuals from the models should constitute a series of random errors with zero mean. Technically such a series is referred to as 'white noise', and implies that any estimated error, say ε_t, is uncorrelated with any other value of ε, past or future.[18] The two series so produced should be purged of any internal correlation, thus when we examine the relationships between the two series the calculated correlation should not display any of the spurious elements referred to above. If we denote the residual from the univariate model for Y_t as ε_t and that for X_t as a_t, a significant correlation between, say ε_t and a_{t-1} may be interpreted as information within a_{t-1} which may be used to model the error from the univariate model for Y_t, namely ε_t. Using the above correlation pattern it is possible to identify and estimate a model between ε_t and a_{t-1}. Substitution into this model for ε_t and a_{t-1} in terms of the original variables then yields a bivariate model structure between Y and X. Similar reasoning would apply to more complicated correlation patterns between ε_t and lagged a_t. The case where a one-way relationship exists between either ε_t and lagged a_t *or* a_t and lagged ε_t is referred to as 'unidirectional causality' whilst the more complicated situation where both ε_t and lagged a_t *and* a_t and lagged ε_t appear associated is called 'feedback'. Thus in terms of the variables under consideration unidirectional causality would exist if either: (i) unemployment is important in determining current or future new firm creation; or (ii) new firm creation is important in determining current or future unemployment. Feedback occurs when both (i) and (ii) are true.

(iv) The unemployment – new company registration relationship We now present the results obtained from carrying out the above type of analysis.

Table 2.1 presents the cross-correlation of the original data. At first sight these would indicate significant feedback between unemployment and new company registrations over quite long lags. However, as indicated above, these correlations cannot be used directly to infer a causal relationship, still less to reflect a lag structure for such a relationship. Indeed, such an interpretation would imply that higher (lower) levels of unemployment cause higher (lower) new company registrations and these in turn cause higher (lower) unemployment.

Table 2.1
Correlation between new company registrations and unemployment 1971–81

(a) Unemployment and lagged new company registrations

Lag	Value
0	0.649
1	0.631
2	0.394
3	0.585
4	0.357
5	0.561
6	0.523
7	0.474
8	0.459
9	0.449
10	0.411

(b) New company registrations and lagged unemployment

Lag	Value
0	—
1	0.644
2	0.638
3	0.624
4	0.611
5	0.601
6	0.595
7	0.587
8	0.573
9	0.556
10	0.541

To remove all internal trending and to reduce each series to stationarity[19] the following univariate models were identified and estimated by means of the Box–Jenkins methodology:

$$(1-0.594B-0.513B^2-0.271B^3)\,(1-B)\,NR_t = a_t$$
$$\quad(0.082)\ (0.086)\quad(0.084) \qquad\qquad \text{MSE} = 603512$$

$$(1-0.509B-0.167B^2-0.194B^3)\,(1-B)\,(1-B^{12})U_t$$
$$\quad(0.09)\quad(0.10)\quad\ (0.09)$$
$$= (1-0.609B^{12})\,\varepsilon_t \qquad\qquad \text{MSE} = 482.26$$
$$\quad(0.08)$$

where NR_t is new company registrations in time t; U_t is unemployment in time t; B is backshift operator; and a_t, ε_t are 'white noise' error series.

Thus the first differences of NR_t are regressed on the three previous differenced values, whilst unemployment is both first and seasonably differenced to produce a stationary series and then regressed on the three previous so adjusted values and a seasonal moving average term.

Whitened series are presented in Table 2.2.[20] These show a completely different picture. On the basis of Table 2.2(b) we may

Table 2.2
Cross-correlations of the univariate residuals

(a) 'Residual new company registrations and lagged residual unemployment'

Lag	Value
0	–0.022
1	–0.382
2	0.022
3	–0.034
4	–0.014
5	–0.049
6	–0.097
7	–0.038
8	0.079
9	–0.126
10	0.031
11	0.2269
12	–0.134

(b) 'Residual' unemployment and lagged 'residual' new company registrations

Lag	Value
0	—
1	–0.0006
2	0.102
3	0.078
4	–0.121
5	–0.048
6	–0.070
7	0.008
8	–0.039
9	0.078
10	0.125
11	–0.119
12	–0.066

reasonably conclude that there is no evidence to suggest that changes in new company registrations 'cause' unemployment, but there does appear some support for the hypothesis that changes in unemployment 'cause' new registration with a lag of one month, Table 7(a), i.e. we have unidirectional causality. Of particular interest is the negative coefficient in this relationship which implies that the residual element of unemployment is negatively related to the residual element of new company registrations with a time lag of one period. There is no evidence of instantaneous causality.

Thus in terms of the errors from the univariate models we may write this relationship as

$$a_t = \rho \cdot \varepsilon_{t-1} \tag{1}$$

where a sample estimate of $\rho \cdot$ is -0.382. A bivariate model, that is, where NR_t is dependent on both lagged NR_t and lagged U_t, may be obtained by substituting from the univariate model into (1). This model may then be estimated by ordinary least squares.

A disadvantage is that this manipulation often produces a pro-ponderence of parameters and explanatory variables. This can be reduced by being willing to omit any variables which have insignificant t-values and looking for common factors in the model.

The final model achieved was, in terms of the original variables:

$$NR_t = 1360.9 + 0.329NR_{t-1} + 0.23NR_{t-3}$$
$$(343.7) \quad (0.077) \qquad (0.076)$$
$$- 5.56 \, (U_{t-1} - U_{t-3}) + 0.806U_{t-12}$$
$$(1.37) \qquad\qquad (0.20)$$

$$\bar{R}^2 = 0.64$$
$$D\text{--}W = 2.083$$

Thus it may be concluded that the level of new business registrations is dependent upon the acceleration of unemployment over the previous quarter. This relationship is negative and this implies that an increase in unemployment would lead to a reduction in new firm formation. There is a small positive seasonal effect.

Conclusions and policy

From the above it is clear that new firms are unlikely to constitute a leading source of economic recovery in a period of severe recession. Market forces, in this situation, tend to draw new entrepreneurs into established and declining industries when a higher proportion of those entrepreneurs will have been pushed rather than attracted into owner-management. Econometric analysis reveals that, *ceteris paribus,* an acceleration in the level of unemployment dampens the rate of new company registration.

On the basis of these conclusions there is no evidence to suggest that there exists a natural mechanism by which economic recovery is caused by the birth of new firms.

Policy should address two main problems: first, the disincentive to enter new 'desirable' industries, and second, the tendency to set prices according to costs irrespective of what the market will bear. The first of these requires policy intervention with a view to both short-and long-term needs. In the short term it is necessary to render product and process innovations more attractive and accessible to new firms. In the longer term there is a need for much greater emphasis upon training, even at school level, and retraining in general. The second requires more basic training for new entrepreneurs in marketing, market appreciation and pricing. This might be better achieved if the multitude of sources of advice were rationalised, better coordinated and more effectively published.

In general, policy designers would be best employed in ensuring that the small-firms sector as a whole is able to meet the demand requirements which would arise in the event of a recovery. In order to do this, it is probably more appropriate to concentrate on overall policies like the Loan Guarantee Scheme, rather than aim to help certain preselected categories of firms. While the former is equally available to all small firms, the latter risks causing the displacement of firms which fail to qualify for aid but are in competition with those who do. In this case, the threat of displacement described earlier would be compounded by policy in the sense that the cost constraints facing some firms are artificially lowered.

It is important that the small-firms sector is able to respond in order to sustain any rise in the level of economic activity. Any constraints upon expansion due to a lack of venture capital, appropriate premises or adequate information and training should be alleviated where appropriate. There is little justification for the implementation of policies, the design of which is based upon the assumption that new and small firms can lead to economic recovery. This merely distracts attention from more realistic sources of economic change.

Notes

1. J.A. Schumpeter, *Capitalism, Socialism and Democracy*, Unwin University Books, London, 1966, p. 83.

2. Firm births are represented by new company registrations and do not include private unincorporated firms. It is assumed that the general pattern of these data reflects that of firm starts in total. Firm deaths are more difficult to measure than births. Many companies cease trading without formal liquidation proceedings. The use of these as a measure of firm deaths therefore involves considerable understatement, but again it is assumed that they reflect the underlying pattern of firm cessations. As a result of these imperfections in the data it is necessary to refer to the trends in firm births and deaths rather than their absolute levels.

3. S. Fothergill and G. Gudgin, 1982, p. 117–19.

4. Examples of the low prices these assets command have arisen from previous work by one of the authors. This research includes that undertaken for the Committee to Review the Functioning of Financial Institutions, in 1978, as detailed in their Research Report no. 3 and the recent ESRC-financed survey of 100 new small firms in the Nottingham area by the Small Firms Unit in the Economics Department at Nottingham University.

5. Cork, Sir Keith (chmn.), *Review Committee, Insolvency Law and Practice*, Cmnd. 8558, June 1982, p. 54.

6. Nottingham University Small Firms Unit, 1983.

7. Mittman and Morrison, 'Bankruptcies: Assets Often Can Be Picked Up at Bargain Prices', *Harvard Business Review* (July–August 1981), p. 155.

8. D.J. Storey, 1982, p. 112.

9. Nottingham University Small Firms Unit, 1983.

10. There is, to the authors' knowledge, no evidence to indicate that this is necessarily higher than that which obtained in the 1960s. Even if a similar proportion did obtain then, there are strong reasons to suggest that the nature of the second-hand capital markets would differ. With fewer liquidations in the 1960s and a buoyant economy, much of the second-hand market would tend to consist of plant and machinery sold by growing firms as they upgrade their stock of capital. This source contrasts greatly with the situation in the late 1970s and early 1980s, when almost all of the second-hand supply results from closures. Firms starting up in the 1960s with second-hand capital would be more likely to be buying into growing and successful industries than those doing the same now.

11. Nottingham Small Firms Unit Working Paper no. 2, "Finance For The New Firm".

12. The difference between receivership and liquidation is that the former is not necessarily final whereas the latter usually is. A firm entering receivership may continue trading in some form or other if its sale as a going concern is judged to be worth more than its liquidation.

13. Let Ω be the set of all available information at time t and $\Omega - \{X\}$ be the set of all information except for past and present values of X_t. Let $F(Y_{t+1}|\Omega)$ and $F(Y_{t+1}|\Omega - \{X\})$ denote the conditional distribution functions of Y_{t+1} for Ω and $\Omega - \{X\}$. We may then say that X causes Y if and only if $F(Y_{t+1}|\Omega) \neq F(Y_{t+1}|\Omega - \{X\})$.

14. The methodology detailed above requires quite large data sets if any form of reliable inference is to be made. A more detailed description of data requirements and the general principles of causality testing may be found in Ashley, Granger and Schmalensee (1980).

15. See R.T. Harrison and M. Hart, 'Factions Influencing New-Business Formation: A Case Study of Northern Ireland', *Environment and Planning* A, vol. 15, (1983), pp. 1400–3.

16. Simple 'eye-ball' inspection of the data suggested that the observations for the three months following the dispute were artificially high. Univariate models were then fitted for the period from January 1971 to February 1979 and from August 1979 to December 1982 to produce the forecasts referred to above.

17. Such models are of the general form $\Phi(B)x_t = \theta(B)a_t + \mu$ where $\Phi(B) = (1 - \Phi_1 B - \ldots - \Phi_P B^P)$, $\theta(B) = (1 + \theta_1 B + \ldots + \theta q B^q)$ and a_t is a random error, μ is a constant, B the backshift operator, such that $B^j x_t = x_{t-j}$ and x_t is a stationary derivative of the original series X_t.

18.
$$E\{\varepsilon_t\} = 0;$$
$$E\{\varepsilon_t, \varepsilon_{t-s}\} = \sigma_\varepsilon^2; \quad s = \emptyset$$
$$= 0; \quad s \neq 0.$$

19. A stationary process will have mean and variance that do not change through time and the covariance between value of the process at two time points will depend only on the distance between these time points and not on time itself.

20. In order to use these values to test hypotheses about causality events it is necessary to know, at least approximately, their sampling properties under the null hypothesis of independence between ε_t, a_{t-k} and a_t, ε_{t-k} over all k. It can be shown that one standard error is approximately $1/\sqrt{n}$, where n is the number of estimated residuals. (Granger and Newbold, 1977). An approximate 95 per cent confidence interval is then given by $\pm 2/\sqrt{n}$ which in the current study is $\pm 2/\sqrt{119} = \pm 0.18$.

References

Ashley, R., Granger, C.W.J., and Schmalensee (1980). 'Advertising and Aggregate Consumption: An Analysis of Causality', *Econometrica*, 48, 1149–67.

Box, G.E.P. and Jenkins, G.M. (1970). *Time Series Analysis Forecasting and Control*, San Francisco, Holden-Day.

Fothergill, S. and Gudgin, G. (1982). *Unequal Growth*, London, Heinemann Educational Books.

Granger, C.W.J., (1969) 'Investigating Causal Relations by Econometric Models and Cross Spectral Methods', *Econometrica*, 39, 424–38.

Granger, C.W.J. (1973). 'Causality, Model Building, and Control: Some Comments', presented at the IFAC/IFORS International Conference on Dynamic Modelling and Control, 9–12 July (University of Warwick).

Granger, C.W.J. and Newbold, P. (1977). *Forecasting Economic Time Series*, New York, Academic Press.

Storey, D.J. (1982). *Entrepreneurship and the New Firm*, London, Croom Helm.

3 The Financial and Capital Environment of the Small Firm

CLIVE WOODCOCK

The financial and capital environment of the small firm in Britain is generally considered to have undergone a vast improvement in the past few years, a view which receives apparent support from the vast range of schemes which has emerged both from local and central government as well as from the private sector. Whether the sheer proliferation of schemes represents a real improvement or whether they are even relevant to the needs of new and developing firms is open to question; what is certain is that this apparent growth in facilities for financing small firms has tended to encourage the growth of the belief that before the dawning of the small-business millenium all was darkness in the world of small-firm finance, that it was an economic dark age lightened only by the presence of the legendary — or mythical — Aunt Agatha, dispensing small but vital packets of risk capital, indeed of equity, to worthy entrepreneurs.

But in fact there has for many years been a substantial capital market for the small firm and indeed Aunt Agatha took many forms. Large numbers of firms came into existence every year, and still do, and they even develop and grow without ever coming into contact with institutional finance. The limited funds needed have come from savings, from relatives, and, probably one of the largest sources of all, the huge amounts of credit from suppliers of which they have been able to avail themselves. It has been estimated, for example, that in the 1970s, before the mushroom growth of schemes for small-firm finance from institutions, around £400 million per year was being raised in new risk funds.

These funds were being raised in the form of ordinary shares and directors' loans, with the cash coming from private investors because there were relatively few institutions actively in the market. There have been many examples of innovative methods of attracting finance, such as the manufacturer of golf clubs who sold shares on which dividends were paid in golf clubs rather than cash.

The delivery mechanism for investments of this kind has always been haphazard and probably always will be, although there are currently several attempts being made to improve upon this situation, the approved funds and investment registers being established in the wake of the Business Expansion Scheme — one of the major government measures in this field — being a good example but one with very considerable weaknesses. The principal weakness is that the funds raised by bringing together numbers of small investors are transformed; institutionalising informal or innovative ways of raising finance tends to narrow the avenues rather than broaden them.

This is because the agglomeration of cash becomes 'big money' and the fund managers look for projects with as little risk as possible and which are in need of relatively large sums of money. The result is that the very market which the Business Expansion Scheme and its predecessor were established to provide for, the firm which wants relatively small sums of money such as under £50 000 or even less than £20 000, is still not being served.

Equally, many of the different schemes from institutions such as banks have been repackagings of products which were previously available — and what was not perceived as being relevant before by the intended customer is still seen as not being relevant. The other aspect is that ingrained attitudes of managers take a long time to alter.

The value of any form of finance depends very much on the economic climate in which companies have to operate and that perhaps has not helped in recent years for either the special schemes or the tax changes to have the kind of beneficial effect which they might otherwise have done. It is debatable whether tax changes really help to encourage initiative and enterprise but taken together with other measures they can, to some extent, help in improving the general climate. The weakness of changes in tax legislation is that they have, almost without exception, been applicable entirely to the corporate small business, ignoring the fact that four out of five small firms are not incorporated and therefore unaffected by the changes.

It can, however, be argued that there has been insufficient time for the various measures which have been enacted — especially given the exigencies of the period — to have manifested their full benefits. Any review of changes in the financial and capital environment for small firms should therefore, first look at what action has been taken by the government — even though the sheer volume of measures may tax the capacity of advisers, trainers, and small-business people alike to absorb.

It may be said that a small company with a competent accountant will not be paying tax anyway but even so, the corporation tax regime is of more than passing interest, indicating as it does a climate of encouragement. Improvements have been made in successive Budgets, with the lower limit below which the special small-firms rate of corporation tax applies being raised to £100 000 with marginal relief up to £500 000 — beyond which companies move onto the full rate which itself will be reduced to 35 per cent by 1987. The rate of tax paid by small companies — a special rate — has been reduced to 30 per cent, at which it is expected to remain at least until 1987, as are the limits for that rate.

The threshold at which traders must register for value added tax (VAT) has also been successively raised but little attention has been paid to the argument that collection costs at the lower levels far outweigh the revenue and that complete exemption of small firms from VAT would be a cost-effective exercise. Relief is also now allowed for inflation when calculating capital gains tax so that a person who has built up a business and wishes to sell it on retirement faces a less punitive tax bill. Changes have also been made to capital transfer tax with higher initial rates as well as subsequent bands for both lifetime and death scales.

Perhaps one of the most important but least mentioned measures was that passed in the Companies Act, 1981, enabling companies to buy back their own shares in certain circumstances. This recognised the difficulties — or at least the perceived difficulties — faced by small unquoted companies in raising equity capital. A proprietor might be reluctant to allow outsiders to share in what he sees as the fruits of his enterprise on a permanent basis and similarly an investor might be reluctant to be locked into the shares of an unquoted or narrowly traded company from which it would be difficult to realise the cash. Letting a company buy back its own shares provides a means of buying out the interest of an outsider. In theory this should make it attractive for new and growing companies to overcome their resistance to balance their financial structure by taking in an appropriate share of equity capital but in practice this has not happened, at least not yet. Even the members of one of the more intelligent lobby groups, representing small to medium-sized firms mainly in manufacturing, have rejected vehemently the idea of equity participation, preferring better loan schemes instead.

In addition to changes in company and tax legislation of this kind the government has launched three major initiatives aimed at encouraging the development of small firms: the Enterprise Allowance Scheme; the Loan Guarantee Scheme; and the Business Expansion Scheme.

The Enterprise Allowance Scheme is an imaginative project — though for many it suffers from an excess of caution in its execution which makes it less effective than it might be — which was developed from a pilot scheme in five areas to cover the whole country from 1983 onwards. One of the main criticisms which has been levelled against it is that insufficient money has been allocated, limiting the numbers who can benefit. People participating in the scheme receive £40 a week for a year to offset less of unemployment or social security benefit while they are establishing their business. Applicants have to be receiving unemployment or security benefit and have been out of work or under notice of redundancy for at least 13 weeks.

One provision which is sometimes criticised is that participants must have at least £1 000 available to invest in the business. It can alarm potential clients but is not an insoluble problem by any means because the promise of a bank loan or overdraft facility for that amount can be considered as an intention to invest that amount in the business. There has also been evidence that the banks have taken a positive attitude towards the scheme in this respect. Places on the scheme are broadly allocated in line with unemployment in the regions. The fact that it has had rather less public attention focused on it than the loan guarantee scheme has probably contributed towards its steady progress and diverted many who might otherwise have drifted into the black economy into legitimate forms of business, encouraging some who might not have tried creating their own jobs at all.

Loan guarantee schemes have been in existence in different countries for some time though Britain did not introduce one until 1981 on a pilot basis for three years and then failed to realise that as a lender of last resort it might suffer losses, with the result that constant attention has been focused on the alleged weaknesses of the scheme and its — relatively small — cost rather than on its strengths. The result of this, with the government being alarmed at what others might consider success, is an uncertain future.

On the other hand, in both the United States and Canada there are moves to reduce activity in supporting small firms through soft loans and loan guarantee programmes, with the Canadian Small Business Minister — who holds Cabinet rank, unlike his British counterpart —

saying recently that he preferred to get out of the way of the businessman and simplify the tax and administrative burden, an example of which was the elimination of two-thirds of the tax laws applying to small businesses. He also said that weak management and the narrow equity base of small firms were rather seen as the major problems of small businesses, a statement which could equally be applied to the United Kingdom.

The UK Loan Guarantee Scheme had an initial allotment of £50 million a year for each of the three years of the pilot scheme but this was quickly raised in response to demand, though both the £75 000 upper limit for loans and the 3 per cent premium charged — with the idea of offsetting the cost of losses — were immediately criticised as being too low and too high respectively. An important characteristic of the scheme is that no personal security is needed, though banks are expected to take any business assets available as security.

For many borrowers this has been a major attraction of the scheme; for the banks, all of whom except the Co-operative Bank were less than enthusiastic about the scheme before it started, the attraction was that the government took 80 per cent of the risk in the event of failure compared with 20 per cent for the banks. During the three-year pilot period nearly 15,000 businesses borrowed almost £500 million, an apparent success, except that instead of being self-financing there was a shortfall of £40 million of premium income over claims, with one in three of those receiving loans failing.

A detailed report by chartered accountants, Robson Rhodes, criticised the handling of the scheme by the banks, saying that their appraisals of applications were not comprehensive enough and that later monitoring was inadequate, even that in half of the failures warning signals were clearly visible even before the guaranteed loans were provided. The banks responded that they were making loans and not equity investments and that criteria for appraisal of these were very different.

That same report was also sharply critical of the role of small firms' advisers, in particular accountants, for failing to educate their clients in the necessity for a balanced financial base on which to operate, and of borrowers themselves for their ineptitude and general lack of understanding of what business is about. It is a criticism which probably has a more general application than might be thought and lends credence to the suggestion that improvements in business knowledge, and financial management in particular, would obviate the need for many of the so-called special schemes aimed at the small business.

In the event, the extension of the Loan Guarantee Scheme brought with it a reduction in the guaranteed proportion of the loan to 70 per cent from 80 per cent and a sharp rise in the premium to 5 per cent from 3 per cent. An obvious result is a sharp drop in applications, both as banks become even less adventurous with more of their own money at risk and the increased cost to the borrower. The banks themselves charge anything from 1.5 to 2.5 per cent above base rate on loans in addition to the premium, making a guaranteed loan a very expensive one — though this is balanced by the fact that the loan might not otherwise be obtainable at all.

Even if the Loan Guarantee Scheme fails to survive — and there are few who would be prepared to lay a wager on its continued existence — it has had beneficial effects, not only as a rather cheap job creation scheme but also in the fact that it has probably helped to spark an entrepreneurial outlook in many who previously have been reluctant to risk everything and who, even though they may have failed the first time around, may have learned from the experience sufficient to enable them to succeed the next time around.

It is frequently said that the main weakness in the financial structure of small firms is their lack of equity finance, resulting in too high a gearing. While persuading small business owners of the benefits of equity investment is necessarily a long-term job, the government has sought to ensure that the funds for such investment are ready in place should the demand arise through schemes such as the Business Start-up Scheme and its successor the Business Expansion Scheme, an imaginative idea which has been slow to move in spite of its advantages over its ill-fated predecessor.

The Business Start-up Scheme (BES) never really got off the ground because it was rendered virtually incomprehensible and inoperable by the restrictions placed round it by the Inland Revenue in an attempt to prevent abuses. The BES, which was introduced in the 1983 Budget, appeared to get off to a good start in its first year by attracting some £40 million from small investors, but mainly into the approved funds set up by a wide range of financial institutions, from merchant bankers to stockbrokers and also including enterprise agencies. But by the second year the approved funds were finding it distinctly difficult to raise money from private investors, and many funds were under-subscribed.

On the whole, the regional and local funds which were expected to develop have so far failed to materialise though there have been one or two. Significantly, some investment management groups have noticed a tendency for potential investors to prefer to search out individual companies themselves instead of putting their money anonymously into a managed fund, to have a sense of participation; Aunt Agatha, it seems, is far from dead.

It is therefore possible that developments in the future will be towards individual investors becoming involved with individual firms or syndicates of the kind which has been set up on Merseyside by the enterprise agency in St Helens, the Community of St Helens Trust, where investments are held by individual members of the syndicate rather than by nominees and therefore retain a real involvement. Investments by this fund are also limited to between £20 000 and £50 000, far below the levels looked for by most approved funds and certainly more in tune with local needs.

An individual may also be inclined to be more adventurous in the choice of investment, a trait which has been noticeably lacking in the approved funds, which have largely looked at solid dependable investments and studiously avoided areas such as high technology.

The essential purpose of the BES is to channel funds from private investors into growing companies by giving substantial tax concessions to the investor, who can offset investments in the equity of most unquoted companies against his or her highest rate of personal tax up to a maximum of £40 000 per year. The investment must be held for at least five years to qualify for relief. A person taxed at the top rate of 60 per cent can therefore invest £20 000 in a qualifying company at a net cost of only £8000. (It is also often forgotten that the minimum sum which can be invested in a company is £500, so quite small investors can benefit from tax relief, too.) The returns from a successful investment can be substantial but even if an investor only receives the original stake back after five years the tax concessions will in fact have given a good return on the money.

For the company in which the money is invested there is the obvious benefit of reduced gearing as there is no pressure to pay dividends on the investment. In addition a firm which is expanding rapidly and using up cash quickly, perhaps on research and development, but which will produce returns much more slowly, could find the five-year time-scale of a BES investment especially useful.

Most of the BES-approved funds aim at realising their capital through flotations on the Unlisted Securities Market (USM); while most of those hopes will probably not be realised the USM has been a major development in capital markets for small firms.

The USM came into being in 1980 for a number of reasons, partly because of rising awareness of the need to give smaller firms access to wider capital markets with less cost and formality than a full Stock Exchange listing and partly because the Stock Exchange itself was concerned at the shrinking number of firms willing to go for a full quotation and at the rapid growth of dealings under its own Rule 163/2. This rule had been in existence for more than 30 years, allowing Stock Exchange members to carry out specific dealings in unlisted shares with prior approval through the normal mechanism of the market but without the company itself having to comply with the usual formalities beforehand.

Traditionally the rule had been used for infrequent dealings in the shares of such organisations as football clubs and small breweries; it had a regional character to it with local stockbrokers using their knowledge of the business scene in their own areas to match buyers and sellers of shares. In the late 1970s the rule began to be used more often as a result of publicity and the response gave rise to concern in the Stock Exchange that a facility for irregular dealings was growing into a substantial but unregulated market for which the Stock Exchange would receive the opprobrium if anything went wrong.

There have been some boom and bust companies in the USM's short history, but, more importantly, a number of companies have progressed on to a full listing on the Stock Exchange while others have found the USM sufficient for their needs and have continued their development within that framework, expanding the financing opportunities open to the smaller company.

The advantages for businesses are obvious, enabling owners or other shareholders to raise cash when the company joins the market and at any subsequent time, either through rights issues or otherwise increasing the equity base; in takeovers the firm can issue shares instead of paying cash or can pay with a mixture of both, reducing the cost of purchase; it can provide valuable incentives for employees through share option schemes. Furthermore, only 10 per cent of the share capital needs to be offered on the USM compared with 25 per cent for a full listing, and there is a huge difference between the cost of joining the USM and a full listing.

Oddly enough, now that the novelty of the USM has worn off there has been a further resurgence of interest in dealings under Rule 163 and activity is once more increasing there. An interesting feature of that growth is that it is being generated largely by regional stockbrokers who, as has been noted, were in any case its traditional users before the advent of the USM.

Another outlet for the firm which wants to raise or realise capital is the over-the-counter (OTC) market which is also experiencing very substantial growth. This was originally mainly the preserve of the investment bankers Granville and Co. (previously known as M.J.H. Nightingale) but they have been joined by several other market makers who have formed the British Institute of Dealers in Securities

(BIDS), under which name they quote share prices. On the OTC market markets for shares are made on a matched bargain basis. One of the advantages of a quotation on the OTC market is that new equity investment in an OTC-quoted company qualifies for tax relief under the Business Expansion Scheme, a facility which is not open to USM investments.

This is obviously a very considerable advantage but the OTC market is unlikely, as perhaps might have been expected, to obtain the bulk of the BES business because, as noted, there is a resurgence of business under Rule 163 — arising from stockbrokers who are bringing their clients together to invest in companies under the BES with the intention that dealings will be done under the 163 regulations. However, the main requirement now is to persuade small business owners of the value of equity participation; the equity capital market exists to provide for the demands.

The development of these markets might be considered as a very real and tangible manifestation of the growth of venture capital markets in Britain — though the definition of just what constitutes venture capital may present something of a problem. In the United States there is a fairly clear definition but in Britain it would not be unfair to say that it covers virtually all investments short of funding major public corporations.

Under this heading it is therefore possible to group the 100 or so organisations which describe themselves as venture capital companies, additional to the trading markets already mentioned. They range from firms backed by multinational institutions like Prudential Assurance such as Prutec and more recently Pruventure, to American venture capitalists bringing the expertise into the UK. Whichever it is, such companies are now investing more than £100 million per year in promising British enterprises. This growth has also really only occurred since about 1980, though there were a number of home-grown financiers before, such as the Small Business Capital Fund and the biggest of them all, ICFC.

The traditional role of merchant banks has been in advising companies and signposting them to appropriate sources of finance — at a price — but they have now moved from that and often instead invest in unquoted businesses themselves or place funds they are managing for institutions such as pension funds. A well-known name in this respect is Lazards, which manages BES funds as well as three regional funds backed by local authority pensions finance.

There is a considerable amount of money available in the venture capital field at present and so far there have not been enough major crashes to cause rethinking about investment in the smaller firm —

though a few nerves were tested by the collapse of a minicomputer firm in Wales with losses of around £8 million.

This perhaps falls into the area of high-technology funding which so many of the Business Expansion Scheme funds are so anxious to avoid. There has in fact been an increase in the number of specialist companies claiming that they have the expertise which enables them to assess proposals more effectively. There is a tendency for them to be associated with larger organisations such as Investors in Industry, Prudential Assurance, British Technology Group, and the Welsh Development Agency.

The one which has been longest in the field is the Ventures Division of Investors in Industry — of which ICFC is also a subsidiary — which has adopted a policy of active involvement in a limited range of high-growth companies, though it has in fact been funding technically based companies for many years under its earlier title of Technical Development Capital. The Ventures Division of Investors in Industry aims to transform promising new ideas into viable commercial products or services with technology-based projects a speciality.

The intention to invest in technological innovation for the benefit of British industry is not always as easy as it might sound, as Prutec, a subsidiary of Prudential, now merged with Pruventure, found, even though that was its original remit. Now it is looking further afield because of the difficulty of finding as many high-growth investments in the UK as it would like. On the other hand, it has had its fingers burned with the failure of the computer firm mentioned earlier. Prutec has two prongs to its efforts: it provides finance for projects in centres of technical excellence chosen for market potential and then places the products devised in host companies for the production and marketing process; and it invests directly at an early stage in high-technology ventures, taking a minority stake in the equity.

The government has, of course, at various stages made efforts to speed up the process of technological development and under the Conservative administration the two arms of this effort, the National Enterprise Board and the National Research Development Corporation were brought together to form the British Technology Group. BTG itself has had its role very much reduced in recent years but still plays a part in funding small firms.

It is also of interest to note that one of the clearing banks has gone further than the conventional response of having a few resident technical advisers to assess technological projects. Lloyds has developed a technology appraisal scheme for which no charge is made to the firms concerned; under this scheme technical and managerial assessments are provided for projects or products, including commercial and financial implications. The technical assessment is done by Cranfield Institute of Technology (CIT) while commercial implications are examined by both the bank and CIT. Whether this is an effective way of reducing the risks of investing in rapidly changing high-technology firms it is as yet too early to make a worthwhile assessment but it does indicate forward thinking in banking circles.

Substantial growth in funding opportunities for smaller firms has also occurred in an area which many often dismiss without full investigation because of imagined difficulties in obtaining it. This is the finance which is available under a number of headings from the European Community. There has been a considerable increase in the number of UK institutions through which funds are made available and also in many cases eligibility has been increased by the elimination of restrictions to assisted areas; furthermore the funds from Europe are often at lower interest rates than would normally be found on the open market. On the other hand, many of the lending institutions do not specifically lend EEC funds at lower rates, saying instead that European funds form a portion of other packages on which terms are easier than they might otherwise have been. Nobody doubts the honesty of the banks in this regard but it is hard not to sympathise with the small business owner who finds it hard to obtain the specific EEC finance which he or she has been told is less costly; it does sometimes seem like a matter of 'now you see it, now you don't'. Finance under all the various schemes is offered by ICFC while the clearing banks and development agencies offer assistance under one or more schemes.

In addition to the Scottish and Welsh Development Agencies European funds can also be channelled through the job-creation arm of British Steel, BSC Industry, which can not only arrange funds but also provides particularly useful advice and help in charting a way through the process of actually obtaining the money. It provides, in certain circumstances, low-cost loans on its own account as well.

The main sources of EEC finance are the European Investment Bank (EIB) and the European Coal and Steel Community (ECSC), though the European Social Fund has become more active, too. Small firms cannot actually deal directly with either the EIB or the ECSC but have to go through the banks and other institutions which act as agents and pay out the funds to qualifying applicants.

The EIB has been the Community's provider of long-term finance from the outset but for most of its life has been involved with funding infrastructure projects. In recent years, however, it has increasingly turned its attention to the encouragement and growth of small firms. Its funds were originally available only to businesses in the assisted areas but this restriction has now been lifted, though there are lower interest rates for those in the assisted areas. Assistance from the ECSC is specifically for projects in those parts of the country where the jobs of coal and steel workers are disappearing through pit and plant closures and contractions. Special emphasis has again been given by ECSC to the smaller firm in recent years. The areas in which its grants and loans are available are still restricted to coal and steel closure areas, but in the interests of flexibility and a genuine desire to help, these coal and steel closure areas have been deemed to extend some surprising distances.

Additionally, the jobs provided in the firms receiving finance have only to be suitable for former coal and steel workers and do not necessarily have actually to be filled by former miners or steel workers. Loans from ECSC are based on £10 000 per job created up to half of the fixed-asset element of a project, and as well as interest rates below market levels, there can be a further reduction in interest charges of 3 per cent for the first five years.

EIB loans at or near market rates are available for sums of between £15 000 and £250 000. The loans are usually available for firms in manufacturing and selected service or tourist activities, though if a tourist project is not in an assisted area it does not stand much chance of succeeding. Attempts to help the gearing of firms are made by waiving capital repayments for the first two years of a loan though the balance has to be repaid in instalments every six months over a six-year period. Many other different types of funds can be obtained from EEC sources, such as training grants, coal conversion loans where a firm converts from oil-or gas-fired boilers to coal, but help is often needed in tracking them all down and working out the best package, which is where the help of organisations such as BSC Industry and the development agencies is invaluable.

Another baffling maze for the small firm operator is the huge array of government aid which still exists in spite of the efforts by the Conservative administration to cut it back. This aid can be in the form of regional assistance or through specific schemes for particular industries or special developments such as microprocessor applications or computer-aided design and manufacturing. Regional aid policies have undergone considerable changes, though they still fall into three broad categories: those related to the location of the project and those which depend on the sector of industry or type of activity involved – but the number of assisted areas have been reduced, while aid dependent on location has been severely restricted.

This, in fact, is probably one area where the market for small-firm finance is changing for the worse, though at the same time it is probably one which has not been much used by the smaller firm in the past because the effort required to obtain it has often not been worth the benefits gained in the end.

No review of the financial and capital environment for the small firm would, of course, be complete without looking at the role of the banks who remain, in spite of all other developments, the major providers of finance for small firms through their huge branch networks in the form of overdrafts and short-, medium-and long-term loans. The banks have not in the past generally been providers of long-term loans but they have moved increasingly into this field and have met a response which indicated that there was a need. Their efforts to move into the provision of equity finance has not made the same kind of impact, however, though this is not entirely surprising in view of the general reluctance of businesses to take in equity partners.

One area into which banks have been moving is joint schemes with local authorities and development agencies such as the Council for Small Industries in Rural Areas (CoSIRA). National Westminster, for example, set up a joint scheme with CoSIRA — which has its own very limited loan fund — under which the agency's clients benefit from a reduction in the rate of interest otherwise payable to the bank and a lower arrangement fee, while the bank benefits from initial appraisals being carried out by CoSIRA as well as monitoring. The Co-operative Bank has been involved in local authority joint ventures incorporating a guarantee element, the guarantee being provided by the local authority, for loans up to £50 000 at preferential interest rates.

One bank scheme which seems to soldier on for ever is National Westminster's Business Development Loan for loans from £2000 up to £250 000 for one to 20 years. Lending on this scheme has now totalled well in excess of £1 billion.

Others may not be able to claim such massive sums lent but new ideas have been developed, for example, by Lloyds which has revised its schemes aimed at the smaller firm and introduced a novel interest-rate conversion option which allows long-term borrowers to switch every five years from fixed rate to a rate linked to base rate or vice versa, combining the benefits of fixed interest rates but without being locked in at that level for the long term when interest rates might be falling.

While banks have always offered a full range of services for exporting companies there have been improvements aimed particularly at the smaller firm, led by Midland and followed more recently by Barclays and the Co-operative Bank. As ECGD policy-holders themselves the banks take much of the administrative work off the company with small or perhaps intermittent export sales and the customer deals simply with his own bank in insuring against the risks of not being paid.

In addition to these sources of finance there has grown up a number of local authority investment funds, sometimes through the economic development companies set up by those authorities and sometimes from their pension funds. Other authorities have developed interest-rate subsidy schemes with financial institutions such as ICFC to help encourage small firms in particular localities, realising that they too have a role to play in job creation.

The more informal providers of finance have also moved heavily into the small business field with finance companies, factors and leasing companies now providing an increasing proportion of the needs of smaller firms, especially as more of these firms attain a greater degree of sophistication in their financial planning. The tendency of customers to become slower and slower payers during the recession has helped many companies to look at the facilities offered by factors, for example; initially they have used it as simply a way of speeding up payments — factoring basically being an arrangement to sell trade debts — but have then moved on to using those services as an integral part of their cash-flow planning. This has been particularly noticeable among fast-growing companies.

Financial and capital markets for the smaller company have expanded substantially in recent years and the supply probably outstrips the demand at present and has not produced the results which might have been expected. On the other hand the major benefits will probably only emerge as smaller companies attain a greater degree of sophistication in financial management generally and learn how to use properly what is available. In the meantime what was previously a lack of knowledge, an information gap, on finance has been replaced by the bewilderment factor as small-firm managers wonder where to start in sorting out what is being thrust at them.

4 Surviving the Financial Stress of Small Enterprise Growth

PATRICK HUTCHINSON AND GRAHAM RAY

Growth often produces financial stress for small enterprises and the objectives of this paper are to consider the effects of growth on the financial management of the small enterprise, to examine the stressful financial profile of 'supergrowth' enterprises, to investigate the role of financial control in dealing with this financial stress and to consider the implications for financial institutions and entrepreneurs. The paper makes use of empirical evidence collected during an SSRC project carried out at Bath University between 1975 and 1979 and seeks to relate this to the general theories of finance and financial control with particular reference to small enterprises. A more detailed account of the financing and financial control of small enterprise development, including the research method for the Bath studies, can be found in Ray and Hutchinson (1983).

The effects of growth on the financial management of the small enterprise

Previous studies

There have been a number of studies which have investigated small firm finance. Some studies by, for example, Singh and Whittington

(1968) and Davis and Yeomans (1974), have explored the issue of size in relation to profitability, changes in government credit policy, and influence on the discounts of issue prices. These studies have, however, been concerned with relatively large quoted companies. Other studies by, for example, Hart with Bates (1965) and Bolton (1971), have looked at unquoted private firms but have analysed the data involved on a cross-sectional basis rather than in terms of changes over time. The more in-depth longitudinal studies that have been conducted by, for example, Stanworth and Curran (1973) have concentrated on behavioural rather than financial aspects.

The Bath studies, carried out between 1972 and 1979, were concerned with the financing and financial control of small, rapidly growing enterprises up to flotation. Whilst not longitudinal in the strictest sense, that is involving a continuous observation of the phenomena concerned, the studies involved a retrospective analysis of the financing and financial control of small enterprises over a period of their lives up to flotation. The final samples taken consisted of 66 firms, 33 of which started small and grew to achieve a London Stock Exchange flotation between April 1968 and March 1973. In order to make the generalisations more meaningful, a matched sample of relatively passive small firms which did not grow to flotation was taken for comparison purposes. The data collected were in the form of sets of financial accounts of the individual firms for each of up to ten years prior to flotation and the replies to a structured interview involving a questionnaire. The purpose of the questionnaire was to provide further details and explanations to the accounts and to raise issues about financing not revealed in the accounts.

The 33 small enterprises in the Bath sample experienced 'supergrowth' in the period up to their eventual stock market flotation. The average (median) total assets for these firms was £110 000 as gleaned from their earliest available accounts up to ten years prior to flotation. Nearly half (16) of the firms had been established with less than £1000 capital. The average sales turnover was £177 000. At flotation the average total assets were £1.5 million and average sales were £2.5 million. Average growth rates become almost meaningless for the sample, including as it did firms which grew from total assets and sales of less than £1000 to millions of pounds. All the firms had growth rates in sales far above those for the Bolton Committee's sample of fast growth firms (15 per cent per annum for manufacturing firms, 10 per cent per annum for non-manufacturing firms).

By comparison the matched sample of firms which did not go public grew from average total assets of £216 000 to £348 000 for the same period. The matched sample sales turnover increased from an average of £336 000 to £437 000. Most matched firms fell within the range between the Bolton Committee's definition of fast growth firms and slow growing firms (stationary or declining sales).

The 'traditional' view

The Bath studies were concerned with testing empirically the traditional view of financing of small enterprises. Table 4.1 shows, in a modified form, the traditional view of the financial life-cycle of the small growing firm, as found in the finance textbook by Weston and Brigham (1978), one of the few finance texts to include a chapter on small firm finance. Table 4.1 identifies the potential financial stress factors which can arise with growth.

Table 4.1
The traditional view of the financial life-cycle of the firm

Stage	Source of Finance	Potential Stress Factors
Inception	Owners' resources	Undercapitalisation
Growth I	As above plus: retained profits, trade credit, bank loans and overdrafts, hire purchase, leasing	'Overtrading' Liquidity crises
Growth II	As above plus: longer-term finance from financial institutions, e.g. ICFC	Finance gap
Growth III	As above plus: New Issue Market	Loss of control
Maturity	All sources available	Maintaining R.O.I.*
Decline	Withdrawal of finance, firm taken over, share repurchase, liquidation	Falling R.O.I.*

* R.O.I. = return on investment

It is important to focus on the stress factors encountered by small enterprises as they grow to flotation since most current issues in finance are concerned with testing theories related to what could be described as the 'mature' firm, namely a large, privately owned company quoted on the stock exchange. In the case of the large firm the main financial issues surround the optimisation of the financial function. This takes the form of the financial management of funds and investments in such a way as to maximise shareholder wealth. This leads to the pursuit of the optimisation of the financing mix, working capital management, investment decisions and dividend policy all with a view of the market assessment of the risk/return profile of the firm as ultimately embodied in the capital asset pricing model. These issues may not have the same significance for small enterprises which may be primarily concerned with the process of raising finance and dealing with the financial stresses of growth.

The representation of the financing life cycle of the firm as shown in Table 4.1, whilst plausible, has not been subject to extensive empirical testing. This traditional view has, however, many implications for what is to be expected in the financial profile of firms as revealed by their accounting data and in their financial experiences. This should be revealed in their accounting ratios in the form of low liquidity, high profitability, high gearing, and so on, and in the nature of their problems in raising finance. The next section provides empirical evidence of the stressful financial profile of rapidly growing small enterprises.

The financial profile of 'supergrowth' small enterprises

In this section the financial profiles of the Bath study's sample of small, 'supergrowth' enterprises is investigated up to the point of their stock market flotation. This profile was established using the questionnaire and accounting data collected from the 'supergrowth' enterprises which went public and the matched sample of small enterprises which did not grow to stock market flotation. In addition comparisons were made with other relevant data from an Industrial and Commercial Finance Corporation (ICFC) report (1970) and the Bolton Committee Research Report No. 16 (Tamari 1972).

The accounting data collected from the firms in the study were analysed using ratios. In selecting the ratios for analysis the objective was to arrive at the minimum number of ratios which provided coverage of the areas of interest and which yielded the maximum useful comparison with other studies. The main areas of interest in this study were liquidity, profitability and gearing.

The ratio chosen for liquidity was the net working capital (current assets less current liabilities) as a percentage of total assets (current assets plus fixed assets less depreciation). Profitability was looked at in three different ways. Profitability in terms of return on investment was measured by calculating earnings before interest and taxation as a percentage of total assets. Profit in terms of income generation was measured by expressing sales as a percentage of total assets. The final measure of profitability was accumulated retained profits (revenue reserves) as a percentage of total assets. This ratio is important for small firms as it reflects the fact that small, growing firms are vulnerable because of lack of equity reserves which reduces their ability to raise finance. Finally financial gearing was measured as the percentage of the book value of the equity to the book value of total debt (long-term and current).

Having arrived at a list of ratios it was necessary to decide what comparisons to make. Comparisons can be made over time and between firms. In this study the comparisons over time were done in two ways. An analysis was made of the ratios aggregated for the firms over a period of calendar years. An analysis was also performed on a 'lifetime' basis for the period up to flotation, counting the figures which covered flotation as being in period nought and counting back to period minus five. The importance of the 'lifetime' analysis is its relevance to testing the traditional view of the financing of the firm which predicts that the financial profile is determined by the stage of development of the firm. The importance of the comparison with calendar year figures is to establish that any trends in the figures for the firms which went public were in fact due to their special situation and not general economic factors.

In making comparisons with other groups of firms the objective was to ascertain the extent to which the profiles of firms which went public were distinctive. The comparisons made were between the matched sample of small firms which did not go public, the Bolton Committee's figures for small fast growing firms and slow growing firms, and the sample of ICFC-financed firms. These comparisons enable the small firms which grew to flotation to be compared with a wide range of other firms.

Table 4.2 provides a summary of the financial profiles of 'super-growth' enterprises along with those of the matched firms and the Bolton and ICFC firms' figures. Also included are figures for bankrupt and non-bankrupt firms taken from Altman (1968) which help provide a perspective on the range of figures possible. In terms of the ratio of net working capital to total assets, the 'supergrowth' firms were more liquid than only Altman's group of bankrupt firms. In fact many of the 'supergrowth' firms had negative working capital during the period. The ratio of retained earnings to total assets shows the 'supergrowth'

Table 4.2
Comparative average ratios (%)

Ratio	Bath Small Firms		Bolton Small Firms		ICFC	Altman's Firms	
	'Supergrowth'	Matched (Passive)	Fast Growers	Slow Growers		Bankrupt	Non-bankrupt
Net working capital/total assets	13	16	22	36	30	−6	41
Retained earnings/total assets	21	27	20	28	31	−63	35
EBIT/total assets	16	10	12	8	11	−32	15
Equity/total debt	92	196	85	172	122	40	248
Sales/total assets	225	182	240	197	165	150	190

firms sharing a relatively low figure with the Bolton fast growing firms ahead of the bankrupt firms. The ratio of EBIT to total assets puts the 'supergrowth' firms at the top of the league. That of equity to total debt again puts the 'supergrowth' firms low down along with the Bolton fast growth firms again ahead of the bankrupt firms. Finally, the ratio of sales to total assets puts the 'supergrowth' firms next highest to the Bolton fast growing firms. The financial profile of the 'supergrowth' firms is therefore established as consisting of low liquidity, low retained earnings and low equity to debt, much closer in this respect to the profile for bankrupt firms than the profile for less rapidly growing small firms. On the other hand, the 'supergrowth' firms are the most profitable.

Since Table 4.2 presents average figures, it conceals much of the data relating to the calendar year and lifetime analysis which were carried out as part of the Bath studies. The following subsections consider these important dimensions.

Liquidity

The traditional view of the financing of the firm suggests that the small growing enterprise will experience liquidity problems because of the lack of access to capital markets. This will cause greater reliance on short-term sources of finance such as trade creditors and bank loans and consequently be reflected in a lower proportion of net working capital to total assets. The 'supergrowth' small firms which went public did have very low liquidity. Indeed, of these 33 firms 18 experienced periods of negative net working capital.

The question that arises is whether the figures for the firms which went public could have been affected by other factors such as general economic climate or by the particular circumstances of the firms. The questionnaire data revealed that the owner-managers of the 'super-growth' firms did not associate financial stress points, resulting in low liquidity, with periods of 'credit squeeze'. The more likely explanation, therefore, lies in the circumstances of these firms which experienced very rapid growth. This was also borne out by the comparisons made with the ICFC companies.

As the traditional view predicts, liquidity was found to be particularly strained in the period up to flotation, improving as the firm achieved a quotation. The trend was different from that for the matched sample of firms but these firms also experienced low average liquidity. The matched sample of modest growth firms which did not go public may have been putting their liquidity under particular strain because of an inability or unwillingness to raise long-term loans. The 'supergrowth' firms, in order to maintain their very high growth rates, not only made maximum use of short-term debt but also long-term debt.

Profitability

In order to grow to reach a stock market flotation a small firm must be profitable. The firms which went public showed a strong upward trend in profitability culminating in a high figure of 21 per cent in the year prior to flotation. It is unlikely that such a trend could be maintained and this could be one of the explanations for a drop in profitability in the year of flotation. The objective of going public at the peak of profitability may well have been pursued by the owners of the 'supergrowth' firms. The drop in profitability in the year of flotation could also have been due to a disproportionate increase in assets when the firms went public and to the costs of flotation.

Accumulated profit, in the form of reserves, is important for small firms. The reserves of a firm will, in part, determine its ability to raise further funds and has been found to be useful in financial analysis in measuring financial stress (Altman 1968). The traditional view suggests that the pressure on retained earnings would occur in the period prior to the run up to flotation. This was borne out in the lifetime analysis, where the effects were seen of the very high profitability catching up with asset growth to improve the reserves of the 'supergrowth' firms. There was a fall in the proportion of retained profits at flotation, again likely to be due to a disproportionate increase in assets, financed by issues of shares and debt finance. The matched sample firms' figures did not show the same trend but fluctuated very gently upwards, as would be expected from modestly growing firms which did not experience the same stresses.

Finally, with regard to profitability, having established the high level of profit generated by the small firms which grew to flotation, it is useful to investigate whether this high profitability was primarily due to high profit margins, high asset turnover, or a combination of high margin and high turnover.

A strong surge in asset turnover was experienced by the 'supergrowth' firms in the years prior to flotation. The asset turnover was well in excess of that for the matched sample, for which sufficient figures were only available for four years prior to flotation, except in the last year before and the actual year of flotation. Whilst the turnover figures declined in the last two years before flotation, the return on investment was maintained up to the actual year of flotation, when it dropped. The reason for this maintenance of high return on investment was a great increase in the profit margin of these 'super-growth' firms which increased to over 10 per cent in the last two years prior to flotation, more than twice as high as for the matched firms. It would appear that, as these firms approached flotation, their profiles changed from fairly high margin and very high turnover to very high margin and fairly high turnover. Whether this is due to any inevitable consequence of the growth process or whether it is due to increased efficiency through greater financial control, cannot be answered from the figures. The issue of the development of financial control systems is, however, discussed in more depth in the following section.

Gearing

The traditional view of the financing of the firm predicts that in order for growth to be sustained the firm will have to raise additional finance. It has already been seen, from the figures for net working capital, that the 'supergrowth' enterprises which went public made extensive use of short-term finance, with the rule of thumb of equal amount of debt and equity being violated by the 'supergrowth' enterprises. The 'supergrowers' made much more extensive use of debt, particularly long-term debt. The reliance of the matched sample on short-term financing was not much less than that of the 'super-growth' firms. The great difference in the relationship between equity and debt, twice as high for the matched firms, was due to the lack of use of long-term debt finance by the matched firms. Indeed, of the 33 small firms which did not go public, 17 firms had no long-term debt whatsoever.

The 'supergrowers' started to make extensive use of long-term debt finance as they approached flotation. From five years before flotation, the great reliance on short-term debt lessened, and the proportion of equity to debt only rose in the year prior to flotation. The explanation lies in the increased use of long-term debt during this period of four years. It would therefore appear that the major difference in financing between the fast growing small firms which achieved quotation and the matched sample of more modestly growing small firms, which did not, lies in the use of long-term debt. The crucial question raised by the traditional view is whether a lack of ability to raise long-term debt finance is a cause of slower growth. In order to answer this question it is necessary to discover whether the matched firms had experienced a 'finance gap'.

The questionnaire data revealed that there was no general com-plaint of the existence of a finance gap, either in terms of availability of funds or financial advice, by either the 'supergrowth' enterprise which grew to flotation or those which did not. The major reason given by the small firms which did not achieve flotation for not so doing was that this would require growth that was not wanted or not feasible.

These findings confirm the view of the Bolton Committee that there was no institutional deficiency in the finance market. To some extent the findings cast doubt on the Bolton Committee's recommendation for the establishment of Small Firms Advisory Bureaux to help remedy the 'information gap' since this gap was not perceived by either the small enterprises which grew to flotation nor by those that did not.

Financial control of 'supergrowth' enterprises

Having now established that the financial profile of the "supergrowth" firms consists of low liquidity, low retained earnings to total assets and low equity to debt, the question arises as to how such firms manage the massive 'overtrading' which, according to prescriptive texts, is a situation to be avoided. In particular, are the characteristics of the financial control system of such firms very different from those of less successful firms? In this section the focus of attention will be on the particular problems involved in designing, developing and maintaining appropriate financial control systems during the development of the small enterprise in order to cope with financial stress.

Financial control systems exist to ensure that the economic resources of an organisation are used effectively and efficiently in the pursuit of the organisation's goals. The financial control system is one of a number of subsystems, such as production, marketing and manpower, which are concerned with administrative control. Each of these subsystems has a structure and process. So far as the financial control system is concerned there is a structure of internal accounting which involves the use of responsibility centres such as company, expense, revenue, profit and investment centres. The process of financial control is the provision of historical and forecasted financial information, usually with a core of balance sheet and profit and loss account data, which concerns the allocation of resources, the measurement of performance and the communication and review of results.

A number of authors, such as Dermer (1977) and Anthony and Dearden (1980), have suggested that financial control systems are situationally determined. This means that the structure and process of financial control systems are variables which are contingent on other factors. Ray (1980) identified seven factors which affected the financial control system, namely: corporate goals, key result variables used to

Table 4.3
Summary of financial control characteristics and contingent factors of entrepreneurial and passive firms

	Entrepreneurial ('Supergrowth')	Passive (Matched)
In pursuit of		
objectives	Maximise profits, increase turnover	Less emphasis on maximising profit more on independence
working through an		
organisational structure	'Tree' organisation, development of teams, 'clover leaf' emerging	'Tree' in well-established firms
with a		
style of management	Autocratic becoming more consultative	Paternal
there evolves a		
structure of internal accounting	Increasing movement to profit centres	Less emphasis on profit centres
which provides		
historical data	Monthly or weekly profit and loss and balance sheet items	Very similar to entrepreneurial firms
and		
forecasted data	Trend to monthly information particularly strong on cash flow	Very little emphasis
which monitors		
key variables	Cash-flow, profitability, sales	More emphasis on supplier relationships

monitor performance, corporate culture, the environment, technology, organisation structure and organisation process.

Whilst the above classification is useful in providing a descriptive contingency framework of financial control it is necessary to have criteria by which financial control systems can be assessed in terms of their effectiveness and efficiency. Ray (1980) suggests four criteria, namely: consistency, consonance, flexibility and educability. An efficient financial control system will be consistent with other sub-systems and will also be internally consistent. In a fully integrated computerised management information system such consistency is an integral part of the design of the system and the output of one suite of programs, for example concerning marketing, becomes the input of a suite of programs covering other operations which in turn produces an output which is the input for accounting routines. There is also a substantial body of research (e.g., Lorsch and Morse, 1974) which provides evidence that when the financial control system is consonant with the factors which impinge on it, such as goals and organisation structure and process, then this leads to more efficient matter/energy processing, more effective information processes and greater stability.

It is conceivable, however, that in the short and medium term a financial control system might be consistent and consonant and yet, in the long term, might not have the capacity to adapt to changing environmental demands. In a turbulent dynamic environment the main criteria for effectiveness are therefore likely to be flexibility and adaptability. Finally, educability is an important criterion in order that errors detected in terms of consistency, consonance and flexibility can, in fact, be corrected.

Table 4.3 summarises the key features of the financial control systems of the 'supergrowth' entrepreneurial firms and the matched 'passive' firms resulting from the Bath studies. The following sub-sections provide an explanation of these results and include observations by the Bolton (1971) on various aspects of financial control.

Objectives and key variables

The evidence of the Bolton Committee Report emphasised the underlying motivation of small businessmen as the 'need to attain and preserve independence', and commented that

> the desire for independence appears to be over-riding and indeed may on occasions even operate against their own economic interest. Many businessmen in small firms recognise that money is not their prime motivation . . . Many owner managers of small

firms recognise that, should their business expand beyond a certain point, they would then be obliged to engage supervisory staff, take a partner and have recourse to external sources of finance, all of which would inevitably lead to some loss of independence.

The passive firms in the Bath study also rated independence highly. The evidence from the 'supergrowth' enterprises is strikingly consistent and, by comparison, strikingly different. The objectives of maximising profits and increasing turnover predominated, and applied just as firmly in the early days when the firms were struggling to avoid making losses, as later when a public quotation had been obtained. The objective of 'being independent' was mentioned by only a small minority of these entrepreneurs, and growth at all times was welcomed as an opportunity and not frowned upon as a threat. The objectives of maximising profit and increasing turnover were accompanied in the entrepreneurial firms with an emphasis on cash-flow, profitability, sales and relations with customers as key variables.

Organisational structure and style of management

The Bolton Committee noted that

> one of the outstanding characteristics of the small firm is the simplicity of its management structure. The typical small firm is directly managed by its owners, who themselves take nearly all important decisions and probably oversee their execution as well . . . Only in the larger firms in our size range is there a subordinate managerial structure . . . This direct dependence on the proprietor in every facet of the detailed running of the business is the source of most of the strengths, and many of the weaknesses . . . They run their business on the basis of their experience and commonsense. This may be effective so long as the scale of the firms' activities remains small enough for one man to control them all effectively, and so long as no serious crisis overwhelms his pragmatic management. Either of these eventualities, however — significant growth or a need to consider drastic changes in the firm's policy — is likely to reveal a need for certain specialist skills which are most unlikely to be found within the average small firm.

Again, the evidence for the 'supergrowth' enterprises is different from the average small firm. From the earliest years a significant number of firms identified their organisation structure to be of the 'tree' type. In other words, at a very early stage, in a minority but significant number of entrepreneurial firms, a subordinate managerial structure existed. This number increased together with those which identified their organisation structure as of the 'clover leaf' type (a more refined structure) during the rapid growth period so that by flotation the 'hub and wheel' structure no longer predominated. The vast majority of entrepreneurial firms identified the creation of a team as a crucial factor in their success, which allowed them to deal with their rapid growth. The evidence suggested that the organisation structure of the entrepreneurial firms, even from a very early stage, was different from the organisation structure of the passive firms for whom the 'tree' type of organisation predominated and unlike the entrepreneurial firms, showed little inclination towards a 'clover leaf' structure.

The Bolton Committee does not give any direct evidence of the style of management practised by the average small business, but we can infer that no evidence was produced for the existence of 'consultative' and 'participative' styles which are often noted in large companies. By deduction, the 'authoritative' and 'paternal' style can be inferred to predominate, and in this regard the small rapid growth firms are not different since these two personal styles predominate up to flotation, and even four years after flotation a bare majority of the firms still identified these as predominating styles of management. However, the style of management in the passive firms was more likely to be paternalistic than in the entrepreneurial firms where the style was more authoritarian, becoming more consultative around the time of flotation.

Structure and type of internal accounting

With regard to the structure of internal accounting, the Bolton Committee reported that

> cost control and cost data are often so poor that management frequently learns of an impending crisis only with the appearance of the annual accounts or following an urgent call from the bank manager. In less serious cases lack of costing data may make it impossible to gauge the effects on profits of different levels of activity or courses of action, especially where there is a variable product mix.

The findings for the entrepreneurial firms showed that from the early

The findings for the entrepreneurial firms showed that from the early years a significant and increasing minority of firms were structured into cost centres and profit centres and, in the period of rapid growth leading to flotation, this applied to a majority of firms. The passive firms made less use of profit centres.

The provision of historical and forecasted information was commented on by the Bolton Committee, which observed that 'credit control and stock control information is often inadequate', and that 'ignorance or mistrust of developments in this field [information use and retrieval] such as the introduction of new simple business machines and the use of data processing bureaux make it difficult for some small businessmen to follow the detailed progress even of their own firm'. From the early years in the entrepreneurial firms, the elements of the historical profit and loss account and balance sheet were reported upon, for the most part, monthly or weekly. In the take-off and rapid growth period prior to flotation this substantial base of regular monthly historical information was reinforced by an increasing tendency to produce regular monthly forecasted information. This substantial base of historical and forecasted information gave sound credit control, stock control, product cost control and, in particular, control over cash-flows, from the early days when many firms were making losses and also during the period of exceptionally rapid growth. The regular supply of this accounting information could not have been achieved without access at a very early stage in development to both data processing facilities and also to an accountant, who first of all acted as a 'scorekeeper' and provided regular and detailed historical information and then, particularly in the take-off period, provided an increasing volume of forecasted information.

The provision of historical information did not differ significantly between the entrepreneurial firms and passive firms but dramatic differences existed in the provision of forecasted information of all types, both for elements of the balance sheet and of the profit and loss account. This can probably be explained by the fact that the entrepreneurs wished to increase market shares; accordingly they set objectives and moved towards them. In these circumstances forecasts were exceedingly relevant. On the other hand, the passive firms tended to assume that they would currently achieve the same as last year; that they would maintain their market share and accordingly relied on historical information. This difference in outlook also showed in the attitude towards prices which the passive firms tended to accept as given by the market whereas the entrepreneurial firms were more inclined to vary contribution ratios in order to move up and down the market.

Conclusions

Implications for financial institutions

The findings concerning the extreme financial ratios manifested by small rapidly growing enterprises do raise the question of how able financial institutions are to recognise firms with growth potential and trade off their high illiquidity and high gearing against their higher profitability.

Two quotations, one from Bates (1964, p. 174) and one from the evidence given to the Wilson Committee (1977, p. 133), illustrate this problem:

> It may be that some lending institutions are too conservative and pay attention to asset cover at the expense of profit potential; in that case part of the answer lies in the institutions changing their ways and this is already happening. But it would be too much to expect that every branch of every bank should have expert financial analysts capable of using the most up-to-date techniques and able to spare the time to carry out detailed analyses of small business proposals with all of their special difficulties.

and

> very often we get a large project, a more important project out of the large companies, with more employment resulting. Such a project can be negotiated more easily, because a large company will have all the information that we require, they tell us what they are going to do and will have the facts and figures which substantiate that ready. We can struggle to provide assistance to a large number of smaller projects and still only have the same effect.

The problem faced by financial institutions is therefore to find a cheap and effective way of evaluating small firms for investment purposes. Accounting data are the most readily available source of information about potential customers. Where the accounts of a small firm indicate high profitability, high liquidity and low gearing the firm is likely to be regarded, prima facie, as a potential customer. Where the accounts show high profit and low liquidity it is often difficult for financial institutions to make a trade-off, particularly if employing rules of thumb (like a current ratio of 2:1) on a univariate basis. From the data collected it appears that small growth firms are highly illiquid and highly profitable. Failed firms also exhibit low liquidity. The question then arises as to how much extra profit can be traded off against low liquidity in establishing whether a firm is likely to be successful or fail. In practice, given the high fixed costs involved in loan evaluation it is likely that many financial institutions would not pursue this question further and reject such an application from a small firm exhibiting this profile. A technique which, using readily available accounting data, could distinguish between the potentially bankrupt and potentially viable small firm could reduce this inhibition to make trade-offs between profitability, liquidity and other key financial variables.

A great deal of research in recent years has been done with multivariate models, using ratios, following on from the earlier work by Beaver (1968) and Altman (1968). Most of this research has been concerned with predicting the failure of quoted companies. The work of Edmister (1972) attempted to predict the failure of small firms, using US Small Business Administration data.

In order to illustrate the use of multivariate techniques in financial analysis, Altman's discriminant function was applied to the data for the sample of 'supergrowth' enterprises which achieved stock market flotation. As shown earlier in this paper, the financial profile of small growth firms exhibits certain characteristics, such as low liquidity and high gearing, which are also characteristics of failed firms. On the other hand the sample of small growth firms was very profitable and would have been regarded, with the benefit of hindsight, as being successful. It was therefore thought to be of interest to see how far Altman's discriminant model would be able to trade off the extra profitability of the sample firms against their low liquidity and high gearing.

The analysis showed that nearly half of the 'supergrowth' enterprises would have been classified as bankrupt at some stage up to their flotation. The matched sample firms which did not grow to flotation had a much lower proportion in this category. This application of Altman's analysis illustrates well the problem of dealing with rapidly growing small firms and shows the need to apply and refine multivariate techniques in the area of financial analysis of small enterprises.

Implications for entrepreneurs

The major implication for entrepreneurs arising from the results of the Bath study concerns their ability to ensure that they maintain financial control of the growth of their businesses.

The criteria of consistency, consonance, flexibility and educability can be related to the financial control systems in entrepreneurial firms. The successful small enterprise will change rapidly in a number of ways in a short period of time. The design problem is that of ensuring appropriate financial control systems for changing circumstances. What is appropriate this week may be inappropriate next month. For example, the rapidly expanding firm runs the danger of inconsistency in that competing information systems may evolve which lead to duplication of information and subsequent confusion.

The major changes will be demonstrated in an increase in the scale of activities. This may be accompanied by changes in organisation structure but usually not without some delay. The problem posed for information systems is how to remain consonant throughout these rapid changes and the solution is concerned with the pursuit of flexibility to these changes. This increase in the scale of activities usually means that the entrepreneur starts off well able to control his affairs by physical inspection but then finds that he must rely to an increasing extent on information supplied in a written form but usually supplemented by verbal briefings by his acolytes.

During a period of growth the danger gradually becomes greater as the reliability and relevance of the information system is questioned and the participants begin to fail to learn fully from the information system. In extreme cases this can lead to complete rejection of the 'official' system and the substitution of a number of competing 'homemade' information systems. This is sometimes categorised into 'formal' and 'informal' systems and is expressed in a way which suggests that informal systems are, by their nature, harmful and disruptive. However, entrepreneurs are likely to put great store on informal information systems, and the problem can be defined as how to ensure that both formal and informal systems operate in a way which ensures that the participants use both to learn about their situation and thereby are better able to control it.

The successful entrepreneur appears not only to have inbuilt sensors which allow him to identify, in the financial control system, inconsistency, dissonance, inflexibility and ineducability which arise from changes in the contingent factors but also the ability to ensure appropriate changes are implemented. A minority of exceptional and outstanding entrepreneurs also tend to be proactive in anticipating these changes and in planning the required adaptations rather than reacting (or not) to evidence of misalignment.

References

Altman, E.I. (1968). 'Financial Ratios, Discriminant Analysis and the Prediction of Corporate Bankruptcy', *Journal of Finance,* September.

Anthony, R.N. and Dearden, J. (1980). *Management Control Systems,* 4th edn, R.D. Irwin, Homewood, Ill.

Bates, J. (1964). *The Financing of Small Business,* Sweet and Maxwell.

Beaver, W.H. (1968). 'Alternative Accounting Measures as Predictors of Failure', *Accounting Review,* September.

Bolton, J.E. (1971). *Report of the Committee of Inquiry on Small Firms* (Bolton Report), Cmnd. 4811, HMSO.

Davis, E.W. and Yeomans, K.A. (1974). *Company Finance and the Capital Market,* Cambridge University Press.

Dermer, J. (1977). *Management Planning and Control Systems — Advanced Concepts and Cases,* R.D. Irwin, Homewood, Ill.

Edmister, R.O. (1972). 'An Empirical Test of Financial Ratio Analysis for Small Business Failure Prediction', *Journal of Financial and Qualitative Analysis,* March.

Hart, P.E. with Bates, J. (1965). *Studies in Profit, Business Saving and Investment in the United Kingdom 1920–1962,* vol. I, George Allen and Unwin.

ICFC (1970). *Small Firm Survey.*

Lorsch, J.W. and Morse, J.J. (1974). *Organisations and their Members: A Contingency Approach,* Harper and Row, New York.

Ray, G.H. (1980). 'The Development of Financial Control Systems', PhD thesis, University of Bath.

Ray, G.H. and Hutchinson, P.J. (1983). *The Financing and Financial Control of Small Enterprise Development,* Gower.

Singh, A. and Whittington, G. (1968). *Growth Profitability and Valuation,* Cambridge University Press.

Stanworth, M.J.K. and Curran, J. (1973). *Management Motivation in the Smaller Business,* Gower.

Tamari, M. (1972). *A Postal Questionnaire of Small Firms: An Analysis of Financial Data,* Research Report no. 16, Cmnd. 4811, HMSO.

Weston, J.F. and Brigham, E.F. (1978). *Managerial Finance,* Holt International Editions.

Wilson, H. (1977). *Committee to Review the Functioning of Financial Institutions: Progress Report on the Financing of Industry and Trade,* HMSO.

PART II
THE SURVIVAL OF
ENTREPRENEURSHIP

Introduction

The economic analysis of the small enterprise, the subject of the papers in the opening section of this volume, does not completely exhaust the behavioural scientist's contribution to the analysis of the small firm. In the next group of papers the focus shifts to the motivational, social and political aspects of entrepreneurship. Why do people go into business for themselves and how do their efforts interrelate with society at large? Attention is also being increasingly directed to the future of small business ownership as we move towards post-industrial society. Will small business owners survive as a stratum or will the twin securities of the Welfare State and the dominant large corporation reduce the incentives to accept the challenge of self-employment?

In the opening paper of this section David Storey[1] makes the link between the economist's interest in the small enterprise and the interests of the geographer, political scientist, policy-maker and sociologist. After a further warning about the problems of definition in the small enterprise sector, he goes on to discuss six major areas of controversy connected with the socioeconomic functions of the small firm in contemporary industrial society: small firms as creators of competition; small firms as generators of employment; small firms as the seed corn of tomorrow's major corporations; small firms as a satisfying work environment for both employer and employee; small firms in the inner city economy; and, finally, small firms and technological change.

Politically as well as economically, small firms are frequently seen as essential to the creation of the climate of competition basic to the functioning of a successful free enterprise economy. Yet, as Storey shows, demonstrating this is more difficult than might at first be thought. He concludes that in most industrial societies small firms do not compete with large firms to any marked degree and that, in fact, most small firms are highly dependent on large firms. Yet, he argues, neither fact necessarily undermines the dynamism or effectiveness of free enterprise economies.

Storey's discussion of the contribution to employment made by the small business sector begins with a careful examination of the well-known American study by Birch. The latter offered a highly optimistic view, subsequently seized upon by many politicians, arguing for more support for the small firm so that it might play a major role in solving current high levels of unemployment. Storey's conclusion is cautious, even sceptical of these claims, a view shared by many other academic specialists in the small business field.

Similarly, the seed corn role of the small firm is seen as easily exaggerated. True, today's large firms were once yesterday's struggling enterprises but most small firms never grow. Indeed, Storey estimates that the probability of a wholly new small firm employing more than 100 people a decade from now is between ½ per cent and ¾ per cent. Moreover, of course, to ensure a sufficient future supply of the relative handful of large enterprises which dominate most economies, only a handful of the hundreds of thousands of new small firms actually need grow.

The contention that small firms provide a pleasant, socially relaxed, satisfying and friendly work environment for all involved has also provoked considerable debate. Storey's paper introduces this debate (which is examined in greater depth in subsequent papers by Curran and Stanworth and also Rainnie and Scott in Volume 2) and impartially concludes that, despite the frequency of these claims, the evidence is at best equivocal.

The role the small firm plays in the inner city has become central to the widespread concern over the accelerating collapse of inner city communities. Small firms have been seen as a powerful antidote for this collapse but, as Storey shows, there is mounting scepticism among researchers. Historically, small firms were the core of the inner city economy and their disappearance was itself a contribution to the inner city crisis. Whether the small firm is likely to return in big enough numbers to counter this decline as well as compensate for the reduction in large and medium-sized inner city firms might be doubted.

Finally, Storey confronts the issue of the role of the small firm in technological change — another issue which is currently generating a formidable literature. As his examination shows, the results of research are very mixed: small firms *have* contributed spectacularly to technological innovation and typically produced a greater return on research and development expenditure than their large counterparts. But, on the other hand, most small firms play little or no part in innovation. A substantial proportion are subcontractors with little will or ability to innovate, run by owners with little understanding of modern technology and who would anyway find it difficult to recruit and retain the much sought after and highly qualified employees required to exploit fully modern technology.

The following paper offers an overview of the psychology of entrepreneurship, a subject which has attracted a great deal of attention from psychologists as well as other behavioural scientists such as economists and sociologists. Elizabeth Chell carefully and critically reviews the main psychological approaches to entrepreneurship — the psychodynamic model, the social dynamic model and, most popular of all, the trait approach.

The psychodynamic model sees the entrepreneur as having an almost deviant personality, the result of family background factors and early deprivations producing a person who finds it difficult to relate to others except in situations where he or she is in full control. Running a business provides autonomy in economic situations and entrepreneurship is the behaviour which creates this personal freedom. Chell is sceptical of this model in its usual form but feels it might be made more plausible if current social and other environmental influences were taken into consideration.

The social development model does stress the importance of situational factors but, in effect, tends to overemphasise them. Advocates of this approach often end up leaving out a proper consideration of the importance of the individual, a curious omission in a theoretical explanation purportedly concerned with the phenomenon of entrepreneurship, acknowledged to be the one economic activity most dependent on individual behaviour.

The trait approach is by far the most popular in the literature on the psychology of entrepreneurship. It seeks to identify a single, or more frequently, a constellation of personality traits or characteristics which distinguish the entrepreneur from others. However, trait theory generally has come in for a lot of criticism in psychology in recent years. There is the problem of tracing the links between so-called personality traits and actual behaviour in real situations as well as the problem of deciding what part situational factors play in modifying the expression of personality characteristics.

Chell goes on to suggest an approach which offers an opportunity to incorporate the varying influences of individual personality and situational influences within a dynamic, interactive relationship. Her approach also has the advantage of permitting analysis of the entrepreneurial role *after* the enterprise has come into existence — an important aspect neglected by most of the previous literature. Overall, this paper demonstrates admirably the complexities and limitations of previous research and thinking on something as seemingly simple as the 'entrepreneurial personality'.

The final two papers in this section are by sociologists. Bechhofer and Elliott concentrate on the historical development of the small business owner stratum or class. They identify this stratum through certain distinctive key characteristics — the use of relatively small amounts of capital to operate directly an economic enterprise adopting simple technology and a relatively unsophisticated form of organisation. As the authors concede, there are problems in making this definition watertight but, as they also stress, it is not merely a shared economic position which marks off the *petite bourgeoisie* stratum but also their shared consciousness. The latter consists of tendencies to display similar beliefs, attitudes and behaviour which, taken together, clearly mark them off from other occupational and social groupings in society.

As Bechhofer and Elliott show, this shared consciousness has important effects outside the purely economic sphere, especially on the political order – an effect paralleled in several industrial societies. For example, small business owners are often seen as automatic supporters of the Conservative Party in Britain or the equivalent in other industrial societies. But, as this paper shows, this picture is incorrect. The consciousness of the *petite bourgeoisie* includes a strong element of being a class apart whose interests do not necessarily coincide with other (large) business owners or other middle class groups. In some industrial societies small business owners have formed their own political parties or have made their support explicitly conditional on their interests being protected. Papers by McHugh and Curran in Volume 2 explore these issues in more detail.

In the final part of the paper Bechhofer and Elliott explore the social dimensions of small business ownership and the survival of the small business owner stratum. They emphasise the cultural significance of the stratum as the embodiment of values central to the free enterprise ethic: hard work, thrift, property as a measure of success, independence and anti-collectivism. No other stratum has a way of life which seeks to embody these values so directly. Indeed, other strata have shown a propensity to drift away from these values even while they continue to pay them lip service.

The final paper in this section, by Scase and Goffee, reinforces the point that the small business owning stratum is very far from homogeneous. This elementary point is often forgotten in discussions on the small enterprise. Not only is the small firm found in every major economic sector — a fundamental source of variation in itself — but there are wide variations in the amount and type of capital assets employed as well as in relations between owner-managers and others, especially employees. Scase and Goffee also note how recent economic and political change has also altered the opportunities for self-employment, diminishing them in some areas but increasing them in others.

Like the previous paper, Scase and Goffee's contribution is concerned with the question of the precise significance of the small business owning class in advanced industrial societies. They examine in detail a number of important recent contributions to this debate. While they offer no solution to these issues they do contribute positively by offering a conceptual clarification of the *petite bourgeoisie* class by diving it into four sub-categories: the *self-employed* who are by far the largest grouping within the *petite bourgeoisie* and who are distinguished by the fact that they employ nobody else; *small employers; owner-controllers* and *owner-directors.* Small employers work alongside their employees but the other two groupings have increasingly distant relations with their employees. Broadly, the four categories also correlate with size of enterprise, with owner-directors usually having the largest.

What is important about this fourfold division of small business owners is that each tends to be linked with distinct managerial, organisational and ideological patterns adopted in the operation of the enterprise and in their membership of society generally. As later papers in these volumes show, this fourfold division is only the beginning, albeit an important one, in the variations which need to be taken into account in understanding the economic and social dynamics of the small enterprise and its owner. Ethnic origin, gender and different forms of organisation such as the co-operative and the franchised small enterprise are also highly significant as sources of heterogeneity, as subsequent papers demonstrate.

Together the four papers in this section share two tasks. The first is to underline the point that the small business owner and the small business must be seen as much more than purely economic phenomena. The economic interrelates with the psychological, social and cultural aspects and only when all these dimensions are brought into the analysis can we begin to understand the complexities of the functioning small firm. Second, this section also introduces the no less important point that the small firm has political, social and cultural interrelations with its wider environment which are as significant as the more commonly discussed economic interrelations. Again, a full understanding of the survival of the small firm needs to take these external relations into account.

Note

1. David Storey took the opportunity to update material from the early sections of his book, *Entrepreneurship and the New Firm*, London, Croom Helm, 1982, when it was edited for the extract published in this volume.

5 Entrepreneurship and the New Firm

DAVID STOREY*

Introduction

In virtually every country in the world the small firm is, and has always been, the typical unit of production. Small firms, however defined, constitute at least 90 per cent of the population of enterprises but in many developed countries the two decades following 1945 saw a decline in the proportion of total output produced by such firms.

There is now evidence to suggest that this decline has ceased and even been reversed. The last ten years have seen the small firm undergo a remarkable metamorphosis. In the 1950s and 1960s the emphasis of government policies in many countries was to create large enterprises which would be able to compete internationally. It was argued that modern industrial development was in industries where economies of scale were of paramount importance. Only large firms could hope to produce output in sufficient quantities to take advantage of these economies. It was believed that scale economies were at the plant (technical) level, so that larger establishments would have lower unit costs of production than small establishments. Managerial diseconomies were thought to be negligible, whereas large firms were more likely to have access to the capital necessary to undertake

* From: Chapter 1, *Entrepreneurship and the New Firm,* Croom Helm, London, 1982.

research and development and to finance advertising. Large firms were likely to be able to borrow money at lower interest rates because they represented a lower risk to the bank than did a small firm. The bank itself was likely to prefer to deal with several large customers since it would find monitoring company developments easier than a portfolio consisting of many small companies.

These factors suggested that the small firm was likely to become progressively less important. Indeed it seemed that the extent to which the small firm sector had declined represented an index of development. The small firm was equated with technological backwardness, and with barely competent management. The manager in the large enterprise, with his DCF, MBO and his job enrichment was contrasted with the 'belt and braces' approach of the small firm owner-manager. In some countries, notably Japan, small firms have always played a central role in economic development, whilst the independence and aspiration of the entrepreneur has always been part of the national culture in the United States. Nevertheless even these countries, as well as those of Western Europe, have seen a resurgence of the small firm in the last decade.

The small firm: definitions, importance and trends

The term 'small firm' is in such common use that the unwary reader might be forgiven for thinking that there was some uniformly accepted definition of what constitutes a small firm. Nothing could be further from the truth! The distinction between 'big' and 'small' is arbitrary and, in those industries where definitions are according to value of work done, vary from year to year because of inflation. Neck (1977) quotes an American study in 1975 of small firm definitions which identified more than 50 different statistical definitions in 75 countries. Not surprisingly Neck suggests the criteria for 'small' vary according to the context, with an upper limit of small for financiers being based on fixed assets or net worth. Other definitions might be based on total employment (including or excluding outworkers), total sales, energy consumption, number of customers, and so on. Clearly firms which are small in some of these contexts are far from small in others.

It is therefore necessary to identify those characteristics of the small firm which epitomise its operations. First, the small firm generally has a small share of the market, although it could also have a large share of a very small market. Secondly, it is normally managed by the owners, rather than by employees on behalf of shareholders. Thirdly, the owners are legally independent in taking their decisions — although in practice probably extremely dependent upon the goodwill of their bankers. Other characteristics are that the small firm normally produces either a single product or a set of closely related products, generally at a single establishment. Its operations are generally local with the obvious exceptions of importing and exporting businesses.

For statistical purposes it is necessary to have definitions of the small firm, but the variety of contexts and uses noted above, means that definitions in most countries vary according to the industry in which the small firm is found (Beesley and Wilson, 1984). In Britain, the Business Statistics Office (BSO) in 1978 identified 1.3 million small businesses, with these constituting 96 per cent of all firms. Only 100 000 small firms were in manufacturing. The BSO definitions illustrate the sectoral variations: in manufacturing a small firm is defined according to whether or not it has less than 200 employees, while in construction the upper limit is 25. In all other sectors the small firm is defined according to turnover; in wholesaling the limit for a small firm is £730 000; in the motor trades it is £365 000, and for all other sectors it is £185 000 (at 1978 prices).

In Australia the small firm is defined as having less than 100 employees in manufacturing and less than 20 employees in all other sectors. The United States uses the 100 employee definition for manufacturing but uses output definitions for other sectors. For Germany the statistical data are on an establishment (plant) basis, rather than upon a single ownership (firm) basis, making comparison even more difficult.

These variations in definition make it extremely difficult to undertake valid comparisons of the importance of small firms in various countries (Storey, 1983). In practice the only meaningful comparisons are between the role of small firms in the manufacturing sector which, at least in Britain, contains under 10 per cent of all small firms.

The role of the small firm

Despite the heterogeneity of the small firm population, such firms are thought to perform a set of common functions:

1   Small firms provide a source of competition (potential or actual) to larger firms in their industry, limiting the latter's ability to raise prices and/or be technically inefficient in the use of factors of production.
2   Small firms have become increasingly acclaimed as major creators of new jobs in developed countries since standardised products,

which have traditionally been produced in large enterprises, are now increasingly produced by the developing countries.

3   Small firms provide the seed corn from which the giant corporations of future years will grow.

4   Small firms can provide a harmonious working environment where owner and employee work, shoulder to shoulder, for their mutual benefit. This is likely to be reflected in fewer industrial disputes and lower absenteeism.

5   The inner city areas of the industrialised nations contain heavy concentrations of the social problems of unemployment, low incomes and poor housing. It is argued that small firms can make an important contribution to the regeneration of such areas.

6   Small firms are likely to be innovative, being found in industries where technical development is essential for survival. The low capital requirements in modern microelectronics make this industry particularly suited, at present, to new small firms.

The extent to which in practice small firms fulfil the roles claimed for them is reviewed in this section. It illustrates the difficulty of deriving testable hypotheses from the above statements. In addition there are several claims made for small firms which seem either to be based on no evidence (other than casual observation) or which are virtually untestable. For example, it is often claimed that major fluctuations in the demand for certain products mean small firms move into and out of these industries with great frequency. They react to the signals of the market-place by taking risks that are unacceptable to larger firms, and by doing so make the market system more responsive to the demands of the consumer. The extent to which localised markets, protected by increasing transportation costs or consumer tastes, have influenced the small firm sector is also frequently debated but rarely quantified.

Small firms as competitors

It is not easy to test the extent to which small firms compete with larger firms so reducing the latter's ability to determine market prices. Davies and Kelly (1971) found that over 50 per cent of small firms encountered their main competition from other small firms, whilst only 28 per cent thought they were competing directly with large firms (the remainder felt their competition came primarily from overseas companies).

Lydall (1958) categorised small firms as either 'jobbers' or 'marketeers'. Jobbers were essentially complementary to, rather than competitive with, large firms since they were producing output for a specific (normally large) customer such as a retail chain or a large firm.

These firms are important in industries such as metal manufacturing, engineering, wood products, paper and printing and, as Lydall showed, the proportion of jobbers increases as firm size declines. The marketeers, on the other hand, compete directly with the large firm. Since Lydall's study there has been a sharp increase in industrial concentration making it likely that the number of marketeering firms will have declined.

The work by Hitchens (1977) on the UK iron foundry industry tends to support these findings. He found, in that industry, that 59.8 per cent of firms viewed themselves as competing with less than ten firms, with this competition coming, in their view, from firms of a similar size. Nevertheless, it is interesting to note that of those firms who felt themselves to be competing primarily with firms of a different size, 78.7 per cent thought their competition was with larger firms and only 21.3 per cent with smaller firms.

In a study of Australian small firms, Johns, Dunlop and Sheehan (1978) found that the most important source of competition for the small manufacturing firm was other small firms in the immediate locality. There were, of course, substantial industrial variations in this pattern, with 51 per cent of the timber firms identifying small local firms as the main source of competition, yet only 21 per cent of chemical and oil firms. In aggregate, 38 per cent of all small firms surveyed regarded their prime source of competition as being from small local firms, compared to 33 per cent who viewed it as coming from large non-local firms.

The dependence of small business upon large customers is, of course, not necessarily an indication of a weakness in the small firm sector. As Anthony (1983) shows, Japan has the highest proportion of total manufacturing employment in small firms of any of the developed countries, yet the majority of these small firms are directly dependent upon the large enterprises for their business. In the immediate post-war years the Japanese motor industry developed primarily upon a subcontracting basis. Yamanaka and Kobayashi (1957), in their study of this industry, found that with fluctuations in demand it was easier for the motor car giants to regulate the need for components if this function was subcontracted to small firms rather than provided within the company. They also found that the subcontractors could employ labour at lower wage rates.

Clark (1979) shows that this relationship has continued to exist in Japan, since 60 per cent of small and medium-sized enterprises are still engaged in subcontracting. He also notes that although major differences exist in value added per capita between small and large firms, the two continue to co-exist even though large food, printing and electrical companies produce an output per capita 2½ times greater than that of small firms employing less than 30 people. Large firms in Japan also maintain their advantage over small firms since the latter, in 1973, had 54 per cent of all current assets financed by promissory notes and bills. Clark believes that this enables large firms more easily to take advantage of suppliers during a credit squeeze by slower settlement of accounts, than in countries where the small firms have access to other sources of funding.

The fact that most small firms do not compete with large firms, and are in fact crucially dependent upon the development of large firms, does not mean that such a sector will show sluggish rates of growth. The example of Japan, where most small firms are jobbers, yet where the small firm sector has made an important contribution to that country's growth, illustrates it is not necessary to have small firms in direct competition with the large firms. It is more important for small firms to offer at least the threat of competition.

Small firms and employment

Birch (1979) showed, from a study of 82 per cent of all manufacturing and private sector service establishments in the United States, that two-thirds of *net* new jobs were created in firms employing less than 20 people. He argued that the small independent business was the prime source of employment growth in the USA, whilst larger firms were redistributing rather than creating employment.

Birch stated that there was an absence of knowledge about which types of companies created jobs, and about which were most likely to respond to government incentives. Consequently, he argued, government had to rely upon aggregate, macroeconomic policies such as tax incentives and alterations in public expenditure, rather than being able to direct incentives towards those companies and individuals likely to be most responsive. Birch examined employment changes in 5.6 million business *establishments* (the number of *firms* or companies was substantially lower) in the manufacturing and private service sectors of the United States between 1969 and 1976. His analysis was conducted by using a components of change or job accounting technique. The technique accounts for net changes in numbers of jobs by isolating the gross components. Jobs are created through expansions of companies plus openings, and lost through company closures and contractions.

Birch's main conclusions for the USA were:

(i) Gross job loss through contraction and closure was about 8 per cent per annum.

(ii) In 'replacing' these jobs — i.e. gross job gains — about 50 per cent were created through expansions of existing companies and about 50 per cent through new openings.

(iii) About 50 per cent of gross jobs created by openings were produced by independent free-standing entrepreneurs (births) and 50 per cent by multi-plant corporations (in moves).

(iv) Firms employing less than 20 people generated 66 per cent of net new jobs in the United States, or 51.8 per cent excluding subsidiaries and branches of larger enterprises.

Birch was impressed by the contribution to employment made by the new, young, small independent firm which was committed to seeking out new and profitable ventures. Such firms created 66 per cent of net new jobs.

The measures used by Birch in determining the contribution of very small firms to job creation are, however, less clear than they initially appear. Two-thirds of *net* new jobs were created in firms employing less than 20 people. It should be apparent that this is not the same as saying either that two-thirds of *all* new jobs or of *gross* new jobs were created in such firms. Many distinguished financial commentators have made this mistake — some indeed have reported that Birch found two-thirds of all jobs were created by small firms.

It is vitally important to distinguish between gross and net job creation, and to understand when either or both are valid measures of the contribution of large and small firms to employment change. Simply stated the rule is that where employment in all size bands increases, the proportionate contribution of small and large firms is validly measured by net changes, but where employment declines, either in total or only in individual size bands, net change may be an invalid measure. The latter is the case for manufacturing employment as reported by Birch for the USA. His data shows that a negative number of *net* manufacturing jobs were created by large firms and a positive number by small manufacturing firms, so it is not possible to determine the *relative* net contribution of large and small firms. This can only be done by examining gross job losses and gross job gains, data which Birch does not provide.

Comparisons of the manufacturing sectors of Britain and the USA have been made by Fothergill and Gudgin (1979). Using data for the East Midlands, which may be reasonably representative of the UK as a whole, they show a startling similarity in terms of job generation by size, between the US manufacturing industry during 1969–76 and East Midlands manufacturing during 1968–75. During these years, in both the USA and the East Midlands of England, firms employing more than 100 workers showed an aggregate decline in employment, whereas the very small firm sector showed an aggregate increase in employment.

These 'tests' of employment change are, however, unsatisfactory because new firms are placed in a size category according to their final year's employment, whereas existing firms are categorised according to a base year and expressed as a percentage of total employment in that size band. This excludes the effect of openings, but gives a more realistic picture of employment change due to expansions, contractions and closures.

Finally, Birch's analysis is conducted primarily on a firm, rather than an establishment, basis (Armington and Odle, 1982). This means that a firm which originally had a single establishment in a prosperous area, but which decides to transfer its manufacturing operations to a less prosperous area, and by doing so reduces its total employment, is classified as a declining firm. Nevertheless, the transferred employment is still a gain to the less prosperous area and may also benefit the prosperous area in terms of reduced pressure on the local labour market. Hence, although large companies are only redistributing operations this may not be undesirable, since it is not only the total employment in an economy which is important, but also its regional distribution.

Birch stated that over eight years approximately 50 per cent of gross new jobs in the US were attributable to openings of new firms and of these, half were generated by independent 'free standing' entrepreneurs, i.e. about 25 per cent of gross new jobs were created by such entrepreneurs.

For Britain, as a whole, it is unlikely that more than 50 per cent of gross new manufacturing jobs per decade are created by wholly new establishments. In the prosperous regions approximately 30 per cent of gross new jobs are created by openings — with half of these being created by wholly new firms (births). In the assisted areas, however, about 70 per cent of gross new jobs are created by openings (30 per cent through expansions) but only about one-fifth of these, i.e. 14 per cent, are attributable to wholly new establishments (births) — the rest are created primarily by existing firms moving branches or subsidiaries into the area. In both the assisted and the prosperous areas, therefore, the proportion of gross new jobs created by new establishments is unlikely to exceed 15 per cent of gross new manufacturing jobs. Fothergill and Gudgin, for example, show for the East Midlands that 15.1 per cent of *gross* new manufacturing jobs per decade are created by wholly new firms, whereas in Cleveland about 12 per cent of *gross* new jobs are created by new firms.

The contribution which small firms can make to job creation in future remains a matter of some dispute. It appears that as a group, small firms may be increasing their labour forces at a time when large firms are decreasing their payrolls. The detailed data on which job accounting can be undertaken are currently available in Europe only for the manufacturing sector which has been a net shedder of labour to the services sector — hence comparisons with the Birch data are difficult. Nevertheless, it seems clear that the contribution which the small firm sector can make to employment generation is nowhere near as high as is suggested by those who misquote the Birch results.

Small firms as seed corn

Today's giant corporations were once back-street enterprises. In most instances they grew as their industry grew, but there are several cases of new firms in a well-established industry growing through their ability either to produce existing products more cheaply or through producing an improved product.

We saw earlier that small manufacturing firms as a group in Britain have been increasing employment since the mid-1960s whilst large firms have declined. However the probability of an individual firm achieving a growth rate, in terms of employment, equal to the arithmetic mean of its cohort is, however, substantially less than 50 per cent. This is because the growth patterns of new firms are positively skewed with a few firms growing rapidly but the majority growing at a rate equal to or less than the mean.

Hence it must be stressed that the performance of the very small firm sector, as measured by its arithmetic mean performance, should not be interpreted as being typical of the small firm sector. Put bluntly, the chances are that today's small firm will show virtually no growth, and that the next most likely outcome is that it will not exist in ten years time. Very few prosper, but those who do can more than compensate both for those which die and those which fail to grow. Using data for wholly new manufacturing firms created in Northern England (Storey, 1985) current estimates suggest that the probability of a wholly new firm employing more than 100 people in a decade is between ½ per cent and ¾ per cent.

The working environment

The conventional view, supported by the Bolton Committee, is that whilst the small firm is not necessarily the most technically advanced, it provides a pleasant environment in which work-place conflicts are minimised.

It is argued that the worker in a small firm has direct access to the boss of the firm who has it within his power to make decisions upon grievances. This contrasts with a large organisation where senior management has little contact with those on the shop floor, since they are 'protected' by intermediaries such as middle management or the foreman. Unfortunately middle management is often insufficiently autonomous to make decisions and hence tends to leave the decision to senior staff who may have less 'feel' for the problem. For his part the worker on the shop floor may feel frustrated that, although the decision may be communicated to him by intermediaries, they are not responsible for the decision. The opportunity for debating the matter is limited to either 'making an issue', with its implications for worker–management relations, or resentfully accepting the decision.

In a small firm there is greater opportunity for face-to-face negotiation. The boss may be approached and he will give a decision which can then be disputed by the workers, leading to a more generally satisfactory compromise. It is important that the work-force see those who are responsible for making decisions and this, it is argued, is more likely to be found in a small than a large firm.

The large organisation is also often characterised by divison of labour which means the work is repetitive, boring and stripped of non-material rewards such as pride in workmanship or recognition of achievement. On the other hand, in the small firm there is less specialisation and hence tasks tend to be complex, with the experience gained representing valuable (yet enjoyable) training.

All these factors suggest that the small work-place is likely to be a more satisfactory environment than the giant enterprise, but the evidence to support this hypothesis is somewhat equivocal. Several forms of testing could be tried. The obvious strategy is to examine the extent to which strikes vary according to the size of the work-force. There appears fairly conclusive evidence that large plants are more prone to strikes than small, even though it is true that collection of data from small plants is less comprehensive.

Yet strikes are only one manifestation of the existence or absence of conflict in the work-place. Since small firms are less unionised than large firms, and since strikes are positively related to the degree of unionisation, then other indices of disharmony may be more relevant. For example, high rates of labour turnover, absenteeism and even accidents at work, may reflect more accurately the nature of job satisfaction in plants of varying size.

The work of Ingham (1970) contrasts with the Bolton notion of small firms as offering much higher non-monetary rewards than large firms. Careful reading of his research results, and his reviews of previous work, suggests that Ingham was, at best, agnostic about the work-place benefits provided by small firms. He finds no clear evidence, either in his study, or in his reviews, of a relationship between size of establishment and various measures of labour turnover. He finds that only in 'exceptional cases' do absentee rates rise with organisation size, whilst the relationships between organisation size and productivity do not show any evidence of greater productivity in small than in large establishments despite small-scale methods and (probably) a low capital intensity of production. Bolton, however, had stated 'the turnover of staffs in small firms is very low and strikes and other kinds of industrial dispute are relatively infrequent'. Bolton attributed this to management being more flexible and direct, with working rules being varied to suit the individual.

Ingham explains his results by suggesting that the motivation of workers in large establishments differs from that in small. In his terms the large plant workers were 'economistic and instrumental in their work orientation'. This means that whilst small firm workers were unlikely to be absent from work primarily through a feeling of 'letting the side down', absentee rates were also likely to be low in large organisations where workers realise that the financial penalty is greater. The congruence of aims in large organisations occurs through the cash nexus, whereas in small firms it occurs through a 'responsibility nexus'. This congruence may in turn be due to the nature of workers recruited, with small firms tending to recruit workers who were more likely to be influenced by considerations of responsibility, and large firms recruiting workers more motivated by financial reward.

The above description illustrates the difficulty of identifying the direction of causation especially when it is shown that small-sized establishments are correlated both with low wage rates and low unionisation. These in turn are correlated with a low propensity to strike, which may be an indication of the quality of industrial relations in a plant.

Curran and Stanworth (1981a) have attempted to overcome these difficulties by interviewing workers in small and large-sized establishments in the printing and electronics industry. They do not find any evidence of employees in small firms being anti-union, and the vast majority would join a union if firms allowed. The main result of their research is that firm size has markedly less influence upon industrial relations than the industry concerned, variations in local and community structures and national political and economic considerations.

In a subsequent paper, Curran and Stanworth (1981b) show that factors such as the age of respondents and their family life-cycle position are important in influencing perceived levels of job satisfaction. Once these and specific industry characteristics are taken into account Curran and Stanworth can find no support for a relationship between firm size and reported job satisfaction amongst the work-force.

Small firms and the inner city

The inner cities of most developed countries exhibit similar characteristics. They have poor housing and social infrastructure, high unemployment and are often populated by unskilled whites and ethnic minorities with low incomes. They have normally been subject to substantial population decline with the more affluent residents having moved out to the suburbs leaving a decaying community which co-exists with high property values because of the industrial and commercial demand for land only short distances away.

It has been strongly argued by Falk (1978) that the small firm is an appropriate vehicle for the regeneration of these areas, even though it is the disappearance of small firms in such areas, together with the declining employment in locally based enterprises such as docks, that is the major 'component' of employment decline. He argues that the small firm has several major advantages over larger firms. The first is that it requires relatively small sites to produce its output and secondly that it uses a relatively labour-intensive production process. The inner city with its expensive sites may be appropriate for firms which require only small amounts of land. The use of labour-intensive production methods means that it is likely to have the maximum impact upon local unemployment. These ideas received official support in the White Paper on inner cities (Department of the Environment, 1977).

Falk also argues that the small firm in the inner city is likely to have easy access to a relatively rich market since transportation costs will be negligible. In addition it is more likely to be able to obtain access to supplies than, for example, the firm situated in a rural town. The small firm may also find there are, in the area, a number of other similar firms, which together create external benefits such as having a financial sector accustomed to particular dealing with specific industries or with skilled labour being available without having to be trained.

The hypothesis that inner city areas would be fertile incubators for new firms was first proposed by Hoover and Vernon (1960) in their examination of New York. They suggested that small firms in certain industries would find it advantageous to locate in high-density metropolitan areas. They identified ladies' clothing, printing, toys and jewellery as industries where the inner city firm may have advantages since these trades carry low inventories and require low mechanisation because of the fluctuations of fashion. Such firms attempt to minimise risk by restricting overheads, but in doing so have to remain very small. Once the firm developed and grew, it was, according to Hoover and Vernon, likely to encounter constraints, notably the difficulty of securing suitable premises in the inner areas, and was likely to move to a suburban or rural location. The hypothesis that the inner areas were attractive to new firms — and that the more successful firms consequently moved out of the area, remained essentially untested, despite popular acceptance, until Leone and Struyk (1976) published their work on five US cities. They found some evidence that the central area of New York had a relatively high proportion of new start-up businesses but the evidence for other central areas was weak. There was very little evidence for the hypothesis that inner city firms wishing to expand, subsequently moved to a more suburban location. In fact they found that such firms normally moved to an alternative location within the inner area.

Further research by Nicholson, Brinkley and Evans (1981) and by Cameron (1980) has also questioned the validity of the 'incubator' hypothesis. Nicholson *et al.* examined new firms in London, but could find no evidence that firms found the inner city a particularly favourable location. Firms indicated that the reason for locating in these areas was the benefits of being close to markets, rather than lower costs of production. Perhaps the only support for an incubator hypothesis was that Nicholson *et al.* support the observation made by Fagg (1980) that new firms tend to locate in old premises — whether in the inner or outer areas — and that since the inner city has a greater concentration of old premises it is likely to be attractive to the new firm.

Cameron (1980) examined the differential location patterns of firms in the inner and outer areas of Glasgow. He found that the birth-rate of new firms in the inner city area was approximately two-thirds of that of the conurbation as a whole. Interestingly neither Nicholson *et al.* nor Cameron find any support for the assertion that firms which are born in the inner areas subsequently move out of the area once they expand, although both studies find that inner area firms are very mobile. Most moves are usually of short distances to other parts of the inner area.

If small firms were particularly suited to the inner areas it would be expected that they could be creating more new jobs, or losing jobs less rapidly than large firms. We have already seen that large manufacturing firms, as a group in the UK, are losing jobs rapidly but there is no evidence that the growth of small firms is concentrated in the inner areas. If anything, the evidence suggests that the shift into the rural areas of population has been accompanied by the creation of new firms which have subsequently shown high rates of employment growth. Fothergill and Gudgin (1982) suggest, in contrast to Falk, that the inner area is a particularly unattractive location for a firm which intends to grow since there is a shortage of space for expansion.

Although certain classic inner city industries may find the central areas attractive, these tend not to be industries which subsequently grow and create large numbers of jobs. Such firms maintain their position by not growing since size reduces their capacity to react to fluctuations in demand. On the other hand, those industries likely to grow are ones with high skill content and are likely to be established by entrepreneurs with high educational qualifications. Such an individual will wish to minimise the distance from home to work, as shown by Cooper (1973), and is more likely to live in the suburbs than in urban areas. These factors, together with the entrepreneur's preference, noted by Nicholson and Brinkley (1979), to locate in a 'green-field' area suggest that a rural town, rather than an inner area, is likely to host the location of those new industries likely to show permanent substantial employment growth.

The inner London Borough of Tower Hamlets, studied by Howick and Key (1980) clearly illustrates these problems. In the borough very small industry is significantly more important than in the UK as a whole since 42.7 per cent of employment is in establishments employing less than 50 people, compared with a UK average of 16 per cent. This high proportion of employment in small establishments has not prevented a massive turnover of firms and net job losses. Between 1973 and 1976 manufacturing employment in the borough fell from 28 024 to 20 910, even though 2 780 new jobs were created. Howick and Key questioned these small manufacturers (dominated by the textile and food and drink trades) on the perceived advantages of an inner city location. Proximity to customers and suppliers was frequently mentioned, but Howick and Key make an interesting distinction between traditional inner city industries such as textiles, printing, furniture, and so on, and those industries attracted to the area by the existence of the docks. The former are satisfied with their location in the inner area, with their precise location being determined by the availability of suitable (cheap) premises. Industries initially attracted by the docks (engineering, metalworking, timber and food), however, showed greater dissatisfaction with the area since during this period dock-related activity declined sharply. These industries also create relatively few jobs per square foot of working space and are more likely to be constrained by the shortage of space in most inner city premises.

The inner city, although it has a higher proportion of employment in small firms, has not prospered. Keeble (1978) showed that for the seven major conurbations in Britain, those which had the largest mean factory size in 1972 were the only ones whose employment in manufacturing had increased between 1959 and 1971. It is unlikely that large numbers of manufacturing jobs will return to such areas by embracing a small firms policy since the main cause of manufacturing job loss has been the closure of large plants and the failure of medium-sized plants to grow.

The small firm and technological change

Although it has proved difficult to measure its contribution precisely, it must be true that technical progress has made a significant contribution to the economic growth of all nations. Improved technology has enabled existing products to be produced with fewer inputs, which can then be used elsewhere in the economy to produce more or different goods. Technology has also enabled wholly new products to be manufactured. Structural problems have, however, occurred in all economies in transferring resources from the declining to the growing industries.

The role which small firms have played, and could play in the future, in stimulating technical change is open to debate. For example a case can be made that in favourable circumstances the small firm could make a major contribution to both technological advance and the creation of new wealth. There are a number of instances where individual firms have succeeded in what appear, otherwise, to be unfavourable environments. Probably the best-known examples of geographical areas where small and new firms have made a major impact is the county of Santa Clara in California (Silicon Valley) and alongside Route 128 in Boston, Massachusetts. According to Little (1977) there were, in 1974, approximately 800 new technology-based firms in Silicon Valley and over 400 in the Route 128 area of Boston, most of them in electrical, instrumentation and information technology. Little also shows that in the United Kingdom in 1976 there were probably less than 200 such firms — of which approximately one-half were too small to be identified. Little suggests that the number of new technology-based firms (NTBF) in the Federal Republic of Germany is, if anything, even smaller.

The importance of small firms in this sector cannot be underestimated. They represent the cutting edge of new technology, they can create jobs, wealth and make a major contribution to exports (Oakey, 1984). For example, seven technology-based companies in the USA, founded between 1900 and 1935 had, by 1974, combined sales of $26 billion and employed a total of 764 000 people. Such firms not only grow rapidly but also have a lower failure rate than other types of firm. Roberts and Wainer (1968) found that only 20 per cent of science-based firms established by ex-Massachusetts Institute of Technology staff failed within the first five years, compared to an average US failure rate of 50 per cent. Some equally impressive growth rates have been shown by two NTBFs in Europe. Racal Electronics, founded in 1951, had by 1975 sales totalling £50 million and employed more than 4000 people. Nixdorf Computer AG, in the Federal Republic of Germany, also showed remarkable growth over a similar period having sales in 1975 of DM633 million and employing 7600 people.

These firms remain very much the exception in Europe, even amongst high-technology firms. In other sectors, studies of the contribution to technological development of small and large firms have encountered a number of measurement difficulties. The first is that it is unclear whether to compare small firms' contribution to technical development with their proportion of expenditure on research and development or with their proportion of total output or employment. Using the former index, Ray (1979) quotes the work of Freeman (1971) showing that small British firms contributed approximately 10 per cent of all post-war innovations — markedly *more* than small firms' share of research and development spending. From this he suggests that the relative absence of small firms in the UK is an important limiting factor upon the ability of the economy to develop and that their spending is highly productive. Ray does not mention, as Freeman does, that whilst small firms contributed 10 per cent of all innovations they produced, over the same period, more than 20 per cent of net output and employed more than 20 per cent of the manufacturing labour force. Thus small firms would appear to produce more innovations per pound spent on research — but produce far fewer innovations per pound of output or per employee.

Secondly, it is unclear what index of technical output should be used. Both Freeman and Ray referred to post-war innovations but innovations are not homogeneous — some are major developments whilst others are merely minor modifications to existing practices. The use of an innovations index may also tend to underestimate the importance of the small firm since, as Jewkes, Sawyers and Stillerman (1969) point out, development tends to be undertaken by the large firm, whereas inventions are more likely to emerge from the unstructured small firm environment. Jewkes *et al.* showed the majority of the 70 major post-war inventions derived either from universities, private inventors or from small firms. It then required the access to funds available to the larger firm before commercial exploitation of the invention became feasible and it is this interdependence, in matters of technological development, between large and small which is stressed by Bolton.

The small firm is less likely to engage in research and development than the large firm. Johns, Dunlop and Sheehan (1978) show that approximately 4 per cent of Australian enterprises employing less than 150 people were engaged in research and development compared with 90 per cent of enterprises employing more than 1500. They also quote Japanese data for 1973 which show that, in each industry, firms with less than 300 employees were less likely to have a research and development programme than were firms of a larger size. In their study, Rothwell and Zegveld (1982) show that most of the innovative ideas for the small firm come from within — normally from the founder himself. They show that 70 per cent of innovative ideas in the small firm are 'in house', compared with only 49 per cent for firms employing more than 1000. Cox (1971), in a study for the Bolton Committee, showed that although small firms in the survey provided 31 per cent of total employment, they provided only 15.5 per cent of employment for qualified scientists and engineers (QSE). Only in electronics did small firms employ a higher proportion of QSEs than their share of total employment.

The relatively low proportion of QSEs employed by small firms is reflected in more recent results provided by Oakey (1979) who examined the data on innovations originally used by Freeman, together with data on the Queens Award to Industry — the latter being a scheme launched in 1965 to recognise outstanding achievement by British industrial firms in either exports or technological development. Oakey contacted 323 firms who had either received the award or who had, according to Freeman, made a significant innovation. He found that an establishment with more than 1000 employees was ten times more likely to have developed and implemented a significant innovation than an establishment employing between 100 and 999 people, thus supporting the original data presented by Freeman. Oakey also showed that there were significant regional differences, especially in establishments employing less than 100 people. In the prosperous regions of the UK — the South-East and the West Midlands — there was one innovating plant for every 540 establishments, whereas in the development regions there was one innovating plant for every 1300 establishments. No account was taken, however, of the structure of industry in the two groups of areas.

Small firms as a group also spend less on research and development per employee than large firms and they produce fewer innovations than large firms. On the other hand, they produce more innovations per pound spent on research and development and almost certainly produce more major inventions than large firms. Their unique contribution to technological change is that they are willing, often at the risk of failure, to develop products which the large firm feels will sell in insufficient quantities, or which the large firm may wish to suppress for fear of competition with existing profitable lines of business. The establishment of a small firm offers an opportunity for a technologist to develop his scientific expertise and to demonstrate the viability of his idea to his former employers. Large firms are now becoming more aware of the effects of losses of good quality staff and are making a greater effort to direct the energies of entrepreneurial scientists into areas which benefit the parent company — see Rothwell (1975).

For every Racal, unfortunately, there are probably several thousand small firms who have no wish to innovate, and a good deal more who are incapable of so doing. In this, as in many other respects, the small firm in the electronics or instrumentation industry bears no resemblance to a firm of similar size in the furniture, printing, food processing or dressmaking industry. The grouping of firms, on the basis of size, is probably less meaningful in terms of innovation than any other aspect of the debate over the merits of small and large firms. The problems which the NTBF faces differ markedly from that of similar-sized firms in more conservative industries. Finally, the importance for technical change of the link between the large and the small enterprise has to be stressed — a link which can be of mutual benefit. The small firm may generate an idea and then require assistance to develop it. This may be provided by the larger firm either through a licensing system or by the acquisition of all or part of the small firm. On the other hand, many ideas developed in the research laboratories of large firms are, from its viewpoint, not exploitable on a sufficiently large scale to merit further development. These may either be developed by an existing small firm, or by the research staff setting up on their own.

References

Anthony, D.W. (1983). 'Japan' in D.J. Storey (ed.), *The Small Firm: An International Survey,* Croom Helm, London, 46–83.

Armington, C. and Odle, C. (1982). 'Small Businesses: How Many Jobs', *Brookings Review,* Winter, 14–17.

Beesley, M.E. and Wilson, P.E.B. (1984). 'Public Policy and Small Firms in Britain', in Levicki, C. (ed.), *Small Business: Theory and Policy,* Croom Helm, London, 111–126.

Birch, D.L. (1979). *The Job Generation Process,* MIT Program on Neighbourhood and Regional Change, Cambridge, Mass.

Cameron, G.C. (1980). 'The Inner City: New Plant Incubator?' in A.W. Evans and D. Eversley, *The Inner City: Employment and Industry,* Heinemann, London.

Clark, R. (1979). *The Japanese Company,* Yale University Press, London and New York.

Cooper, A.C. (1973). 'Technical Entrepreneurship: What Do We Know?', *R & D Management, 3* (2), 59–64.

Cox, J.G. (1971). *Scientific and Engineering Manpower and Research in Small Firms,* Committee of Inquiry on Small Firms, Research Report no. 2, HMSO, London.

Curran, J. and Stanworth, M.J.K. (1981a). 'The Social Dynamics of the Small Manufacturing Enterprise', *Journal of Management Studies, 18* (2), 141–58.

Curran, J. and Stanworth M.J.K. (1981b). 'A New Look at Job Satisfaction in the Small Firm', *Human Relations, 34* (5), 343–65.

Davies, J.R. and Kelly, M. (1971). *Small Firms in the Manufacturing Sector,* Report of the Committee of Inquiry on Small Firms, Research Report no. 3, Cmnd 4811, HMSO, London.

Department of the Environment (1977). *Policy for the Inner Cities,* Cmnd 6845, HMSO, London.

Fagg, J.J. (1980). 'A Re-examination of the Incubator Hypothesis: The Case of Greater Leicester', *Urban Studies,* 17, 35–44.

Falk, N. (1978). *Think Small,* Fabian Society Tract no. 453, London.

Fothergill, S. and Gudgin, G. (1979). 'The Job Generation Process in Britain', *Centre for Environmental Studies,* Research Series no. 32, November.

Fothergill, S. and Gudgin, G. (1982). *Unequal Growth,* Heinemann Educational Books, London.

Freeman, C. (1971). *The Role of Small Firms in Innovations in the U.K. since 1945,* Committee of Inquiry on Small Firms, Research Report no. 6, HMSO, London.

Hitchens, D.M. (1977). *Business Efficiency in Iron Founding,* Technicopy, Stonehouse, Gloucs.

Hoover, E.M. and Vernon, R. (1960). *The New York Regional Study Plan,* Harvard University Press, Cambridge, Mass.

Howick, C. and Key, A. (1980). 'Small Firms and the Inner City: Tower Hamlets', *Centre for Environmental Studies, Policy Series no. 9.*

Ingham, G.K. (1970), *Size of Industrial Organisation and Worker Behaviour,* Cambridge Studies in Sociology no. 1, Cambridge University Press, Cambridge.

Jewkes, J., Sawyers, D. and Stillerman, R. (1969). *The Sources of Innovation,* 2nd edn., Macmillan, London.

Johns, B.L., Dunlop, W.C. and Sheehan, W.J. (1978). *Small Business in Australia: Problems and Prospects,* George Allen and Unwin, Sydney.

Keeble, D. (1978). *Industrial Location and Planning in the United Kingdom,* Methuen, London.

Leone, R.A. and Struyk, R. (1976). 'The Incubator Hypothesis: Evidence from Five SMSA's', *Urban Studies, 13* (3), 325–32.

Little, A.D. (1977). *New Technology-Based Firms in the United Kingdom and the Federal Republic of Germany,* Wilton House, London.

Lydall, H.F. (1958). 'Aspects of Competition in Manufacturing Industry', *Bulletin of the Oxford Institute of Economics and Statistics, 20* (4), November, 319–37.

Neck, P.A. (ed.) (1977). *Small Enterprise Development: Policies and Programmes,* Management Development Series no. 14, International Labour Organisation, Geneva.

Nicholson, B. and Brinkley, I. (1979). 'Entrepreneurial Characteristics and the Development of New Manufacturing Enterprises', paper given at CES (Centre for Environmental Studies) conference on 'New Firms in Local and Regional Economies', October.

Nicholson, B., Brinkley, I. and Evans, A.W. (1981). 'The Role of the Inner City in the Development of Manufacturing Industry', *Urban Studies, 18,* 57–71.

Oakey, R.P. (1979). 'An Analysis of the Spatial Distribution of Significant British Industrial Innovations', CURDS (Centre for Urban and Regional Development Studies), University of Newcastle upon Tyne Discussion Paper no. 25.

Oakey, R.P. (1984). 'Innovation and Regional Growth in Small High Technology Firms: Evidence from Britain and the USA', *Regional Studies, 16,* (3), 237–51.

Ray, G.F. (1979). 'Comment on Technical Innovation and British Trade Performance' in F. Blackaby (ed.), *De-industrialisation,* Heinemann/NIESR Policy Papers no. 2, London, 73–7.

Roberts, E.B. and Wainer, H.A. (1968). 'New Enterprises on Route 128', *Science Journal,* December, 78–83.

Rothwell, R. (1975). 'Intracorporate Engineers', *Management Decision, 13* (3), 142–54.

Rothwell, R. and Zegveld, W. (1982), *Innovation and the Small and Medium Sized Firm: Their Role in Employment and Economic Change,* Frances Pinter, London.

Storey, D.J. (1983). *'The Small Firm: An International Survey',* Croom Helm, London.

Storey, D.J. (1985). 'Manufacturing Employment Change in Northern England' in D.J. Storey (ed.), *Small Firms and Regional Economic Development: Britain, Ireland and the United States,* Cambridge University Press, London.

Yamanaka, T. and Kobayashi, Y. (1957). *The History and Structure of Japan's Small and Medium Industries — With Two Specific Surveys,* The Science Council of Japan, Division of Economics and Commerce, Economic Series no. 15, Tokyo.

6 The Entrepreneurial Personality: A Review and Some Theoretical Developments*

ELIZABETH CHELL

The nature of the entrepreneurial character is a continuing theme which has threaded its way through the small business literature raising spectres of what constitutes entrepreneurship, without reaching any definitive conclusions (Deeks 1976). As with a change in fashion, different propositions have been put forward at different times, although it is now clear that the wealth of research investigations can be boiled down to a rather more modest number of conceptual models. The models of *psychological* interest are (i) the psycho-dynamic model of Kets de Vries (1977); (ii) the social development model of Gibb and Ritchie (1981); and (iii) the trait approach which characterises the efforts of many researchers intent on discovering a trait or cluster of traits which uniquely distinguish the entrepreneur from other groups (for example, McClelland, 1961; Brockhaus, 1980; 1982).

The psychodynamic model

Kets de Vries paints an extremely powerful, if not poignant, portrait of the entrepreneurial personality. This includes a family background

---

* A modified version of this paper was published in the *International Small Business Journal,* vol. 3, no. 3 (1985).

'more often than not filled with images of endured hardships' (1977, p. 45). Such experiences 'may leave . . . the adult troubled by a burdensome psychological inheritance centred around problems of self esteem, insecurity and lack of confidence' and with 'repressed aggressive wishes towards persons in control' (p. 46). The upshot of such a background may be problems concerning occupational identity and choice which may persist throughout life. The entrepreneur thus becomes the deviant, drifting from job to job unable to 'fit in' and who develops a rebellious, non-conformist stand. Moreover, 'driving ambition may be viewed as a need to contradict strong feelings of inferiority and helplessness. Hyperactivity becomes a way of covering up passive longings. Passivity changes into activity as a reaction against anxiety' (p. 49).

Thus early life experiences are said to shape prominent patterns of behaviour amongst entrepreneurs. They include a sense of impulsivity, a persistent feeling of dissatisfaction, rejection and powerlessness and lowered self-esteem. The entrepreneur is under constant stress and is plagued by feelings of guilt and anxiety. 'Distrust and suspicion of everyone in a position of authority force the entrepreneur to search for non-structured situations where he can assert his control and independence' (p. 49–50). The consequence of all this is that 'it is extremely hard, if not impossible for individuals with an entrepreneurial disposition to integrate their personal needs with those of organisations. To design one's own organisation . . . often becomes the only alternative' (p. 50).

In summary, this model of the entrepreneur is of a person whose family background and other deprivations have been formative in shaping a somewhat deviant personality: one which is insecure and unable to operate effectively in an imposed and structured environment. He or she is hostile, aggressive and impulsive, and has many personality characteristics which, in the longer term, it is suggested, may jeopardise the success and even the viability of the business. Kets De Vries sees the solution in terms of the need for the entrepreneur to change; others might see it in terms of a problem of selection — whom to involve or otherwise in new start-ups (see Casson 1982).

What evidence is there to suggest that the entrepreneur can be characterised as a personality 'type' fitting this particular description? Many 'type' approaches do not take into account environmental circumstances. At least, Kets de Vries has provided an account of the entrepreneur's formative years and their implications in terms of learnt or adopted behavioural coping patterns. However, this has proved insufficiently convincing to many researchers; as Gibb and Ritchie (1981) suggest:

the stereotyped notion of the prospective entrepreneur being a behaviourally deviant employee proved of very limited applicability . . . Similarly, there were few who could be regarded as opportunistic and loosely committed rapid 'job changers' unable to follow given job and career lines . . . *In overall terms, the research does not support the view of these being people substantially disillusioned with their current work environment.* (1977, pp. 195–6) (emphasis added).

The main theoretical problem with the type approach is that it tends only to describe accurately the extremes of a given population and leaves the vast majority untouched (Robbins, 1979, p. 69). The Kets de Vries model may thus only be applicable to those entrepreneurs with particular backgrounds and life experiences and may not apply to entrepreneurs in general. Indeed, it may be that the description does not even differentiate a particular type of entrepreneur from individuals from other walks of life with similar deprived backgrounds. This implies that the avenue into entrepreneurship may be, in Freudian terms, merely a sublimation activity on the part of those individuals, enabling them subconsciously to resolve their inner conflicts and tensions by creating an environment with which they can cope. Why not also become an academic or a criminal? Each of these 'occupations' is worked out in a sufficiently unstructured environment to enable a deviant so described to resolve his or her inner feelings of distrust to authority, inability to 'fit in', and so on.

Other evidence with which to evaluate this particular model of the entrepreneur can be gleaned from the sociological literature (see, for example, Bechhofer and Elliott 1976; Scase and Goffee 1980; Stanworth and Curran, 1973, 1976). In this regard, it is important to consider, not only the characteristics of small businesses, but also the reasons and motives of small business people for starting up (Boswell 1973).

The argument concerning the characteristics of small businesses and of their owners is more complicated than might first appear, because it is entirely dependent upon the definition of what constitutes an entrepreneur, and what typifies a small business. The extremes of this conceptual morass range, for example, from the notion of the *petite bourgeoisie*, the distinguishing features of which are small scale, low technology, high turnover of businesses, deep antipathy to bureaucracy, personalised service, need to perpetuate traditional ways of doing things and the market conditions in which the 'little man' can succeed (Bechhofer and Elliott, 1976) to that of 'product innovator' where a person with a good idea for a new product can mobilise resources and skills to bring about a new product launch. Such entrepreneurship could conceivably characterise existing personnel *within* a company, and may have little or nothing to do with ownership or managing one's own business (Monds, 1984). One way round this problem may be to attempt to categorise business enterprises (see Scase and Goffee, 1980, p. 23) and to take a large statistical sample, as suggested by Brockhaus (1982).

Moreover, if the psychodynamic model were valid, it should be possible to identify a set of reasons (consonant with the deviant stereotype) which typify the entrepreneur. However, all the evidence suggests that the motives for starting a business are diverse (Boswell 1973; Chell and Haworth 1985; Haworth and Chell 1985; Scase and Goffee 1980; Watkins 1976). Certainly, the 'myth' of the 'profit maximiser' is not borne out, rather there is a mixture of psychological reasons and, in some cases, the attribution of luck or good fortune, which determine the business venture.

Despite the differences in the particular reasons for start-up, there are two general and highly plausible explanations of this event. For instance, Shapero's model of the factors that determine company formation consists of four aspects (Shapero, 1971). These are: (i) *displacement*, which describes the inertia of being in a comfortable rut and the absence of any external impetus to shift the person into self-employment or entrepreneurial activity; (ii) *an apparent disposition to act* such as might arise from the desire for independence or autonomy; (iii) *credibility*, depicted as the need for admiration or peer approval; and (iv) *the availability of resources*. The utility of this model lies in the realism of the need for several things to 'fall into place' before the individual takes the major step of setting up on his or her own.

A second source of explanation which is compatible with the Shapero model is the social marginality thesis (Dickie-Clark 1966; Stanworth and Curran 1973, 1976; Scase and Goffee 1980). This thesis suggests that there is a perceived incongruity between the individual's personal attributes and the role(s) he or she plays in society. This relative deprivation may thus provide the necessary impetus for such individuals to become self-employed. For such people, there is clearly the 'pull' of assuming a more attractive, socially esteemed role in society, and the 'push' of reducing the incongruity between self-image and socially conferred role image. This social marginality thesis can be applied, not only to minority groups within a society, but also at the micro-level to individuals within an organisation. In the latter case, such individuals may give negative reasons for starting up, ('push' rather than 'pull'), in terms of their dislike of working for someone else, feelings of being exploited and undervalued, and having low or no promotion prospects.

There are two further points which may be made about this particular thesis before leaving this section. They are: (i) it makes no attempt at universality, that is, it may provide a coherent account of why some groups and some individuals set up in business, but leaves open the possibility that there are other motives (within the displacement and disposition categories) for start-up; (ii) it stresses the importance of the social situation in the account of the start-up process, rather than focusing upon the psychodynamics of the individual, though it most certainly includes a psychological component to the start-up process.

The social development model

Gibb and Ritchie (1981) argue that the traditional view of entrepreneurship has been to assume in-born character traits which differentiate the entrepreneur from other groups or individuals; that this view largely ignores environmental influences and in sum assumes that 'entrepreneurs are born and not made' (p. 182). This view may be termed the trait approach and is discussed more fully in the next section.

Gibb and Ritchie propose an alternative model which suggests that 'entrepreneurship can be wholly understood in terms of the types of situation encountered and the social groups to which individuals relate' (p. 183). The model assumes that individuals change throughout life and it is the individual's transactions with specific social contexts and reference groups that shape the person. The model assumes 'the formative nature of early life experience in creating basic traits and drives', but 'it places *equal* emphasis on the way adulthood itself may shape new entrepreneurial ideas and ambitions' (p. 185; emphasis added). People change throughout their 'life course' and it depends at what point in the life-cycle the individual makes the decision to enter the small business world as to what this action *means* to him or her.

In order to cope with a complex labyrinth of data, Gibb and Ritchie propose a fourfold typology which spans the life-cycle and suggests certain key influences at each stage. Thus, the *improvisors* typify the small business owner at the early stage of his or her life and career: the *revisionists* are slightly older and near to mid-career; the *superceders* are into the second half of their life and a new career; and in the final stage of the life-cycle come the older, late and post-career *reverters*.

It is undoubtedly true that social pressures and circumstances change throughout one's life and that these are influential in terms of one's behaviour, freedom of movement and so on (Levinson *et al.*, 1978; Levinson, 1980). Indeed, it has been argued by some psychologists (notably Sheehy 1976) that there are particular turning points throughout the course of the life-cycle, where individuals work through personal transitions in order to satisfy and reconcile their own changing goals, needs and ambitions with the opportunities, circumstances and situations which they currently find themselves in.

The problems with the Gibb–Ritchie model would appear to be these:

(i) Although it claims to recognise the importance of early life experience in forming basic traits, and so on, it is to all intents and purposes an entirely 'situational' model, that is, it would appear to lose sight of the person by describing behaviour as a function entirely of social influences.

(ii) Although they criticise the 'traditional' view of the entrepreneur as a stereotype with limited applicability, these authors would appear to have substituted four stereotypes in its place. Again, the argument against the type approach made in the above section applies in this context also.

(iii) On empirical grounds the generalisations made from this research were put forward on the basis of a limited, untypical collection (that is, not a statistically valid sample) of would-be entrepreneurs. This casts doubt on the generality of the findings. Indeed, Cromie (1984) had difficulty in applying his findings either to the Gibb–Ritchie model or to the traditional view of entrepreneurship.

(iv) The reasons for starting a business which were discussed in the previous section may be applicable at any point in the life course of the entrepreneur. The implications of the social development model as stated are: depending upon the age or stage of life of the entrepreneur at the start-up, he or she will (a) bring to bear varying amounts of experience to enable business development; and (b) be constrained in his or her propensity to take risks as a result of other commitments and responsibilities. This is no doubt true and may add yet another dimension to the account of why people start their own business. However, it is also somewhat trivial, for it does nothing to help differentiate between the successful and unsuccessful small business owner, nor does it enable one to predict which are likely to become successful.

The trait model

Probably by far the greatest proportion of investigators of entrepreneurship have attempted to discover a single trait or constellation of traits which they could claim differentiated the entrepreneur from other groups (see Brockhaus 1982, for a review). This approach has met with limited success. For example, Lynn (1969) suggested that 'one of the underlying personality traits [of the entrepreneur] could be anxiety or neuroticism' (p. 152). McClelland's work in the 1960s suggested that achievement motivation was a primary characteristic of the entrepreneur (McClelland 1961), whilst Schrage (1965) found that 'veridical perception' was more important than either achievement or power motivation in distinguishing the *successful* entrepreneur. Hornaday and Bunker (1970) attempted to discover whether 21 different characteristics applied to the entrepreneur. In a follow-up study, it was suggested that the characteristics of 'achievement', 'support', 'independence' and 'leadership' differentiated the successful entrepreneur from a control group (Hornaday and Aboud 1971). Timmons, Smollen and Dingee (1977) also suggested that there were more than 20 characteristics which discriminate between entrepreneurs and others. Pandey and Tewary (1979) have provided evidence that people with high 'internal scores' are more likely to be successful entrepreneurs.

In a more recent study, Cromie and Johns (1983) argue that entrepreneurship is a personality variable. They suggest that entrepreneurs display greater achievement motivation, achievement values, persistence and self-confidence than other groups in society. Moreover, they will hold stronger economic values and possess internal rather than external locus of control over life events. In terms of a comparison with a group of senior managers, Cromie and Johns found that the only apparent significant differences were (a) the primacy of the business (that is, the entrepreneur not surprisingly felt that the business dominated his life more than did senior managers); and (b) the entrepreneurs were found to be more internal than the group of managers. Interestingly, these researchers did discover significant differences between a group of 'aspiring' entrepreneurs and the established ones on three 'key entrepreneurial characteristics' — achievement values, locus of control and economic values.

There are two observations which may be made at this juncture:

(i) The original 'locus of control' concept of Rotter (1966) was that of a 'learnt behavioural response', that is, not a trait, although it has been used subsequently by others as a trait concept. This suggests that it may be important to discover what are the stimulus conditions which may cause the development of this particular response in a large proportion of entrepreneurs. Brockhaus (1982, p. 45), having reviewed the evidence on the role played by the 'locus of control variable' concludes:

> An internal locus-of-control belief may therefore be associated with a more active effort to affect the outcome of events. This internal belief and the associated greater effort would seem to hold true for both successful entrepreneurs and successful managers. Therefore, it fails to uniquely distinguish entrepreneurs, but holds promise for distinguishing successful entrepreneurs from the unsuccessful.

(ii) To what extent were the 'aspiring' entrepreneurs acting out their own stereotypic concept of the entrepreneur? This possible explanation is given credence by the fact that the established entrepreneurs had few so-called entrepreneurial qualities which could distinguish them from a control group of senior managers. From the above analysis, it would appear that three lessons can be learnt from this study: (a) at what point in time do you measure the so called traits of the entrepreneur? (b) how enduring are these traits? and (c) how appropriate is it to think of entrepreneurship *entirely* as a personality variable?

There would seem to be a great deal which is equivocal and inconclusive about the trait approach to entrepreneurship. This may be considered as not surprising if we take a wider view of trait approaches in general. In psychology, the trait approach to personality has come under heavy attack in recent years (see Chell, 1985, for a more detailed discussion of this theme).

The main criticisms of trait theory are:

(i) There appears to be a very low correlation between the assessment of the trait and actual behaviour.

(ii) If there is no physico-chemical or neurological basis to traits what are they?

(iii) The underlying assumption of trait theory is that of individual consistency in expressing the trait. But how consistent are people? Could it be that we see people performing a very narrow range of activities in a limited number of situations and environments and assume that they behave similarly across a much wider range of situations?

(iv) How far does the impact of various situational factors modify an individual's behaviour?

The upshot of arguments such as these was to suggest to some (for example, Rotter 1964; Argyle and Little 1972; Bowers 1973; Harré 1979; Mischel 1973, 1981; and Jones and Nisbett 1972) that the measurement of traits alone was an inadequate basis for the prediction of behaviour. Assessment of both person and situation variables should enable the psychologist to predict behaviour with greater accuracy (Argyle, Furnham and Graham 1981).

The major successor to trait theory was interactionism. This can be neatly summarised in the Lewinian formula $B = f(P, E)$, where B is behaviour, P is personality and E is environmental factors (Ekehammer 1974). There are two possible interpretations which can be placed on the term 'interaction'. In the case of physical interaction, person and situation variables (the independent variables in this model) give rise to (cause) the behavioural response (the dependent variable). It is then a case of deciding what might count as the operative person and situation variables (see, for example, Newton and Keenan 1983). On the other hand, *psychological* interaction between person and situation variables assumes that how the person perceives and cognises the situation is paramount. In this interpretation, it is the *meaning* which person holds for the situation which 'causes' him or her to behave in a particular way, and thus it is the cognitive constructs of the person and the symbolic meaning signalled by the situation which 'shapes' behaviour.

The interactionist model has the advantage of maximising the variability between person and situation factors on subsequent behaviour. For example, some situations may be extremely powerful, and this may result in insignificant individual differences; whereas, in other circumstances, people might vary their behaviour according to the situation they are in (Argyle and Little 1972). As Argyle and Little recount, much of the recent interactionist research has been aimed at apportioning the variability due to P, E and $P \times E$ factors, using, principally, analysis of variance techniques. One of the objectives of the studies was to demonstrate that, while some of the variance could be explained by P and E factors, by far the most variability was due to $P \times E$ interaction. Such results were interpreted as demonstrating considerable support for the theory.

Recently, one of the drawbacks to the theory has been identified as the poor vocabulary and methodology which we have for analysing and describing situations (Frederiksen 1972; Argyle *et al.*, 1981). It is suggested that until theorists and researchers can more accurately classify situations (i.e. not only in terms of their physical dimensions but also in terms of how individuals interpret those situations) then the

ability of interactionists accurately to predict behaviour will also be severely limited (Bem and Allen 1974).

Towards a reconceptualisation of entrepreneurship

The Gibb and Ritchie paper (1981) is rich in suggestions of environmental factors which might influence the small business person at the start-up stage, although clearly it is important to document systematically those environmental factors which affect the behaviour of the established entrepreneur and consequently the growth of his or her business.

In terms of appropriate person variables, the trait approach would appear to have thrown up nothing but equivocal findings. An alternative way out of this impasse might be to conceive of a collection of different person variables. Mischel (1973) has suggested a set of 'cognitive social learning variables'. These are 'the products of each individual's total history . . . that in turn regulate how new experiences affect him or her' (Mischel, 1981, p. 345). Moreover, they 'should suggest useful ways of conceptualising and studying specifically how the qualities of the person influence the impact of stimuli ('environments' or 'situations') and how each person generates distinctive complex behaviour patterns in interaction with the conditions of his or her life' (ibid.).

These variables are:

(i)   *competencies,* that is, skills or abilities of the person;
(ii) *encoding strategies and personal constructs* which describe the different ways people represent, symbolise and think about environmental stimuli, in-coming information or particular aspects of the situation they are in;
(iii) *expectancies* suggest that how a person performs in a given situation depends in part on what he or she *expects* might happen; there may be different behavioural possibilities and the person will weigh up the alternative courses of action open to him or her;
(iv) *subjective values* suggest that people may choose different courses of action because the outcomes of such actions have different values for them;
(v)   *self-regulatory systems and plans* is another way of saying that people have different goals and standards which they try to maintain and/or achieve. They adopt contingency plans and rules in order to attempt to reach their goals and this activity alone specifies the sequencing and organisation of their behaviour. Importantly, this aspect of a person enables him or her to

overcome the 'power of situations': 'We can actively *select* the situation to which we expose ourselves, in a sense creating our own environment, entering some settings but not others, making decisions about what to do and what not to do' (Mischel 1981, p. 350).

How can such a set of *person variables* be translated into a more concrete set of variables to be applied to entrepreneurial behaviour? First of all, we can ask (i) what skills and abilities does the entrepreneur have or need in order effectively to run his or her business? (ii) how does the small business person perceive his or her environment; what are the salient or influential dimensions of the environment which affect his or her behaviour? (iii) given the type of business he or she is in, his or her assessment of the business environment, its markets, customers, and so on, what are his or her expectations of the viability of the business, its future growth or expansion? (iv) what outcomes does he or she value — for example, is growth and/or expansion of the business a valued target? (v) what are his or her goals and objectives and how does he or she intend to achieve those goals? Such questions clearly distinguish between entrepreneurs in different sorts of business, for example, in construction (Norris 1984) and in research and development (Schrage 1965) or high technology.

It is possible to develop this model further in terms of the roles and functions performed by the entrepreneur. The role and function models are largely derived from the economists. They have suggested that the entrepreneur performs three key roles: those of innovator, risk-taker and a 'manager-coordinator' role (Kets de Vries 1977). Current thinking suggests that entrepreneurs are not necessarily innovators as such, but are more likely to be exploiters and developers of ideas which have been developed by larger firms. Furthermore, the idea of the entrepreneur as a risk-taker has also been brought into question. Brockhaus (1980), for example, could find no evidence with which to distinguish entrepreneurs from other managers on this dimension. Thirdly, as regards the managing-coordinating role, a similar conclusion was reached; as Kets de Vries puts it: 'here the distinction between the entrepreneur and the business executive becomes blurred' (1977, p. 37).

Although it would seem that there are no distinctive roles which the entrepreneur might play, this concept of 'role' does enable one more closely to relate those person variables which we have discussed above to the situations which the entrepreneur, in his or her daily routine of running a business, may encounter and must negotiate or avoid. According to Harré's situation-act model, it is the *meaning* of the situation to the individual which is of key significance (Harré, 1979;

112

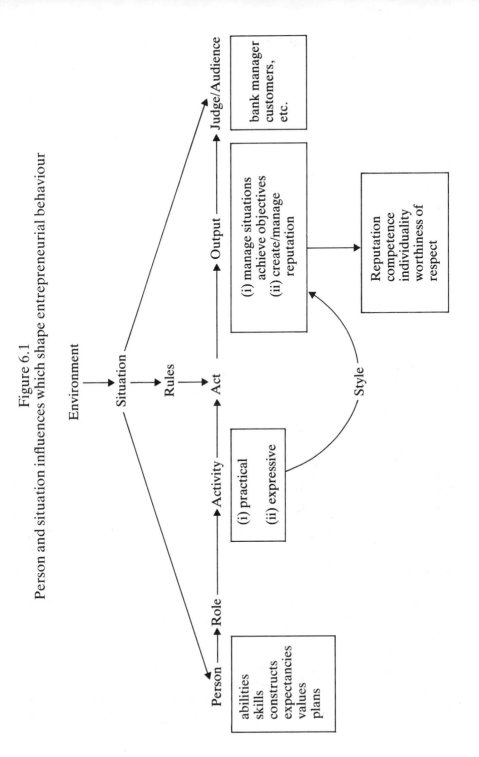

Figure 6.1
Person and situation influences which shape entrepreneurial behaviour

Branthwaite, 1983; and cf. Stanworth and Curran, 1976). The individual learns how to handle or manage situations by learning the rules which govern them. The model can be applied to the world of the small business person as shown in Figure 6.1.

The explanation of Figure 6.1 is as follows. Both the internal and external environments of the business create situations which the incumbents have to deal with or ignore. Situations, according to Harré, are rule-governed and prescribe the 'acting out' of appropriate roles. The entrepreneurs, bringing his or her own set of person variables to bear on each situation, may or may not have the appropriate repertoire of behaviours to cope with and deal with the situations he or she encounters. Indeed, it is common knowledge that the entrepreneur often has to play multiple roles — chief executive, production manager, sales executive, general 'dogsbody', and so on.

In the early stages of the start-up process, the entrepreneur is unlikely to have all the role behaviours and skills necessary to cope. Once the business is established a critical point may occur where the entrepreneur must decide whether to expand the business or maintain a steady state. Some small business men (for example, in the construction industry) do not want growth (Norris 1984). It is argued that the reason for this is that they do not want to relinquish control over any part of the business. However, another way of looking at this may be in terms of their information processing capabilities. McGaffey and Christie (1975), for example, argue that there is a relationship between the information processing attributes of entrepreneurs and the complexity of the organisations they develop. Translated into the model being developed, this suggests that the limiting factors on growth of the business are the entrepreneur's capabilities in terms of having the necessary skills to cope with increased information which will arise from the greater number and variety of situations which he or she will encounter and need to negotiate if the business is to grow and/or be at all successful. Another factor, of course, is the need for *some* entrepreneurs to maintain total control and not to delegate. This analysis gleans some support from the work of Casson (1982) who presents a functional analysis of the role of the entrepreneur in terms of the qualities required for effective decision-making. Due to the skewness in distribution of some of these qualities, the possession of such scarce qualities thus confers an advantage on some people in becoming an entrepreneur.

In acting out appropriate roles, the entrepreneur engages in various activities. These activities, according to Harré, have two main functions: (i) a *practical* function — to manage the situation and fulfil the individual's needs; (ii) an *expressive* function — to convey impressions to others. In terms of the latter, this contributes to the central function of human social activity, which is to develop a *style* and a *reputation*. Actions are often carried out with particular judges and audiences in mind. For example, in dealing with customers, the business person may attempt to please, and convey an impression of reliability, friendliness, orderliness and general business capability in order to win orders. The manner with which he or she deals with customers will affect the maintenance and longevity of the relationship, future orders and whether the business is recommended to others, and so on.

The modified situation-act model of Harré applied to the world of the small business person is thus highly appropriate in that it provides a general model of the broad dimensions of what the entrepreneur brings to each situation and suggests how the meaning of the situation translates into practical activities of learning the rules governing each situation, developing and exercising skills and building up a reputation.

Finally, it is worth noting that this particular thesis has similarities with the sociological 'social action perspective' of the small firm (Stanworth and Curran 1973, 1976). These authors argue that

> the key to growth lies in the meanings attached to participation in the firm by the actors involved . . . A social action perspective . . . links the meanings and actions of the small firm's participants with their wider social environment . . . An interpretation of the social situation is based upon a knowledge of both internal and external forces influencing the situation . . . Of particular importance [to the key role of owner-managers] are the new owner-manager's reasons for going it alone. Understanding this aids an understanding of attitudes towards growth later in the firm's life (Stanworth and Curran 1976, pp. 100–1).

Summary, conclusions and implications

There has been a great deal of 'mythology' surrounding the role of 'entrepreneurship'. Several models have been put forward but all appear inadequate under close scrutiny. For example, the psycho-dynamic model of Kets de Vries reduces to a stereotypic image of the entrepreneur as a deviant unable to fit comfortably into organisational life. The social development model, on the other hand, stresses the differential importance of various social influences at significant points in the individual's life cycle with its consequent effect upon the start-up process (Gibb and Ritchie 1981). This model was eventually reduced to that of substituting four stereotypes of the would-be entrepreneur in place of the one. The third significant approach was to discover those traits which were peculiar to the entrepreneur and would thus distinguish him or her from members of other groups. The 'trait approach' resulted in equivocal findings with no firm evidence of any single trait which could be applied to entrepreneurs generally.

An attempt at reconceptualising entrepreneurship suggested that what was needed was a model which encapsulated, in general terms, appropriate person variables, and took account of the variability in behaviour due to differences in persons and situations. This further suggested a combination of Mischel's social learning person variables incorporated into a modified version of Harré's situation-act model.

Using this model, we might speculate that if a systematic study of the influences which affect the success or effectiveness of small business people were carried out across a sample of entrepreneurs selected at random (i.e. from a diverse range of industries) then it might be possible to suggest: (i) under what circumstances (i.e. in what environments) entrepreneurs were most effective; (ii) what person variables (in terms of their orientation to their environment) were salient in determining the success of a small business; (iii) to what extent the interaction between person and environmental variables are of overriding importance in affecting the success of the small business; (iv) the nature of the roles the entrepreneur adopts and his or her skill requirements in negotiating typical business situations; (v) differences between industries in terms of the appropriateness of particular person variables associated with the entrepreneur's capability to abstract the meaning from a diverse range of situations and deal with them effectively; (vi) differences between entrepreneurs and their situation or circumstances which influences the size and rate of growth of the business.

The practical and policy implications of this analysis are considerable: (i) in terms of understanding the key aspects of the small business environment; (ii) in understanding how the small business manager perceives, and operates within, that environment; (iii) in determining what aspects of the environment need to be manipulated or changed in order to make the business more effective; (iv) in terms of the training and personal development of the entrepreneur. This could include the need to realise his or her own inadequacies (i.e. skill deficiencies — see Welsch and Young 1984); to acquire and develop new skills (cf Casson 1982); to broaden the individuals conceptual framework in order to assess and evaluate the environment; to develop a wider range of action alternatives, the ability to assess his or her long-term goals and strategy and to plan effectively to realise those goals.

References

Argyle, M., Furnham, A. and Graham, Jean A. (1981). *Social Situations*, Cambridge: Cambridge University Press.

Argyle, M. and Little, B. (1972). 'Do Personality Traits Apply to Social Behaviour?' *Journal for the Theory of Social Behaviour 2*, 1, 1–35.

Bechhofer, F. & Elliott, B. (1976). 'Persistence and Change: The Petite Bourgeoisie in Industrial Society', Archives Européenaes Sociologic, XVII, 74–99.

Bem D.J. and Allen, A. (1974). 'On Predicting Some of the People Some of the Time: The Search for Cross-situational Consistencies in Behaviour', *Psychological Review, 81*, 6, 506–20.

Boswell, J. (1973). *The Rise and Decline of Small Firms*, London: George Allen & Unwin.

Bowers, K.S. (1973). 'Situationism in Psychology: An Analysis and a Critique', *Psychological Review, 80*, 5, 307–36.

Branthwaite, A. (1983). 'Situations and Social Actions: Applications for Marketing of Recent Theories in Social Psychology', *Journal of the Market Research Society, 25*, 1, 19–38.

Brockhaus, R.H. Sr. (1980). 'Risk Taking Propensity of Entrepreneurs', *Academy of Management Journal, 23*, 3, 509–20.

Brockhaus, R.H. Sr. (1982). 'The Psychology of the Entrepreneur', in C.A. Kent, D.L. Sexton & K.H. Vesper (eds), *Encyclopedia of Entrepreneurship*, Englewood-Cliffs, N.J.: Prentice-Hall.

Casson, M. (1982). *The Entrepreneur*, Oxford: Martin Robertson.

Chell, E. (1985). *Participation and Organisation: A Social Psychological Approach*, London: Macmillan.

Chell, E. & Haworth, J.M. (1985). 'A Study of the Factors Affecting the Sales Performance of Independent Retail Newsagents', in A. Gibb *et al.* (eds), *Small Firms Growth and Development*, Aldershot: Gower.

Cromie, S. (1984). 'Motivations of Aspiring Male and Female Entrepreneurs', paper presented at the 1984 UK Small Business Policy and Research Conference, 5–7 September, Trent Polytechnic, Nottingham.

Cromie, S. and Johns, S. (1983). 'Irish Entrepreneurs: Some Personal Characteristics, *Journal of Occupational Behaviour, 4*, 317–24.

Deeks, J. (1976). *The Small Firm Owner-Manager*, New York: Praeger.

Dickie-Clarke, H.P. (1966). *The Marginal Situation*, London: Routledge & Kegan Paul.

Ekehammer, B. (1974). 'Interactionism in personality from a historical perspective', *Psychological Bulletin, 81,* 12, 1026–48.

Frederiksen, N. (1972). 'Towards a Taxonomy of Situations', *American Psychologist* (February), 114.

Gibb, A. and Ritchie, J. (1981). 'Influences on Entrepreneurship: A Study over Time', paper presented to the 1981 Small Business Policy and Research Conference, 20–21 November, Polytechnic of Central London.

Harré, R. (1979). *Social Being,* Oxford: Basil Blackwell.

Haworth, J.M. and Chell, E. (1985). 'An Application of Latent Class Analysis to the Measurement of Motivation', *Journal of the Market Research Society, 27,* 2, 131–46.

Hornaday, J.A. and Aboud, J. (1971). 'Characteristics of Successful Entrepreneurs', *Personnel Psychology, 24,* 141–53.

Hornaday, J.A. and Bunker, C.S. (1970). 'The Nature of the Entrepreneur', *Personnel Psychology, 23,* 47–54.

Jones, E.E. and Nisbett, R.E. (1972). 'The Actor and the Observer: Divergent Perceptions of the Causes of Behaviour' in E.E. Jones *et al, Attribution: Perceiving the Causes of Behaviour,* Morristown, NJ: General Learning Press.

Kets de Vries, M.F.R. (1977). 'The Entrepreneurial Personality: A Person at the Crossroads', *Journal of Management Studies,* (February), 34–57.

Levinson, D.J. *et al.* (1978). *The Seasons of a Man's Life,* New York: Knopf.

Levinson, D.J. (1980). 'Toward a Conception of the Adult Life Course' in N.J. Smelser and E. Erikson (eds), *Theories of Work and Love in Adulthood,* London: Grant McIntyre, pp. 265–90.

Lynn, R. (1969). 'Personality Characteristics of a Group of Entrepreneurs', *Journal of Occupational Psychology, 43,* 151–2.

McClelland, D.C. (1961). *The Achieving Society,* Princeton, N.J.: Van Nostrand.

McGaffey, T.N. and Christy, R. (1975). 'Information Processing Capability as a Predictor of Entrepreneurial Effectiveness', *Academy of Management Journal, 18,* 4, 857–63.

Mischel, W. (1973). 'Toward a Cognitive Social Learning Reconceptualisation of Personality', *Psychological Review, 80,* 4, 252–83.

Mischel, W. (1981). *Introduction to Personality,* 3rd edn, New York: Holt, Rinehart and Winston.

Monds, F. (1984). *The Business of Electronic Product Development,* London: Peter Peregrinus.

Newton, T.J. and Keenan, A. (1983). 'Is Work Involvement an Attribute of the Person or the Environment?', *Journal of Occupational Behaviour, 4,* 169–78.

Norris, K. (1984). 'Small Building Firms — Their Origins, Characteristics and Development Needs', paper presented to the Small Business Policy and Research Conference, 5–7 September, Trent Polytechnic, Nottingham.

Pandey, J. and Tewary, N.B. (1979). 'Locus of Control and Achievement Values of Entrepreneurs', *Journal of Occupational Psychology, 52,* 107–11.

Robbins, S.P. (1979). *Organizational Behaviour,* Englewood Cliffs, N.J.: Prentice Hall.

Rothwell, R. & Zegveld, W. (1982). *Innovation and the Small and Medium Sized Firm,* London: Frances Pinter.

Rotter, J.B. (1964). *Clinical Psychology,* Englewood Cliffs, N.J.: Prentice-Hall.

Rotter, J.B. (1966). 'Generalised Expectancies for Internal versus External Control of Reinforcement', *Psychological Monographs, 80,* no. 609.

Scase, R. & Goffee, R. (1980). *The Real World of the Small Business Owner,* London: Croom Helm.

Schrage, H. (1965). 'The R and D Entrepreneur Profile of Success' *Harvard Business Review, 43,* 6, (November/December) 56–69.

Shapero, A. (1971). *An Action Program for Entrepreneurship,* Austin, Texas: Multi-Disciplinary Research Press.

Sheehy, Gail (1976). *Passages: Predictable Crises of Adult Life,* New York: Dutton.

Stanworth, M.J.K. & Curran, J. (1973). *Management Motivation in the Smaller Business,* Aldershot: Gower.

Stanworth, M.J.K. & Curran, J. (1976). 'Growth and the Smaller Firm — An Alternative View', *Journal of Management Studies* (May), 95–110.

Timmons, J.A., Smollen, L.E. and Dingee, A.L.M. (1977). *New Venture Creation,* Homewood, Ill.: Irwin.

Watkins, D. (1976). 'Entry into Independent Entrepreneurship', paper presented to EIASM Seminar, Copenhagen, May.

Welsch, H. and Young, E. (1984). 'Male and Female Entrepreneurial Characteristics and Behaviours: A Profile of Similarities and Differences', *International Small Business Journal, 2,*4, 11–20.

7 Persistence and Change: The Petite Bourgeoisie in Industrial Society

FRANK BECHHOFER AND BRIAN ELLIOTT*

The petite bourgeosie is a stratum that has attracted little academic study. Historians have given it short shrift and they are not alone in their neglect, for in economics, political science and sociology there is a similar disdain for those who cannot be cast in the hero's role in any of the major developments of Western capitalism.

However, in some recent work there are signs that the conventional disregard of those who operate small businesses, in manufacturing, retailing or service sectors of the economy is giving way to some curiosity about the emergence of this stratum and about the role which it has played and is playing in the capitalist societies.[1] Certainly there is evidence of a new interest in the political power of the stratum, particularly at the level of local municipal politics[2] and this is related to the need, perceived by sociologists and historians alike, to explore in more detail the processes of social differentiation which industrialism engendered. If processes of class formation and more specific concern with the power of the stratum have been two of the major sources of interest to date, there is a third matter which stimulates enquiry and that is the stubborn, almost incomprehensible persistence of the stratum in all industrial capitalist societies (and some socialist ones, too).[3]

---

* Abridged from: *European Journal of Sociology,* vol. XVII, no. 1 (1976.)

Inevitably the attempt to talk about the petite bourgeoisie raises problems of definition and the familiar difficulties of establishing adequate boundaries to this stratum. The common-sense view would obviously focus upon that motley collection of occupations to which reference is made when people speak of the 'small businessmen'. So, the stratum is thought to include the small manufacturers, the keepers of minor enterprises of all kinds from simple retailers to those who offer services rather than commodities — the restauranteurs and café proprietors, the bookmakers and garage owners, the keepers of small hotels and publicans and landlords. If we ask what it is that these diverse individuals have in common, the traditional and still most serviceable answer is found in a single word: capital.[4] Whether we think of the buildings and plant of the manufacturer, or the housing rented out by the landlord or the workshop of the self-employed tradesman, the fact remains that all these occupations may be distinguished from those of the working class by their employment of capital (albeit in small measure) to obtain their income. But while this is a necessary element in any definition of the petite bourgeoisie, we would argue that it is certainly not sufficient. To define the petit bourgeois as one who operates a small business with modest capital would force us to include a good many of the small firms which have been set up purely to exploit some very recent technological innovations, the firms which are the 'spin-off' from centres of technical research and development. Those who run concerns like these are trading more on their skill and esoteric knowledge than on the advantages of capital, and with their sophisticated education and the lifestyles and tastes of a scientifically qualified élite they would seem to have little in common with the other occupations mentioned above. Indeed, there are those who would regard this educated élite as part of a new class.[5] In fact it seems to us characteristic of the petit bourgeois that the means which he employs to win a livelihood are typically rather traditional and subject to little alteration. Thus, a second element in our definition of the stratum would stress the dominance of relatively low technology. Finally, we should consider that in such enterprises we would expect to find weakly developed forms of differentiation. Typically, we find a situation in which low *material* technology is accompanied by what Burns[6] once referred to as low *social* technology. These enterprises employ small labour forces — and that after all is the most common basis for distinguishing the *small* business stratum in all the official reports and enquiries. Thus, the social organisation of work is simple, the span of authority small, the petit bourgeois concern cannot be given a bureaucratic structure. Taken together, these three elements, of low capital and simple material and social technology, serve to define the occupational base of the stratum.

Inevitably though, there are problems, for our criteria would exclude some, like clerical and routine administrative workers who are regarded by some neo-Marxist writers[7] as petits bourgeois. Undoubtedly, there are some similarities in attitudes and values; certainly both are distinguishable from working class occupations; but these factors should not obscure the fundamental economic differences between them. The small businessman gets his living by mixing his own labour with his own capital. The clerical and administrative workers do not, consequently they have significantly different interests. An essentially similar point can be made when we consider the relationship between highly skilled artisans and the petits bourgeois. If the tradesman is self-employed, if he uses his skill along with a little capital to build up his own business, then in our scheme he would rate as petit bourgeois. If, on the other hand, he simply sells his labour to an employer then his situation does not differ in kind from that of the mass of manual workers.

The use of the term 'petit bourgeois', defined in the way outlined, serves to distinguish a specific set of occupations with broadly common market and work situations and essentially similar interests. It helps to disaggregate that vague category 'the middle class' and just as the petite bourgeoisie is distinguishable from the routine clerical workforce, so a *grande* or *haute* bourgeoisie is separable from the professionals, the senior administrators and bureaucrats.

Some indications of the interests, allegiances and affinities of the emerging petit bourgeois stratum are found in the fragmentary records of their political sympathies. At the turn of the century we find that shopkeepers, for example, appear on a number of occasions as 'radicals' embroiled with artisans and others in a variety of political activities aimed at changing the traditional patterns of British politics. Along with the small masters and tradesmen they seem to have sought a new independence, a freedom from 'patronage, bribery and deference'.[8] Then, too, we find them described by Thompson as 'intractable jurymen' in the political trials of the 1790s, and by 1807 they are triumphantly carrying through the streets the Radical MPs for Westminster. The precise nature of their radicalism is difficult to ascertain, for radicalism then as now came in many forms and at this point had to encompass the discontents of the minor gentry as well as those of the artisans and petits bourgeois. But certainly much of this radicalism was influenced by Painite ideas. Paine built upon the Christian views asserting the dignity of man, 'the first unit-idea of individualism' as Lukes put it,[9] and in the name of liberty attacked the principle of hereditary privilege. He defended the rights of private property in ways which appealed very obviously to the unrepresented tradesmen and minor manufacturers, and wove together strands of individualism which formed the intellectual roots of liberal democracy.

Not only is it doubtful whether there was ever real unity of political view among the diverse occupations which made up this stratum but only a few years later individuals from the same shopkeeping sector of the petite bourgeoisie appear on the side of those who opposed the radicals at Peterloo. Wanting political advance for themselves the petits bourgeois found little difficulty in defining the 'rights of man' so that they referred to 'men like themselves'. Indeed, before the middle of the century was reached the 'rights of man', had, at least for this sector of the population, become the 'rights of property'. The desire to expand their own political power went hand in hand with the denial of similar rights to those deemed 'inferior' and the creation and development of such distinctions was made progressively easier by the changes in technological and economic structure of the period. The old bonds between the artisans and some of the small business elements were becoming increasingly frayed. In many trades the days of the independent craftsmen were fast disappearing and while most found themselves increasingly drawn into factories, a few avoided the rigours of industrial discipline by acquiring a little capital and setting themselves up as petty capitalists, merchants or retailers.[10] Thus the years of rapid urban and industrial growth, the 1820s and 1830s, saw progressive differentiation of the working population, and while it is right to see this as a step in the making of the working class, it should also be recognised as a move in the creation of the petite bourgeoisie.

In the rapidly growing urban economies the craft-like elements in manufacturing and retailing steadily declined and the opportunities for commercial activities and speculative ventures in land, housing and the provision of services for the swelling populations of the cities greatly increased. The occupations of the petite bourgeoisie became more exclusively concerned with profit, less concerned with specific skills — more involved with customers and clients, less involved with the craft. The work situations remained as they had always been, small in scale, highly personalised, lacking the opportunities for sharing work experiences with large numbers of others and equally innocent of any sophisticated distribution of authority. As more joined the ranks of the small business stratum and as new occupations of this kind were generated, the units of work remained essentially similar — small, independent family concerns. Then, as now, the autonomy of those who ran such enterprises and the social detachment forced upon them by the long hours and restricted social contacts helped to reinforce their commitment to specifically individualistic ideas.

Across the country as a whole, the power of the petit bourgeois stratum in local politics was obviously considerable in the mid-nineteenth century. Following the Municipal Corporations Act of 1835 the small masters, shopkeepers and publicans were frequently found on the town councils of provincial Britain. The property qualifications and the lack of payment for municipal office ensured that this stratum provided a prime recruiting ground for local politicians. Few other jobs provided the opportunities for such involvement and few, perhaps, were so closely affected by many of the municipal decisions, especially those which imposed significantly higher rates. Although the peculiar advantages of independent, self-employed men ensured that some of their number would remain the key figures in radical politics — the Chartist councillors in Leeds in the 1840s and early 1850s, for example — the small businessmen became more generally associated with the activities of the local Economist parties. As Hennock's work[11] makes clear, the political history of many towns shows a conflict between the growing stratum of educated, ambitious professionals and the small-scale business groups. The occupational complexion of the council in Birmingham changed considerably between 1839 and the end of Queen Victoria's reign, for at the beginning of this period 54.7 per cent of councillors belonged to the petit bourgeois stratum, but by 1896 this figure had declined to 15.3 per cent. The shift against the small man was, however, by no means a simple, steady erosion of his power. As Hennock's data on council membership show, a rise in the proportion of small businessmen in 1856 reflected the victory of an Economy party intent on curbing the ambitious and expensive municipal schemes which the more professional groups in local politics favoured. It is likely that the pattern was a common one. The growth of professionals and big businessmen in municipal affairs was frequently accompanied by major investments in city improvements, but the cost of these civic adventures was felt acutely by the retailers and dealers whose capital and income was small. Often they would react by attempting to assert or reassert their views in the town halls and were elected on programmes of municipal economy. Thus in Leeds in 1868 we find the Municipal Reform Association seeking changes in local government and specifically urging a reduction in the rates. It is hardly surprising to learn that the leaders of this movement were overwhelmingly shopkeepers or estate agents.[12] And so the pendulum swung between expenditure and economy — between successful businessman or highly educated professional and the petty retailer or small landlord. But from the 1860s onward the sallies of the petite bourgeoisie never won back the heights of municipal power which they had held in earlier decades. Increasingly, their political position became narrow, parochial and conservative, preoccupied with defending the interests of petty property. With the appearance of working class councillors their position became even more tenuous and the manner in which they were 'squeezed' between professionals and the working class more obvious.

The history of local politics makes one basic point very neatly. It can be shown that in terms of interests and commitments, the petite bourgeoisie has changed very little, yet we find that in pursuit of these interests, the 'labels' which they wear must change from 'radical' to 'liberal' to 'conservative'.

The remarkable persistence of ideas and values reflects the relatively unchanging nature of the working life of the small businessman. The social and economic conditions under which he operates, and the ideological commitments which these enjoin, appear extremely durable — what changes is the broader structure of the economy and the relative power of new classes and strata. By the 1870s the petit bourgeois was likely to find that at the national level his particular economic and political philosophy, which stressed the rights of the minor property holder, which extolled independence and personal ambition, was best expressed by the Liberal party. Certainly it was this party which had most carefully elaborated a vision of the good society in which rational, free individuals should pursue their own interest. From the idea of 'autonomy', the belief that a man is really himself when he employs his own judgement, liberalism derived its radical edge, for such a notion does not encourage the easy or automatic acceptance of authority or superiority. Indeed, it conduces to a kind of 'political protestantism'.[13] Such a view eased the transition from Radical to Liberal politics for it retained one aspect of the highly individualistic, almost anarchic, vision to which members of the petit bourgeois stratum had once been committed. It was the Liberals who had the most explicitly formulated views on the importance of private property, a thing which they regarded as the key to real social progress and the cornerstone of their economic individualism.[14] The recognition that there were frequently gross inequalities in the distribution of private property in capitalist societies encouraged the Liberals to consider that the state might occasionally be forced to intervene to remedy the worst inequalities, but it did not shake their basic belief in the desirability of private property. There can be little doubt that the articulation of a variety of essentially individualistic beliefs in the political philosophy of late nineteenth-century liberalism established a close affinity between that party and the values and aspirations of many petits bourgeois. And for them the attractions of Liberalism assumed a new power in 1875 when the radicalism of the working class acquired a champion in the form of the Labour Party. Thereafter the principal quest for political reform would embody collectivistic commitments which were anathema to the stubborn independence of the small self-employed man, to the man of modest property.

The fact that virtually all workers lived in privately rented housing at this point in time, together with the growth in residential segregation, meant that class relationships were sharply drawn.[15] The power of the petite bourgeoisie over the workers revealed itself partly in the small businessman's role as employer, more markedly in his capacity as provider of basic necessities, like food, but also in his control over housing. For the businessman, housing was a form of productive property and with it he was able to shape and influence the lives of the poor. The involvement of the petits bourgeois in the building and renting of housing was yet another way by which their fortunes and interests and those of the mass of workers became progressively separated. The ownership of this form of property also reinforced the concern of the small business stratum with local politics, for they saw in the city improvement schemes or the decision to spend large sums of money for any civic purpose a potential threat to their economic interests. This dispersal of property ownership among many small bourgeois created serious obstacles to solving the housing problems of the poorest sectors of the community, for though by the early years of this century it was obvious that some form of state and municipal planning was required, proposals for adequate planning legislation foundered on the issues of compensation and compulsory purchase. The almost sacred rights of the property holder were, in fact, sustained until after World War I when the planning law of 1919 was put on the statute book.[16]

The period following World War I also saw a most important political change for, in the general election of 1923, the Liberal party was crushed and the Labour Party emerged as the alternative to Toryism. The effect of this was to drive the petite bourgeoisie further into the arms of the Conservatives, for now there was no real choice of party affiliation. Thus, the Tories inherited the support of the petits bourgeois and thereafter had to give at least the appearance of promoting the interests of the small independent traders and manufacturers. The support of these groups for the Conservatives, though well established and consistent, was not given ungrudgingly, for that party was too well identified first with the traditional aristocratic interest, and latterly with the requirements of big business. Therefore, the petite bourgeoisie increasingly found itself in a curious position where the persistence of its economic and political individualism found no very sincere or enthusiastic support from either major party.[17]

In the years between the two World Wars the depressed state of the economy encouraged state intervention on an unprecedented scale and though such action may not have enjoyed the encouragement of small business interests, the effect in many instances was to allow this stratum to survive and even flourish. In fact the 'hard times' of the years before 1939 saw the establishment of a great many new businesses frequently set up with only the most limited capital. Doubtless many represented nothing more than desperate attempts to make a living by those who had lost their jobs. Many were superfluous and doomed to failure but certainly as far as shops are concerned, these lean years produced not a contraction, but an increase in the petite bourgeoisie.[18]

Since the end of World War II the story has been rather different, for these 30 years have seen considerable change in the nature of Western economies. There has been much rationalisation, particularly in the area of retailing. The growth in scale of marketing operations has produced the large, comprehensive food stores and the sizeable economies of bulk purchase. In most sectors of the economy, as the power of oligopolistic corporations has grown, so it has seemed that the 'little man' must everywhere be under pressure and unlikely to survive. Indeed, it is easy to show that there has been a noticeable reduction in the numbers of small businesses in some sectors,[19] but the high mortality rates tend to be concentrated in some very specific areas of trading. The attention paid to these enterprises distracts attention from the generation of a whole new series of trades and services which have developed in this period of comparative affluence.[20] Even the process of merger and capital concentration does not lead simply to the death of businesses, for the 'fusion' process sometimes produces 'fission' and new small enterprises are created as the old ones are swallowed up.

Tracing the history of the small business group enables us to see more clearly the ways in which its marginality has developed. It can be depicted as in some sense 'peripheral' in a modern capitalist system because technological changes have produced important shifts in the occupational structure. The formation of a working class with its own institutions, political parties and culture has isolated small business proprietors. And their marginality is made starker by the growth of white collar work, for as the clerical and administrative posts increase it becomes more and more obvious that the petits bourgeois have little prospect of alliance with these workers. Theirs is the world of the bureaucracy, the rule book, the submerging of the individual in the impersonal ethos of the large organisation. The routinisation of work in tightly bounded 'offices', the subordination of individual initiative in the interests of predictability and other aspects of bureaucratic structure are conditions that could hardly be further removed from those of petit bourgeois employment.[21] Then too, there is the need for new and continuously revised forms of technical competence and the corresponding need for specialised training which marks out the growing sector of technicians, scientists and professional workers. In this part of the occupational structure, 'knowledge' goes a considerable way towards supplanting capital as the basis for individual life chances. The effect of these major changes is to give the appearance that the petit bourgeois is marking time while all around him the work situations and job relationships are altering rapidly.

The technological changes which produced the shifts in occupational structure also encouraged another familiar trend in advanced capitalist countries — the growing centralisation of authority. As the industrial and commercial enterprises grow larger, as capital becomes more concentrated, so economic decision-making becomes more highly centralised. This process in turn encourages the tendency for centralisation of political authority already demanded by the commitment to a Welfare State and regular intervention in the economy in order to safeguard employment or regulate aggregate demand. Thus, the flourishing of industrial bureaucracies is matched by those of the state and municipality and each reinforces the imprint of that rational, impersonal style characteristic of this mode of organisation.[22] The small business, like the individual, is largely impotent against the weight of bureaucracy. In this growth of centralised authority, and the burgeoning of both commercial and governmental bureaucracies, the petit bourgeois locates much of the responsibility for his present condition. In almost all that he does, the small businessman sees himself as struggling against the prevailing currents. The small scale on which he operates contradicts the cult of bigness; his personalised relationships with employees stand out against the contractual, anonymous character of much contemporary life, but most of all, his insistent self-reliance runs counter to the pervasive commitment to collective organisation, associations and unions as the appropriate representatives of occupational interests. The current sabre-rattling by the National Federation of the Self Employed or the militant statements of the Middle-Class Association are not without precedent,[23] but for most of the post-war years small businessmen in Britain have been characterised by a stubborn refusal to use collective methods of gaining economic power. Their individualism and sense of competition have militated against the success of most petits bourgeois associations. As compared to many working class unions and to many professional bodies, the organisations of small businessmen have conferred little in the way of economic advantage.

That the small business stratum has declined in economic and political power is not due solely to the competition of other classes and strata. Its present situation is not entirely explained by structural changes all around it for in some ways it can be seen as the prisoner of its own ideology. The independence, the insistence on autonomy and the determination to go on dealing in fairly traditional ways, severely limit its capacity to adapt to the changing social and economic structure of society. If autonomy matters more than profit, if personal control matters more than growth, if stability is more important than innovation, if local issues transcend wider concerns — then the small business stratum as a whole will continue to face a decline in its political and economic influence and many of its individual members will inevitably fail.

In fact, in the ideology of the petite bourgeoisie we find a nice paradox, for those very elements outlined above which contribute to individual failure make for its persistence as a stratum. It survives by a continuous process of replacement.[24]

There are always new recruits lured by their hope of gain and by their commitments to these key values of independence and self-reliance. It is probable that the pattern we found in our study of shopkeepers[25] holds for other sectors of this stratum, and the high turnover of businesses is concentrated among a minority of concerns through which a large number of aspiring petits bourgeois pass. Some enterprises exist in the most precarious position, never producing an adequate return and in consequence being bought and sold with some frequency; other concerns disappear altogether and are replaced by new ones. So, one most important kind of replacement within the petite bourgeoisie consists of those who believe in the ideology but lack the business skill or adequate capital and who keep propping up very marginal concerns. But there is also replacement of another kind. The stratum survives because technological change, urban development and many other factors produce new opportunities for small business. The evidence is all around us. The expansion of the tertiary sector of our economies has produced a rich crop of entirely new concerns. This undoubtedly complicates broad arguments about the role of the petite bourgeoisie as a whole for it raises the thorny issue of 'structural equivalence'. Are we, in fact, comparing like with like when we consider changes over a considerable period of time? It seems to us that in most important respects the new enterprises *are* essentially similar to those which they replace. For the most part they do operate with comparatively little capital, they do not usually depend on very sophisticated technology and they rarely have large work-forces. The boutique is not the same as the cobbler's shop which it replaced, the firm manufacturing window frames is not the same as the joiner's business from which it began, the small property company is not the same as the individual landlord it supplanted, but the essential structural conditions show a basic consistency. A living is still made through petty property and there is good reason to suppose that the basic ideological commitments of the new bourgeois are very similar to those whose place they take.

This ideological stability is a matter of considerable interest for it enables us to offer explanations of why people take on risky business ventures against all advice or common sense. The attraction of being a self-employed businessman remains as it has always been, firmly rooted in the individualistic aspects of Western culture. These extol the virtues of winning material and social success by your own efforts — they offer a vision of the good society where government exists simply to enable the resourceful individual to prosper, the heroes are free and independent men whose success is symbolised by private property. Indeed, property is always seen as central in the petit bourgeois ideology, essential for the health of individuals as well as that of the state.

The negative elements of this ideology are equally familiar. The dominant motif is anti-collectivism. From the mid-nineteenth century, the petit bourgeois opposition to collectivism becomes steadily more sharply focused, progressively able to address itself to more concrete and specific targets as the pressure for collective responses mount. It was not only against the trade unions or the socialists that the petits bourgeois inveighed, but also against the mounting efforts of municipalities and state to address the problems of the poorer elements in the society by collective means.[26]

As politics in most Western societies has become more sharply polarised between socialist and conservative views, as the political and economic philosophy of late nineteenth-century Liberalism has been dismembered and variously and sometimes reluctantly incorporated in the programmes of the two big political blocs, so the petite bourgeoisie has provided a consistent, if not very effective, opposition to collectivism whether sponsored by 'right' or 'left', providing a fertile ground for ideas opposing further bureaucratisation and always ready to support the individual against the state. In Britain, there has been no very well-articulated expression of these concerns outside the conventional party system, but in France and Belgium, Poujadism and associated ideas have enjoyed very well-organised support. It is not fanciful to see in the most recent manifestation of petits bourgeois interests in Britain an attempt to create a similar movement in that country.

An interesting argument about the importance of the stratum is that which presents small enterprises as essential for the health of a capitalist economy. There are two themes here. First, there is the claim that small business ensures the continuance of industrial capitalism by providing a pool from which larger and more powerful enterprises grow. Without continuous replacement, the system would ossify. Thus, it is held that some reduction in the size of this sector may be consistent with the maintenance of the current economic system provided that the number of concerns developing out of this pool and growing to medium or large size does not contract proportionately. Any very large drop in numbers is, however, argued not to be in the national economic interest. Secondly, there is the perception of the small firm as the source of innovation. The idea enjoys wide currency, appearing in Marxist analyses where small innovative businesses figure as the prey of the monopolistic corporations,[27] as well as more conservative economic accounts.[28] The small independent enterprise is depicted as flexible and able to exploit or generate new processes, products and ways of trading. Its scale gives it agility to respond rapidly to changed circumstances and to take risks in the hope of profit. It could also be argued that the continuance of some small business is ensured through the activities of large firms. Certainly, in specific areas of retailing, it is possible to show that big business positively encourages the maintenance of large numbers of small outlets.[29] The relationship is not simply predatory or conflictual.

Thus, examination of the economic role of the petite bourgeoisie has led some recent commentators to the conclusion that its contribution is far from 'petty'. As the Bolton Report has it: 'To ask whether there is a future for the small firm in the age of giant companies, international combines and universal intervention by Government, is therefore, tantamount to asking whether the future of private enterprise capitalism as we have known it in [Britain], is threatened'.[30] The idea of their 'centrality' and indispensability also appears in the political behaviour and commitments of the petits bourgeois. In Fascism and in Poujadism there was the promise to reinstate a 'traditional' order, a social world in which the man of modest wealth was respected and emulated and his values accorded legitimacy.[31] These movements pledged themselves to put the small businessman back where they thought he belonged: in the centre of the economic and political map. In less dramatic ways we find in Britain, too, the notion that this stratum is 'the backbone of the nation', and we are currently witnessing a renewed defence of the independent business-man and his values by the present Conservative Party leadership.

However, there is reason to suppose that whatever its level, the petit bourgeois support for Toryism is less than wholehearted. The party has not constantly and successfully defended the small business interests over the past 30 years; in fact, it has often accepted particular measures of nationalisation, promoted other forms of state inter-vention and centralised decision-making which generally are anathema to this stratum.[32] In addition, the development of a 'liberal' Tory philosophy in the 1950s and early 1960s has meant that it has seldom identified itself with the more individualistic petit bourgeois values. Moreover, such is the strength of the 'independence' idea among this group that all central authority is regarded with suspicion, and most state intervention, no matter how well intentioned, construed as 'interference'. The commitment to independence produces an incipient anarchism which moderates enthusiasm for the Tory party and its political programmes. Indeed, it breeds scepticism of politics and government generally. And this is a point brought out in one of the research reports produced for the Bolton Report:

> The powerful underlying need to maintain and preserve inde-pendence and the strong feelings of personal satisfaction derived from one's own achievement go a long way to explaining the attitudes to outside help and assistance. Government assistance was seen as leading to Government intervention . . . Having rejected 'the boss', respondents didn't want to suffer the paternalism of Government or anyone else for that matter.[33]

There is, of course, a piece of conventional wisdom about the petits bourgeois which relates their Conservatism to their alleged authoritar-ianism. As Hamilton and Eberts[34] noted, it is widely assumed that small businessmen adopt hard-line illiberal responses to most social issues. The Tory party with its traditional emphasis upon 'order' is more likely than Labour to offer 'firm', even 'tough', measures to deal with matters like crime and delinquency. Given the paucity of evidence, this line of reasoning is little more than plausible hypothesis.

The petite bourgeoisie has never been a dominant force in national politics in Britain, and such power as it did have has been eroded over the years. Its position on the 'party' dimension has changed. The small shopkeepers and local businessmen continued to have representation and influence in the City Chambers (and probably they are still overrepresented), but the reduction in their local political influence from the heady days of the 1840s, 1850s and 1860s, seems fairly well established. Even at the local level, politics has become more tightly organised, more firmly based upon mass national parties and though the 'ratepayer' interests do not go unvoiced, they are forced very often to set themselves within the framework of a national party and can seldom be presented adequately by a loose coalition of petits bourgeois.

Finally, we should consider the *social* significance of this stratum. In advanced capitalist societies it has become the custodian of beliefs which form very important parts of the prevailing bourgeois ideology. Above all others, there is this belief in the moral superiority of 'independence', and the virtue that attaches to success won by your own efforts. Hard work and the satisfaction of seeing your labour rewarded, thrift, together with the security and developmental potential which it brings, are central, as is the belief in the value of prompt payment and the avoidance of financial entanglement which might threaten maximal autonomy.[35] It is not simply the attachment to these ideas that matters. After all, that hardly makes the petite bourgeoisie distinctive, for they are entertained and held in varying permutations by a great many who live under capitalism. What gives the petits bourgeois their special relationship to their values is the fact that they have chosen and are able to *live* by them. Indeed, the conditions of their work generally ensure that they are able to sustain them and even increase their commitment to them. Given the ways in which work is now commonly organised, this is not the case for most people. Relatively few in fact can structure their work lives around such ideas. Thus, the petit bourgeois stratum serves to keep alive values and beliefs which, in earlier phases of capitalism, provided much of the impetus for commercial and industrial development, and contributed a good deal to the formation of capitalist ideologies.

One should also consider the relationship of this stratum to petty property for, historically, this has played a major part in shaping its interests and its politics. Not only does the petit bourgeois live by property, but he employs it in ways which sometimes blur the conventional distinction between the 'productive' and the 'non-productive' forms. For instance, the propensity (at least traditionally) to acquire housing or land reflected the desire for a safe and profitable investment but it also reflected the fact that such property could be 'consumed' in part by some family member who lived there. Property, in the families of the petite bourgeoisie, is so enmeshed with domestic affairs that its status as an element of 'production' or 'consumption' is frequently changed. And beyond that it has to be recognised that, especially in its more visible and tangible forms, property is a means of signalling success. In a capitalist order, property is a societally sanctioned reward for conformity[36], and property which appears simply as an item of consumption may also carry a potential as a form of security or as the means of establishing the financial soundness valuable in business dealings. Property gives a man a stake in the system, gives him interests which many have seen as leading to caution and conservatism.

Property has helped shape the individualistic ideas which have always informed petits bourgeois politics. 'Middle class' associations to impede the progress of organised labour and to fight for the rights of property were formed in the late nineteenth and early years of the twentieth century, as well as in the 1970s.[37] The idea of property is crucial to the development of these commitments, for property as an institution is profoundly and essentially anti-collectivist. As it has developed in capitalist cultures, property has become a bundle of rights defining a man's capacity to *exclude* others from the use of or access to his possessions. It thus becomes a rich source of values and beliefs opposing collectivism in all its forms.

The stratum has symbolic significance in contemporary Western societies. Most obviously it can be claimed that the ideas and beliefs held by these small businessmen have a central, almost sacred quality within our culture. Thus, insofar as they help to keep alive such notions, they act in an almost sacerdotal way, sustaining values which shape and integrate society. The petit bourgeois becomes then a symbol, and threats to his survival represent serious challenges to the entire edifice of private enterprise. And this is recognised, perhaps cynically, by representatives of monopoly capital who from time to time make public demonstration of their support for small business. In doing so, they may hope to sustain the illusion of a traditional competitive market. Politicians, too, find occasion to exploit the symbolic importance of this stratum incorporating in their rhetoric the idea that the small business is somehow at the heart of our economic system.

But that is simply to point up one side of the argument, for ideas or objects or, indeed, groups may have symbolic value of quite another kind. In a class-fractured, conflictual society the values represented by a stratum may be seen in a powerfully negative way by some sectors of the population. And that is precisely what happens. In left-wing views the small businessman is frequently taken to represent the exploitative, oppressive aspects of the social and economic order. Storekeepers are depicted as unsympathetic rogues, as in some of the social realist literature of the last century[38] or, more soberly, as individuals with considerable economic influence over the lives of the poor.[39] Perhaps most obvious of all is the characterisation of the landlord:

typically petit bourgeois, bent on exploiting the working class, a parasite whose power lies in his property. Here we are dealing with powerful stereotypes. In Britain the term 'Rachmanism' has passed into common parlance and in North America 'slumlord' has become a popular and emotive word. So, this stratum is depicted not only as the guardian of some central values, but also as the carrier of ideological elements which are anathema to the left. Thus, the small businessmen become actors, albeit reluctant ones, in many political rituals. It is the ease and frequency with which the petits bourgeois can be employed in the 'mobilisation of political bias'[40] and taken to represent particular economic and political paradigms which provides the surest confirmation of their symbolic value.

So long as Western societies retain their essentially capitalist form the petite bourgeoisie will continue as a distinct stratum. In all these societies at the present time small business is under threat, both from the general effects of inflation and often from specific fiscal and other acts of governments, but there is little danger that it will disappear. As ever, individuals will fail and withdraw but the stratum will doubtless adapt, find new niches in the economic structure and continue to hold the same belief that a man should make it by himself.

Notes

1. Among the neo-Marxian writing we find concern with the place of the petite bourgeoisie in contemporary capitalism. See N. Poulantzas, *Classes in Contemporary Capitalism*, translated by D. Fernbach (London, New Left Books, 1975); and C. Baudelot, R. Establet and J. Malemort, *La petite bourgeoisie en France* (Paris, Maspero, 1974). For historical perspective see T.J. Nossiter, *Influence, Opinion and Political Idiom in Reformed England* (London, Harvester Press, 1975); and R. Gellately, *The Politics of Economic Despair* (London, Sage Publications, 1974). More generally see: M.J.K. Stanworth and J. Curran, *Management, Motivation and the Smaller Business* (Epping, Gower Press, 1973); J. Boswell, *The Rise and Decline of Small Firms* (London, Allen and Unwin, 1973); *Report of the Committee on Small Firms* (Bolton Report) Cmnd. 4811 (London, HMSO, 1971); J. Bunzel, *The American Small Business* (New York, Knopf, 1962); C. Mayer and S. Goldstein, *The First Two Years* (Washington, US Government Printing Office, 1961); J.D. Phillips, *Little Business in the American Economy*, Illinois Studies in the Social Sciences, vol. XLII (Urbana, University of Illinois Press, 1957–9).

2. E.P. Hennock, *Fit and Proper Persons: Ideal and Reality in*

Nineteenth-century Urban Government (London, Edward Arnold, 1973).

3. See K. Marx, 'The Manifesto of the Communist Party' in K. Marx and F. Engels, *Selected Works,* vol. I (Moscow, Foreign Languages Publishing House, 1951); and the well-known work by C.W. Mills, *White Collar* (Oxford, Oxford University Press, 1951). Recent comment which seems to us to assess the situation shrewdly is found in S. Michael Miller, 'Notes on Neo-Capitalism', *Theory and Society,* II (1975), p. 15.

4. For a more extended discussion, see our earlier paper. F. Bechhofer and B. Elliott, 'An approach to a Study of Small Shopkeepers and the Class Structure', *European Journal of Sociology,* IX (1968), pp. 180–202. For essentially the same view see *Bolton Report,* p. xv.

5. A. Touraine, *The Post-Industrial Society* (London, Wildwood House, 1974). For an excellent discussion, see A. Giddens, *The Class Structure of the Advanced Societies* (London, Hutchinson, 1973), chapter XIV.

6. T. Burns, The Sociology of Industry, in A.T. Welford *et al.* (eds), *Society, Problems and Methods of Study* (London, Routledge and Kegan Paul, 1965).

7. Our view is at odds with that of some neo-Marxists who insist that technicians, office workers and many other 'non-productive' workers be treated as part of the petite bourgeoisie. Though they distinguish these 'new' members from the 'traditional' small business fractions of the class they claim an overall unity for these diverse occupational groups which we find unconvincing. See Poulantzas, *op. cit.,* and Baudelot *et al., op. cit.*

8. E.P. Thompson, *The Making of the English Working Class,* (London, Gollancz, 1963).

9. St. Lukes, *Individualism* (Oxford, Oxford University Press, 1973), p. 48.

10. The process is well described in the famous survey made in 1849 by the *Morning Chronicle;* see P. Razzell and R. Wainwright, *The Victorian Working Class* (London, Frank Cass, 1973), p. 509.

11. Hennock, *op. cit.*

12. Ibid.

13. Lukes, *op. cit.*

14. M. Forsyth, *Property and Property Distribution Policy* (P.E.P. Broadsheet 528, July 1971); R. Schlatter, *Private Property: the History of an Idea* (London, Allen and Unwin, 1951).

15. Vincent has a neat statement about this; see J. Vincent, *The Formation of the British Liberal Party, 1857–68* (Harmondsworth,

Penguin Books, 1972), p. 23, n. 18; more conventional sources are H. Dyos, *Victorian Suburb* (Leicester, Leicester University Press, 1961); and D.A. Reeder, 'A Theatre of Suburbs: London 1801–1911, in H. Dyos (ed.), *The Study of Urban History* (London, Edward Arnold, 1968).

16. See J. Cullingworth, *Town and Country Planning in Britain* (London, Allen and Unwin, 1972), chapter I; W. Ashworth, *The Genesis of Modern British Town Planning* (London, Routledge and Kegan Paul, 1954); D. Read, *Edwardian England* (London, Harrap, 1972), pp. 38–9.

17. The political 'marginality' of this stratum has, of course, been frequently discussed in the context of European political movements, from Fascism to Poujadism.

18. See our discussion in F. Bechhofer, B. Elliott and M. Rushforth, 'The Market Situation of Small Shopkeepers', *Scottish Journal of Political Economy*, XVIII (1971), p. 163.

19. Bolton Report, Tables 5.1, 5.2 and 5.3.

20. For some indication that the number of self-employed persons and the income from such work has shown some increase in recent years, see the *Royal Commission on the Distribution of Income and Wealth*, Report no. I, Cmnd. 6171, para. 98–99.

21. See for instance the discussion in Giddens, *op. cit.*, especially chapters II and X; D. Lockwood, *The Blackcoated Worker* (London, Allen and Unwin, 1958); Mills, *op. cit.;* M. Crozier, *The World of the Office Worker* (Chicago 1971).

22. From a vast literature, see, for instance: J.K. Galbraith, *The New Industrial State* (London, Hamish Hamilton, 1967); P.A. Baran and P.M. Sweezy, *Monopoly Capital* (Harmondsworth, Penguin Books, 1968); R. Miliband, *The State in Capitalist Society* (London, Weidenfeld and Nicholson, 1969); P.M. Sweezy, *Modern Capitalism and Other Essays* (New York, Monthly Review Press, 1972).

23. See for example, N. Soldon, 'Laissez-faire as Dogma: The Liberty and Property Defence League, 1882–1914', and K.D. Brown, The 'Anti-Socialist Union, 1908–49', both in K.D. Brown (ed.), *Essays in Anti-Labour History* (London, Macmillan, 1974).

24. Many have noted the high failure rate but curiously little attention has been paid to the processes of replacement which this implies; see Mayer and Goldstein, *op. cit.;* Bunzel, *op. cit.;* and Bolton Report.

25. See our discussion in F. Bechhofer, B. Elliott, M. Rushforth and R. Bland, 'Small Shopkeepers: Matters of Money and Meaning', *Sociological Review*, XXII (1974), pp. 465–82.

26. Hennock, *op. cit.*

27. Baran, *op. cit.*, chapter I.

28. Boswell, *op. cit.,* chapter I.

29. This is most plainly seen in the policies of the cigarette companies and the confectionery firms.

30. Bolton Report, p. xix.

31. In Germany the political mobilisation of the small businessmen, particularly the retailers, had already taken place in the early years of this century; see Gellately, *op. cit.*

32. Phillips, *op. cit.,* in one of the few studies to examine the matter carefully, suggests that in the US most of the so-called small business legislation has benefited only the larger concerns and failed to assist the great majority of those included in the category 'small business'.

33. Bolton Committee, *Research Report no. 7,* Cmnd. 4811, p. 5.

34. R. Hamilton and P. Eberts, 'The Myth of Business Conservatism', mimeographed (1964).

35. For a discussion of this in the case of small retailers, see Bechhofer, Elliot, Rushforth and Bland, 'Small Shopkeepers'; and Bechhofer, Elliot, Rushforth and Bland, 'The Petits Bourgeois in the Class Structure: The Case of the Small Shopkeepers' in F. Parkin (ed.), *The Social Analysis of Class Structure* (London, Tavistock Press, 1974).

36. A. Gouldner makes the point nicely in *The Coming Crisis of Western Sociology* (London, Heinemann, 1971), pp. 304–26 *passim.*

37. Papers cited in Brown (ed.) *op. cit.*

38. See, for example, A. Morrison, *A Child of the Jago* (1896, reprinted London, MacGibbon and Kee, 1969).

39. See R. Roberts, *The Classic Slum* (Harmondsworth, Penguin Books, 1973); and G.S. Jones, *Outcast London* (London, Oxford University Press, 1971).

40. See S. Lukes, 'Political Ritual and Social Integration', *Sociology,* XIX (1975), pp. 289–308, where the cognitive role of political rituals and the 'mobilisation of bias' is discussed.

8 Class Analysis and the Entrepreneurial Middle Class

RICHARD SCASE AND ROBERT GOFFEE*

At the most general level, the entrepreneurial middle class consists of several diverse groupings which, nevertheless, share a common feature: their ownership of capital assets. These are typically exploited for productive purposes by use of the proprietors' and others' labour. However, the relative mix of labour and capital is highly variable. Thus, there can be instances when income is derived from property ownership (as with small *rentiers*), when income is primarily acquired through the exercise of labour (as with craftworkers and freelance professionals), and other cases where there is a *mixture* of both elements (as with shopkeepers, garage proprietors and restaurant owners). In general, discussions of the entrepreneurial middle class have focused upon specific groups where property ownership is the more important component.

In Britain, for example, Bechhofer and Elliott have investigated Edinburgh shopkeepers[1] and small landlords[2] while more recently, Newby and his associates have studied East Anglian farmers.[3] In addition to differences in the proportionate use of capital and labour, a further source of variation derives from the *size* of businesses which proprietors own. A small shopkeeper not employing labour, a farmer

* From Richard Scase and Robert Goffee, *The Entrepreneurial Middle Class*, London, Croom Helm, 1982, pp. 10–31.

with a thousand acres and five or six employees, and a manufacturer with fifty workers, all actively use their own capital assets for the purposes of personal profit and are, therefore, all members of the entrepreneurial middle class. This, in turn, leads to another source of internal differentiation; namely, the *type* of capital assets employed. Whereas for farmers it may be land, it is machinery for industrial employers and simple hand tools for independent tradesmen.

Thus, empirically, the entrepreneurial middle class is a 'mixed bag', consisting as it does of proprietors who actively use their capital for a variety of purposes within different sectors of the economy. It is not surprising, then, that their location within modern society is conceptually problematic. Indeed, the entrepreneurial middle class has been regarded in at least three distinct ways. First, as 'separate' and 'removed' from the two major classes of capitalist society. Secondly, as part and parcel of an emerging 'post-industrial' or 'service' society. Finally, as a legacy of an earlier or pre-capitalist stage of production.

The first perspective regards certain groupings within the entrepreneurial middle class such as small-scale manufacturers, traders and shopkeepers, as an independent 'stratum' — the petty bourgeoisie — which is separate from both the bourgeoisie and the proletariat. Bechhofer and his colleagues, for example, have argued that they represent a stratum which is 'in some sense marginal or detached from the major classes and interests of contemporary industrial societies'.[4] At one point, this leads them to suggest they are *'outside'* the class structure, whilst at another, they sit 'uneasily *between* the major classes' (emphasis added).[5]

Notwithstanding this, Bechhofer and his colleagues regard the petty bourgeoisie as fulfilling important ideological functions within contemporary society if only because they are the custodians of certain 'core' capitalist values. They claim that an overriding value of many small business owners is *independence;* the appeal is to be 'your own boss' and, thereby, avoid the constraints of employment associated with large-scale corporations. The strength of this appeal is sufficient to compensate for frequently long and arduous working hours; indeed, their 'autonomy' often turns into 'serfdom' such that 'theirs, it seems, is a freedom to establish an extraordinary form of self-exploitation'.[6] Despite this, most remain firmly committed to notions of 'individualism' and 'independence' and this is reflected in their attitudes, life styles and patterns of consumption. In sum, society is seen to be 'open' and it rewards those prepared to work hard and make the necessary self-sacrifice.

Even though the development of large-scale corporations and the growth of the state have fundamentally altered the structure of the economy, such beliefs reinforce the desirability of capitalism as a socioeconomic system. The persistence of small-scale enterprises — whether in farming, commerce or industry — preserves an *image* of competition, the market and opportunity behind which the growing domination of large-scale monopoly enterprises is concealed. In fact, research suggests that small business owners have only a limited awareness of the growing market control of national-based and multinational corporations and of the extent to which their own trading prospects are increasingly dependent upon them.[7] This is so, even for those small enterprises which operate as the suppliers of commodities and services to one or a few large customers which determine their economic survival.

If this view suggests that petty bourgeois elements persist in a 'marginal' sense, a second — but related — approach argues that the entrepreneurial middle class will fulfil an increasingly important function in an emerging post-industrial society.[8] Several factors are said to underlie this trend. Some writers have claimed that as a result of a growing concern with the 'quality of life' the number of independent small-scale enterprises is likely to expand.[9] Within this argument a heavy emphasis is placed upon the growing 'diseconomies' and 'dysfunctions' of large-scale bureaucratic organisations which are said to produce inferior-quality goods under conditions that lead to work dissatisfaction amongst employees. Thus, 'small is beautiful' since it encourages the production of goods and services in the context of more 'meaningful', and, therefore, less alienating, work environments.[10]

Employees who choose to set up their own businesses are helped, it has been argued, by recent technological developments which are encouraging the growth of the domestic economy. The micro-computer, for instance, allows relatively sophisticated software to be purchased cheaply and used in the home. This has led Martin and Norman to speculate that 'we may see a return to cottage industry, with the spinning wheel replaced by the computer terminal'.[11]

Clearly, if these predictions prove to be correct, there could be a substantial potential for the expansion of independent, small-scale production. Some commentators have argued that such opportunities will be increasingly exploited if only because of the marked decline in 'formal' employment over recent years which has forced many to consider alternative forms of making a living.[12] Consequently, the growth of 'informal' economic activity has attracted much attention and Pahl, for example, has claimed that 'the substitution of informal, household production of services for the purchase of services from the formal economy' could serve as the basis for an alternative means of income.[13]

If 'informal' work in the 'cash economy' is increasing while 'formal' employment declines, this, too, could provide new avenues for small business formation and growth. It has been suggested that this trend is further encouraged by the increasing 'burden' of state regulations, controls and taxes.[14] Taken together, these changes are leading, so it is claimed, to a fundamental alteration in both the pattern and nature of economic activity within modern societies. As such, they constitute the basis for a *regeneration* of the entrepreneurial middle class in the developing 'post-industrial' society. Such a view stands in distinct contrast to the classical Marxist position which is the basis of the final interpretation that is now considered.

Thirdly, there are then, those who regard some sectors of the entrepreneurial middle class as the legacy of an earlier type of production which persists within present-day society. The Marxist approach suggests that, in the long run, the development of capitalism will lead to the *dissolution* of the entrepreneurial middle class within the bourgeoisie and the proletariat.

This prediction is based upon an analysis of the capitalist mode of production which distinguishes the stages of *co-operation* and *manufacture* from *modern industry*.[15] Under conditions of co-operation the worker is an autonomous craftsman, but with the development of capitalist manufacture a division of labour emerges and he becomes a specialist in one rather than in a number of activities. To quote Marx, 'each workman [becomes] exclusively assigned to a partial function, and that for the rest of his life, his labour power is turned into the organ of this detail function'.[16]

With the development of modern industry, characterised by mechanised factory production, the worker 'becomes a mere appendage to an already existing material condition of production'.[17] As a 'machine minder' his conceptual capacity is further reduced, whilst at the same time the amount of capital required for production becomes greater. Under these circumstances few workers will become capitalists and, furthermore, few small-scale producers will be able to compete with the production methods of modern industry which inevitably become 'the general, socially predominant form of production'.[18] Thus, 'the larger capitals beat the smaller' causing 'the ruin of many small capitalists, whose capitals partly pass into the hands of their conquerors, partly vanish'.[19] The growth of modern industry, then, restricts the opportunity for workers to function as independent tradesmen or to become business owners while, at the same time, it destroys the capital of existing small-scale producers and manu-facturers.

Given these developments in the capitalist mode of production, the entrepreneurial middle class is typically viewed by Marxists as the legacy of either an earlier stage of *capitalist* production, as with small-scale capitalists, or of *pre-capitalist* simple commodity production, as with the self-employed and the 'traditional' petty bourgeoisie. Thus, although the capitalist *mode* of production may be dominant in a social formation, prior *forms* of non-capitalist production may persist within it.[20] Similarly, the existence of large-scale capitalist enterprises in the present stage of 'monopoly' capitalism does not preclude the persistence of small-scale capital units characteristic of 'competitive' or 'private' capitalism. However, to claim that sectors of the entrepreneurial middle class represent a legacy of declining importance does not explain *how* or *why* they are currently reproduced.

Poulantzas, for example, who defines the 'traditional' petty bourgeoisie as the *self-employed* and those *'not chiefly involved in exploiting wage labour'*,[21] (emphasis added) merely states that 'the contemporary existence of the petty bourgeoisie in the developed capitalist formations . . . depends on the perpetration of this form in the extended reproduction of capitalism'.[22] This is cumbersome description rather than explanation and is indicative of the fact that Poulantzas sees this class as a declining vestige of the simple commodity form 'which was historically the form of transition from the feudal to the capitalist mode'.[23] Similarly, Wright tends to ignore the actual mechanisms which account for the persistence of small-scale commodity production in contemporary society.[24] He defines the petty bourgeoisie as 'those who either work for themselves or, despite the employment of some labour, generate the bulk of surplus value'.[25] In his terms, the petty bourgeoisie have *full* economic ownership of the means of production and *full* control over the allocation of their resources and yet they control little or no labour power. As such, he regards their class position as unambiguous.[26]

But obviously, if members of the petty bourgeoisie produce commodities they *are* affected by the conditions of the market as they exist under monopoly capitalism. Thus, the constraints exercised by, for example, financial institutions and large-scale capitalist enterprises may severely curtail the real control that 'independent' small-scale producers are able to exercise over the use of their investments and resources. If 'economic control' is diminished, on Wright's criteria, the class location of the petty bourgeoisie in contemporary capitalist society cannot be regarded as 'unambiguous'. Indeed, any analysis which views petty commodity producers as representative of a surviving 'simple' or 'feudal' form which somehow persists within contemporary capitalism is of questionable value.

The Marxist interpretation of small-scale capitalists is rather different. They, unlike the petty bourgeoisie, own and control larger capital assets and employ more sizeable work-forces. They are, for example, the owners of family firms and of medium-sized, non-monopoly enterprises in general.

If this type of small-scale capital is representative of an earlier *competitive* stage of capitalism it is, nevertheless, seen to be shaped by the contemporary forces of *monopoly* capitalism. Consequently, Poulantzas suggests a number of functions which small enterprises fulfil in the modern economy. They often operate, for example, in sectors characterised by low profits and high risks, and those which 'service' large corporations. They may also function as a 'staging post in the process of subjecting labour-power to monopoly capital', and as a means whereby prices may be set at a level which allows monopoly capital larger profit margins because of its cheaper production costs.[27]

Poulantzas further argues that the apparent independence of small-scale capital is constrained by monopoly standardisation of products, the patenting of technological innovations and the 'leonine controls' imposed by finance capital as a condition for extending credit.[28] Consequently, the *real* economic boundaries of small-scale, non-monopoly enterprises — so clearly defined in *legal* terms — become increasingly indeterminate. In contrast to the petty bourgeoisie, Poulantzas emphasises that 'the criteria by which non-monopoly capital is defined are always located in relation to monopoly capital . . . There is in no sense a simple "co-existence" of two separate watertight sectors.'[29] Thus, the relationship between the two forms of capital is variable and dependent upon 'the phase of monopoly capitalism and its concrete forms (branches, sectors, etc.) within a social formation'.[30] Despite the extent to which monopoly capital reduces the economic viability of small-scale enterprises, then, Poulantzas recognises their continuing *functional* importance and, hence, their persistence within contemporary capitalism.

To sum up, there is among these writers a neglect of the *actual* dynamics whereby the petty bourgeoisie and small-scale capitalists are reproduced under the conditions of monopoly capitalism. This is the result of excessively abstract analyses which assume their progressive decline and fail, therefore, to study specific empirical processes.

Westergaard, in assessing recent contributions, has professed to be:

both puzzled and disturbed by contemporary western Marxist

work in which the concrete differential impact of capitalist economic processes on people's lives and prospects . . . seems to recede into remote distance . . . or to be brought into the picture only in a context of abstraction which, untranslated, leave the reality of human experience difficult to recognise.[31]

Even Wright, who is committed to the idea that 'Marxist theory should generate propositions about the real world which can be empirically studied',[32] and who attacks abstract class definitions which relegate the complexities of 'concrete social structures' to a secondary role, does not consider it necessary to 'discuss contradictory locations that occur because an *individual* simultaneously occupies two class positions within social relations of production' (emphasis added).[33] He argues that dual class membership, although of significance 'in certain historical circumstances', does not present 'the same kind of analytical problem as positions which are themselves located in a contradictory way within class relations'.[34] Once again, then, the discussion of class *actors* — despite the professed importance of class *struggle* rather than class *structure* — is deemed to be of less significance than that of abstractly defined class locations.

Clearly, the reproduction of the petty bourgeoisie and small-scale capital within economies characterised by the dominance of large monopoly enterprises requires detailed *empirical* study. Abstract analyses that attribute priority to *modes* and *stages* of production, and to class *positions* rather than to class *actors* fail to account sufficiently for the mechanisms whereby the entrepreneurial middle class is reproduced in present-day society. If, as in most Marxist analyses, the distinction between *actor* and *position* is too sharply drawn, then areas of the class structure within which there is a significant degree of social mobility may be inadequately understood.[35] Poulantzas acknowledges that some manual workers and artisans become petty bourgeois producers and small capitalists but he overlooks the actual material processes which allow this mobility.[36]

Although, therefore, at the theoretical level the simple commodity form *can* be distinguished from the pure capitalist mode of production, this type of analysis detracts from the study of empirical relationships. Thus, while the petty bourgeoisie is seen to be fairly 'insulated' from the capitalist mode of production, small-scale capitalists are described in a functional manner by reference to the 'needs' of monopoly capital. This means that the concrete relationships between petty bourgeois producers and small-scale capitalists on the one hand, and the interconnections between these and large-scale corporations on the other, have been relatively unexplored. Further, there have been hardly any sociological studies of the processes whereby *actors* can experience upward mobility through the small-scale accumulation of capital.

A satisfactory analytical framework must take account of the fact that small-scale enterprises *are embedded within a general process of capital accumulation*. Although this assumption is explicit in, for example, Lenin's discussion of the development of capitalism in Russia, it is largely absent in present-day work.[37] Even though the possibilities for actors to become proprietors of small businesses are generally less now than during earlier stages of capitalism, they are certainly greater than is widely assumed. As such, they constitute avenues for individual mobility of a 'non-career' or 'non-meritocratic' kind. Whereas studies of upward mobility have stressed the acquisition of educational and technical qualifications and then promotion within and between hierarchically organised corporations, little attention has been devoted to small-scale capital accumulation as an alternative channel for personal success.[38] Thus, managerial, professional and manual employees can, in various ways and for different reasons, become small-scale proprietors. As Crossick has suggested:

> The lower middle class plays a very specific role in the process of social mobility, whether of a career or inter-generational type. It is available for those seeking to rise out of the working class, whether into white collar occupations by means of a fairly rudimentary education, or by small capital accumulation into the petty bourgeoisie.[39]

Similarly, Mayer has argued that the entrepreneurial middle class functions as:

> A buffer between capital and labour . . . [and] as a bridge and mediator between them. Moreover, the petite bourgeoisie is the predominant channel for social mobility; skilled manual workers can and do move into it from below, while from within its bulging ranks it raises its own spiralists to higher rungs on the income and status ladder. This lower middle class also serves as a net that cushions the fall of the skidders and the superannuated of both the higher middle class and the grande bourgeoisie.[40]

In this manner, the reproduction of the entrepreneurial middle class must be regarded as *integral* to contemporary class dynamics; it cannot be explained solely by reference to earlier *stages* or *forms* of production.

This, then, completes our review of the three major analytical approaches to the entrepreneurial middle class. In Marxist accounts, the class does not, as such, exist; instead, as we have already shown, there is only the petty bourgeoisie and non-monopoly capitalists. In the other two more empirically based orientations, reference is usually to a *mélange* of petty proprietors such as, for example, farmers, small manufacturers, hoteliers and self-employed artisans. But none of these approaches are entirely satisfactory. The composition of the entrepreneurial middle class needs to be more precisely defined and the interrelationships of its constituent groupings more clearly delineated if its reproduction, and the processes of individual mobility through small-scale capital accumulation, are to be better understood.

As we have already stated, the entrepreneurial middle class consists of those who own property which, together with their own and others' labour, they use for productive purposes. More specifically, it can be defined as consisting of *four* sub-categories, each of which is distinguished by differences in the relative mix of capital utilised and labour employed. This, in turn, tends to be associated with the nature of the proprietors' functional contribution to their enterprises. In these terms it is possible to regard the entrepreneurial middle class as consisting of the self-employed, small employers, owner-controllers and owner-directors.

The *self-employed* constitute the largest proportion of small business owners.[41] By definition, they formally employ no labour. They are, however, generally dependent upon the unpaid services of their families and the utilisation of domestic assets for business purposes.[42] In most discussions they are normally seen as having a strong commitment to 'good workmanship'.[43] They regard their work as a way of 'earning a living' without experiencing the constraints usually associated with employment. As such, they are said to emphasise the intrinsic satisfactions which they derive from self-employment, the pride in the quality of goods and services they produce, and the working autonomy which they are alleged to enjoy.[44] Many regard themselves as 'tradesmen' rather than 'businessmen' since they are often more interested in personal work satisfaction than business growth; consequently, most of the self-employed choose to remain as such.

Thus, the self-employed are 'marginal' within the entrepreneurial middle class. If self-employment offers opportunities whereby manual workers can 'escape' from the employment relationship, and thereby enjoy social prestige and economic gain, there are, nevertheless, forces conducive to their reversions to employee status. The self-employed are, for example, vulnerable to the vagaries of the market while, at the same time, their personal skills are likely to deteriorate through ageing. As a result, earnings tend to decline over time and there are normally few capital assets which can be inter-generationally transmitted. Although some of the self-employed may, then, accumulate capital, many others become proletarianised.

Small employers work alongside their employees and, in addition, perform administrative and managerial tasks.[45] They both labour and *own* their means of production and yet, at the same time, employ wage labour. They are *directly* involved in the production of goods and services and, in this way, personally contribute to the creation of profit. Small employers are often skilled manual or technical workers who began their business careers as self-employed. However, the employment of labour introduces a range of novel problems with which, from occupational experience alone, they are often unable to cope. Employees have, after all, to be recruited and trained, organised and controlled, insured and paid. In other words, in order to operate efficiently, small employers must be able to *manage* both finance and labour and, at the same time, do 'a day's work'. Many adapt by either working excessively long hours or by making use of family assistance. As with the self-employed, then, the family and the domestic sphere represent an integral, indeed, inseparable part of the business enterprise. Similarly, small employers are subject to considerable market uncertainties which, together with their heavy dependence upon personal skills rather than capital assets, can make their proprietorship vulnerable.

Their position within the entrepreneurial middle class, therefore, is tenuous, though less marginal than that of the self-employed. In fact, there is a significant degree of mobility — in both directions — between these two categories. It is only when small employers accumulate considerable capital assets that their membership becomes more firmly structured.[46] Only a minority, however, are able to accumulate sufficient assets to become owner-controllers, while many others revert to self-employment or become employees.

Owner-controllers do not work alongside their employees but, instead, they are singularly and solely responsible for the administration and management of their businesses. They are, perhaps, the closest present-day approximation to the classical entrepreneur and, as such, they are more likely to adopt a rational, cost-effective approach.[47] They, too, are subject to market fluctuations, but whereas the self-employed and small employers attempt to protect themselves by cultivating networks of regular customers, the generally larger size of owner-controllers' businesses prevents them adopting this strategy. At the same time, their market position is more vulnerable than that of larger enterprises since the latter often have access to greater cash and credit resources which enable them to 'ride' periods of trading difficulty.

Unlike the self-employed and small employers, owner-controllers depend primarily upon personal managerial and financial expertise rather than purely trade-based skills. This category, therefore, includes individuals with prior managerial experience as well as those who have been upwardly mobile through small-scale capital accumulation. Because owner-controllers do not work alongside their employees they must consciously develop systems of supervisory control. Further, obtaining worker commitment is more problematic than for small employers who are able to dictate work performance by personal example. The owner-controller's more calculative approach is reflected in the greater separation of business and domestic spheres. Unpaid family labour, characteristically important in smaller businesses, is no longer significant. However, enterprises of this sort are usually family-owned and, because they have greater tangible capital assets, can be transmitted between generations. This acts as a buffer against downward mobility of the kind which is often experienced by the self-employed and small employers; as such, owner-controllers are more firmly rooted within the entrepreneurial middle class.

Owner-directors control enterprises within which there are managerial structures.[48] Administrative tasks are subdivided and delegated to executive directors and other senior staff. In other words, the scale of business activities is such that the owners are no longer able *personally* to perform all the functions of supervision and control. Within this category, there is a diversity of trajectories to proprietorship; some may have inherited businesses from their fathers, while others will have founded their own enterprises or purchased them from the owners.[49] Consequently, managerial practices vary. In confronting the common problem of delegation, some owner-directors implement formalised, quasi-bureaucratic decision-making practices while others rely upon more personal systems; for example, the cultivation of an ethos of paternalism within which employee commitment is obtained. As with owner-controllers, the ownership of substantial capital assets firmly entrenches owner-directors within the entrepreneurial middle class. As a hedge against business failure a substantial degree of product diversification often occurs. However, despite differences in managerial strategies, all owner-directors are confronted with a common problem; the need to *delegate* control and yet *retain* personal ownership. Those who, through business growth, fail to do this, often have to 'go public'. They thereby threaten their position as active proprietors.

149

These, briefly, are the four types of business proprietor which constitute the entrepreneurial middle class. The problems confronting individuals who experience mobility on the basis of small-scale capital accumulation rather than through organisational careers are unknown. There is also a general ignorance of the attitudes and beliefs found among different sectors of the entrepreneurial middle class and the extent to which these are shaped by varying material circumstances.[50] Further, little is known about the ways whereby petty capital accumulation is related to different family and employment relationships.[51] In addition, the linkages that develop between small and large-scale business enterprises are largely unexplored.[52] These sociological issues have received scant attention since most analyses have typically regarded them from an almost entirely financial or economic perspective.[53] Until further research is directed to these areas, the reproduction of the entrepreneurial middle class will remain unchartered.

Notes

1. See F. Bechhofer and B. Elliott, 'An Approach to a Study of Small Shopkeepers and the Class Structure', *European Journal of Sociology,* vol. 9 (1968); F. Bechhofer, B. Elliott, M. Rushforth and R. Bland, 'The Petits Bourgeois in the Class Structure: The Case of the Small Shopkeepers' in F. Parkin (ed.), *The Social Analysis of Class Structure,* London, 1974; F. Bechhofer and B. Elliott, 'Persistence and Change: the Petite Bourgeoisie in Industrial Society', *European Journal of Sociology,* vol. 17 (1976); R. Bland, B. Elliott and F. Bechhofer, 'Social Mobility in the Petite Bourgeoisie', *Acta Sociologica,* vol. 21 (1978).
2. B. Elliott and D. McCrone, 'Landlords in Edinburgh: Some Preliminary Findings', *Sociological Review,* vol. 23 (1975); B. Elliott and D. McCrone, *Property and Power in a City,* London, 1980.
3. H. Newby *et al., Property, Paternalism and Power* London, 1978; H. Newby, *Green and Pleasant Land,* London, 1979.
4. Bechhofer and Elliott, 'Persistence and Change', p. 77.
5. Bechhofer *et al,* 'The Petits Bourgeois', p. 123; F. Bechhofer and B. Elliott, 'Petty Property: The Survival of a Moral Economy' in F. Bechhofer and B. Elliott (eds), *The Petite Bourgeoisie,* London, 1981, p. 183.
6. F. Bechhofer, B. Elliott, M. Rushford and R. Bland, 'Small Shopkeepers: Matters of Money and Meaning', *Sociological Review,* vol. 22, 1974, pp. 473–4, 479.

7. It is control by the state rather than big business which attracts most opposition from small business owners. See the contributions in, for example, R. King and N. Nugent (eds), *Respectable Rebels*, London, 1979; and F. Bechhofer, B. Elliott and D. McCrone, 'Structure, Consciousness and Action', *British Journal of Sociology*, vol. 29 (1978).

8. For a discussion of the economic changes underlying this trend see J. Gershuny, *After Industrial Society*, London, 1978.

9. This argument is summarised in J. Boissevain, 'Small Entrepreneurs in Changing Europe: Towards a Research Agenda', unpublished paper presented at the European Centre for Work and Society, Utrecht, 1980.

10. See, for example, E.F. Schumacher, *Small is Beautiful*, London, 1973; K. Kumar, *Prophecy and Progress*, Harmondsworth, 1978.

11. J. Martin and A.R.D. Norman, *The Computerized Society*, Englewood Cliffs, New Jersey, 1970, p. 32.

12. For empirical evidence see F. Blackaby (ed.), *De-industrialisation*, London, 1979; R. Pahl, 'Employment, Work and the Domestic Division of Labour', *International Journal of Urban and Regional Research*, vol. 4, (1980).

13. Pahl, 'Employment, Work and the Domestic Division of Labour', p. 4.

14. See R. Scase and R. Goffee, *The Real World of the Small Business Owner*, London, 1980.

15. See K. Marx, *Capital*, (vol. 1), London, 1954.

16. Ibid., p. 320.

17. Ibid., p. 364.

18. Ibid., p. 478.

19. Ibid., pp. 586–7.

20. The Marxist concept of 'mode of production' refers to an abstract combination of relations and forces of production. A 'social formation' is comprised of several modes and forms of production although one mode will be dominant. When Marx analysed nineteenth-century England the capitalist mode was predominant and all other types of productive activity were subordinate to it. At any particular stage the dissolution of prior modes of production may reach the point where only forms or elements of that mode persist. For further discussion of these points see N. Poulantzas, *Classes in Contemporary Capitalism*, London, 1975; and A. Friedman, *Industry and Labour*, London, 1977.

21. Poulantzas, *Classes in Contemporary Capitalism*, p. 151.

22. Ibid., p. 286.

23. Ibid., pp. 285–6.

24. E.O. Wright, *Class Crisis and the State*, London, 1978, chapter 2.

25. Ibid., pp. 79–80.

26. Wright's schema is summarised in *Class, Crisis and the State,* pp. 61–83.

27. Poulantzas, *Classes in Contemporary Capitalism.*

28. Ibid., p. 147.

29. Ibid., p. 140.

30. Ibid.

31. J. Westergaard, 'Class, Inequality and "Corporatism"' in A. Hunt (ed.), *Class and Class Structure,* London, 1977, p. 168.

32. Wright, *Class, Crisis and the State,* p. 10.

33. Ibid., pp. 74–5, n. 67.

34. Ibid.

35. For recent discussions of this distinction and the implications for research into social mobility and class structure see R. Blackburn, 'Social Stratification', unpublished paper presented to BSA (British Sociological Association) Conference, Lancaster, 1980 and A. Stewart, K. Prandy and R. Blackburn, *Social Stratification and Occupations,* London, 1980.

36. Poulantzas, *Classes in Contemporary Capitalism,* p. 329.

37. V.I. Lenin, *The Development of Capitalism in Russia,* Moscow, 1956.

38. Most social mobility studies assume that the pre-eminent channel for upward movement is through occupational positions within large-scale bureaucracies on the basis of meritocratic criteria. For a recent review of such work see A. Heath, *Social Mobility,* Glasgow, 1981.

39. G. Crossick, *The Lower Middle Class in Britain,* London 1977, p. 35.

40. A.J. Mayer, 'The Lower Middle Class as Historical Problem', *Journal of Modern History,* vol. 47, 1975, p. 432.

41. It is extremely difficult to present accurate statistical data in support of this assertion. Definitions of 'small businesses' and 'self-employed' vary (the latter often including those who formally employ others). Further, as recent discussions of the 'informal' economy suggest, many self-employed proprietors are not 'officially' recognised or, therefore, counted. Nevertheless, most aggregate data on the small firm sector strongly suggest that 'the vast majority of small firms are very small indeed'. *Report of the Committee of Inquiry on Small Firms,* (The Bolton Report), p. 3.

42. See the evidence reported in F. Bechhofer *et al.,* 'Small Shop-keepers'; H. Newby *et al., Property, Paternalism and Power;* R. Gasson, 'Roles of Farm Women in England', unpublished paper, 1980; C. Delphy and D. Leonard, 'The Family as an Economic System', unpublished paper presented to Institutionalisation of Sex

Differences Conference, University of Kent, April 1980.

43. This is particularly the case in discussions of independent craft-workers. See, for example, W.M. Williams, *The Country Craftsman,* London, 1958.

44. See, for example, the discussion in C.W. Mills, *White Collar,* London, 1951.

45. A substantial proportion of the Edinburgh shopkeepers and East Anglian 'family' and 'active managerial' farmers studied, respectively, by Bechhofer *et al.* and Newby *et al.* would fall into this category.

46. For a recent discussion of the 'marginal' and 'established' components of the 'old' middle class see J.H. Goldthorpe, 'Comment', *British Journal of Sociology,* vol. 29, (1978).

47. For discussions of the historical role of the entrepreneur see, for example, M.W. Flinn, *Origins of the Industrial Revolution,* London, 1966; and J. Boswell, *The Rise and Decline of Small Firms,* London, 1973. Entrepreneurial ideology is discussed in T. Nichols, *Ownership, Control and Ideology,* London, 1969.

48. The historical emergence of such structures is examined in A. Francis, 'Families, Firms and Finance Capital', *Sociology,* vol. 14 (1980) and S. Nyman and A. Silbertson, 'The Ownership and Control of Industry', *Oxford Economic Papers,* vol. 30 (1978). For contemporary analyses see M. Stanworth and J. Curran, *Management Motivation in the Smaller Business,* Epping, 1973 and Boswell, *The Rise and Decline of Small Firms.*

49. See Boswell, *The Rise and Decline of Small Firms.* One particular trajectory (inheritance) and one particular managerial style (paternalism) is discussed in G.M. Norris, 'Industrial Paternalist Capitalism and Local Labour Markets, *Sociology,* vol. 12 (1978).

50. Notwithstanding the various contributions of F. Bechhofer *et al.,* H. Newby *et al., Property, Paternalism and Power,* as well as R. King and N. Nugent, *Respectable Rebels,* London, 1979.

51. These issues are discussed in Boswell, *The Rise and Decline of Small Firms* and Boissevain, 'Small Entrepreneurs in Changing Europe'.

52. See, however, Friedman, *Industry and Labour.*

53. This emphasis is reflected in much of the recent debate concerning the role of small businesses in the economy. For a critique of many contemporary assumptions of this sort see R. Scase and R. Goffee, *The Real World of the Small Business Owner,* London, 1980.

PART III
CONTEMPORARY VARIETIES
OF SMALL ENTERPRISE

Introduction

Discussion of 'the small firm' often turns out on inspection to constitute discussion of a single kind of small firm, very frequently the small manufacturing firm. Partly, this results from the tendency to equate the economy as a whole with manufacturing, reflecting a nineteenth-century picture of industrial societies but, in fact, manufacturing represents a shrinking proportion of the economies of all advanced industrial societies. Industrial societies of the future will be based to a far greater extent upon the manipulation of information and the development of services.

Small firms reflect this restructuring in their own distribution across the economy. Binks and Coyne[1] suggest, for example, that under 10 per cent of Britain's small firms are in the manufacturing sector and that under a third of those employed in small enterprises work in small manufacturing firms. Indeed, it can be argued that part of the resurgence of the small firm over the last decade or so is a result of this restructuring since many of the new expanding sections of the economies of advanced industrial societies offer increased opportunities for small enterprise because the minimum scale of profitable operation is often lower than in manufacturing.

Perhaps the second most common stereotype of the small business, in both popular and academic discussion alike, is the corner shop. However, as Kirby's opening paper in this section demonstrates, at best, only 15 per cent of Britain's small enterprises reside in the retail sector and, again, this is a sector where the small enterprise has not fared well in recent decades. In other words, the 'typical' small business in a statistical sense does not exist; rather it is the heterogeneity of the small business sector that needs highlighting.

This section contains five papers devoted to examining in detail different kinds of small enterprise. It begins with a discussion of the small retail outlet and then moves on to papers looking at ethnic small business, producer co-operatives, female-owned small enterprises and, finally, the franchised small business. These last four are less familiar in research terms although, as the papers demonstrate, all may be expected to become more important in the future.

Kirby begins by looking at the numbers of retail outlets and confirms widely accepted views that there has been a sharp decline in recent years and that ownership of this variety of enterprise is typically poorly rewarded as well as insecure. But the paper goes on to argue much more positively (and less fashionably) that there is a role for the small store in a modern distribution system which will continue into the foreseeable future. This argument, it seems, can be applied to most industrial societies, questioning any inexorable trend towards a retail distribution system based solely on large units.

The creation of a stable, small-scale retail sector functioning in a complementary role to large retail outlets requires, however, change among both small retailers and policy-makers. Retailers need greater training and a more aggressive, effective approach to marketing. Policy-makers need to create a more favourable environment by, for example, subsidising small retail outlets to preserve local communities and protect the disadvantaged. Governments could also promote retailer training which, according to Kirby, need not be long or elaborate to dramatically improve the performance of the typical small retailer.

Cornforth[2] examines producer co-operatives in the second paper in this section. This form of small enterprise has expanded enormously in Britain in recent years and there are now at least 800 (and probably many more) in existence. Other advanced industrial societies have proportionately more co-operatives on the whole than Britain. Most are small by conventional definitions though there are also examples of successful large enterprises based upon the co-operative principle in Britain and elsewhere.

Like other forms of small enterprise, co-operatives do not form a single category and Cornforth identifies five types although some of these contain only a handful of examples. The most common variety, and the one which has grown most in recent years, is what he terms the 'alternative' co-operative. These mainly have their origins in the alternative social movements of the 1960s and 1970s and their members are usually relatively well educated and middle class. Their co-operatives are most commonly found in retailing (health foods and bookshops, for example) and craft activities.

The problems faced by producer co-operatives are surprisingly similar to those faced by other, conventional small enterprises — lack of capital, problems in finding suitable premises and inadequate management skills — although, of course, they also have to cope with the demands of maintaining their co-operative ideals. There are indications, however, that external help agencies such as local Co-operative Development Agencies are now emerging to provide support and expertise for new co-operatives. Contrary to some expectations, the survival rate of producer co-operatives appears at least as high as conventional small enterprises.

Jones and McEvoy, in a paper specially written for this collection, critically examine the role of the ethnic small enterprise in Britain's economy. Popular and media views stress the dynamism and hard work of ethnic small business owners, especially those from the Asian community. But, as this paper trenchantly argues, these views add up to just another myth about the small enterprise. Far from being a typical occupational destination for ethnic minority members, small business ownership is relatively uncommon. Nor does the typical ethnic small business owner appear markedly more successful than his white counterparts. In fact, what struck these researchers was not the differences between ethnically owned small businesses and the white-owned variety but their marked similarities.

The authors conclude that rather than being a sign of some inborn entrepreneurial talent, small business ownership among ethnic community members is more often just simply a way of coping with the social and economic disadvantages of living in a racially discriminating society. Finding it difficult to obtain secure, well-paid employment, self-employment is accepted as an alternative. But it is an alternative offering no magical escape from disadvantage. The enterprises ethnic small business owners operate are generally in the least profitable and most marginal areas of the economy. At best, small business owner-ship offers 'a short ladder giving access to longer ladders' allowing parents to provide an environment for their children to be socially mobile through education.

Women small business owners have received very little attention from researchers although women are well represented in many areas of small enterprise ownership such as hairdressing (as well as providing crucial support to their spouses who operate male-owned small firms).

The Watkins and Watkins study reported in the fourth paper in this section compares samples of female and male small business owners. In some respects, such as the importance of independence needs as a motivation for self-employment, female small business owners were remarkably similar to their male equivalents but in others they differed greatly. For instance, less than half the female owners were married or in a similar stable relationship unlike virtually all the males. Nor were husbands as supportive as wives have been shown to be of husbands running a small business.

The data suggest women not only suffer from the cultural bias which defines women as not 'business-minded' but they have fewer opportunities to acquire the educational experience likely to be helpful in running a small enterprise. What is more, they tend to enter self-employment at a younger age than the male small business owner although it might be argued that this may be no disadvantage in the long term. The authors conclude that only fundamental change, particularly in the field of education, will allow women more opportunities to enter into entrepreneurial roles. It might be added that the cultural changes in advanced industrial societies which are beginning a substantial redefinition of gender roles will also contribute to the development of the greater experience and assertiveness which goes with self-employment.

The final paper in this section discusses the franchised small enterprise. This form of small business, long seen as especially characteristic of the United States, is now widespread in most other advanced industrial societies. In Britain, for example, it is estimated that over 350 separate companies franchise at least part of their activities and the British Franchise Association, the industry's trade association, claims that 15 per cent of all retail sales now occur through franchised outlets. (In the United States the proportion is double this, according to the United States Department of Commerce.)

The franchise relationship involves one company (the franchisor) establishing contractual relations with other, independently owned enterprises (franchisees). These are usually small firms who undertake to produce and/or market a product or service according to a strict format devised by the franchisor. The central issue analysed in Stanworth, Curran and Hough's paper is whether the franchised small business is genuinely independent. Sceptics claim that, in reality, franchisees are managers of outlets effectively owned by the franchisor and hence this is a pseudo small business.

The authors note that the notion of 'independence' is a slippery concept in relation to the small business. Many conventionally small firms are very closely linked to other often larger firms, for example.

Despite the formal and detailed specification of the franchisor's control over the franchisee, the data suggest that, in practice, franchisees have more autonomy than many might expect. Without such autonomy the franchisor would not achieve the advantages of franchising, a local outlet operated by a highly self-motivated, hard-working individual willing to make decisions to ensure the local market is fully and effectively exploited.

The five varieties of small enterprise examined in this section emphasise the superficiality of attempting to discuss small firms as a homogeneous category — something which appears to come only too easily even to those who ought to know better. The absence of a contribution on the small manufacturing firm is deliberate. This is the most studied of all small enterprises — indeed, it might be said to be the most over-studied given the overall trend to deindustrialisation now manifested in every advanced industrial society. The characteristic shared by all the varieties of small enterprise discussed in this section is that they are predominantly located in the emerging service and tertiary sectors which will dominate post-industrial society.

Notes

1. Binks, M. and Coyne, J., *The Birth of Enterprise,* Hobart Paper no. 98, Institute of Economic Affairs, London, 1983.
2. Chris Cornforth has updated some of the figures for this abstract from his original paper 'Some Factors Affecting the Success or Failure of Worker Co-operatives: A Review of Empirical Research in the United Kingdom', *Economic and Industrial Democracy*, vol. 4, no. 2 1983.

9 The Small Retailer

DAVID A. KIRBY

Introduction

Traditionally, in most countries, retailing has been one of the main outlets for entrepreneurial talent, and the small retailer is a characteristic of most industrialised economies. While much of this paper relates to small-scale retailing generally, many of the examples are taken from Britain, where, with the exception of retail pharmacies, there are no barriers to entry other than the capital to purchase a business. Indeed, in most countries retailing remains one of the easiest trades to enter and despite several decades of decline, small-scale retailing remains an important element in most distributive systems. In Britain in 1980 there were something in the order of 220 000 independent stores accounting for approximately 34 per cent of all retail sales (Table 9.1). Clearly not all independents are small. Independent retailing is a form of business organisation and the term can refer to a variety of retail forms which range from the traditional corner shop to singly-owned supermarkets, discount stores, department stores, and so on, and even chains of up to nine retail branches. With sales of approximately £160 000 per annum, however, the turnover of the average independent retail trader is well below the upper small shop ceiling of £200 000 prescribed by the Wilson Committee in 1979[1] and considerably below the co-operatives (£249 000) and the multiples

(£261 000). Since the mid-1970s, it has been possible to distinguish between single retail outlets (independents with only one branch), small multiples (with between two and nine branches) and large multiples (with ten or more branches). In 1980, there were 197 884 single outlets, accounting for 57 per cent of the total number of stores and 31 per cent of the retail market. Once again, the single outlets could be large stores but in 1980 turnover averaged £91 559 compared with £109 867 for the small multiples and £432 470 for the large multiples. Most of these single-outlet stores were small, unprofitable businesses employing few, if any, staff and generating low returns on investment. In 1980, for example, the average single outlet employed 4.3 persons and had a gross margin of £21 634 (24 per cent) which it achieved only by being open extremely long hours.[2] Long working hours and meagre profits are a characteristic of small-scale retailing as are inadequate cash reserves, and it is hardly surprising that over one-third of all small traders surveyed in a study undertaken in 1976 were experiencing financial difficulties.[3]

Table 9.1
Importance of independent retailing, 1950–80

	No. of Shops ('000)	Proportion of Retail Sales (%)
1950	450	64
1961	445	57
1971	390	50
1980	220	34

Source: *Census of Distribution,* 1950, 1961, 1971; Retail Inquiry, 1980.

This pattern of trading is, in part at least, a result of the lack of entry barriers to retailing and the low levels of managerial competence in this sector of the distributive system. Characteristically, small-scale retailers have received no formal training in retailing and left school at or before the age of 16. While formal school education has been found not to be an important factor in determining business success,[4] previous business experience is significant and in a study undertaken in 1976,[5] it was discovered that only about one-third of all prospective entrants to retailing had any prior knowledge of the trade. In the majority of cases, this was as a shop assistant. This survey not only confirms the conclusions drawn from studies of existing retailers, but points out that in nearly half of the cases surveyed, the jobs of the prospective new entrants had no relevance whatsoever to small-scale retailing. Thus it would seem that many new entrants have little or no conception of the workings of, or problems involved in owning, a small retail business. Many (perhaps between one-quarter and one-third) are 'seduced by the prospect of being able to make their own decisions, or of having to answer to no one but themselves',[6] while others remain attracted by the hope that they will earn a good living from their enterprises. Very frequently, however, the reality of the situation is very different. Bankruptcies and business failures in retailing remain high[7] and small-scale retailing is 'one of the easiest ways of losing the savings of a life-time'.[8]

Characteristically the first two years of trading are notoriously difficult for most small businesses and it is estimated that it takes between two and five years for a small shop to make any reasonable profit. Inevitably, many new businesses fail before this period has elapsed. The sector is characterised, in fact, by a high rate of turnover and Bechhofer et al.[9] discovered in the early 1970s that 'approximately 20 per cent of Edinburgh's shops closed or changed hands at least once every six to twelve months'. Traditionally, however, there has been 'no lack of individuals prepared to risk their capital for the envisaged freedom of running their own business'.[10] More recent studies have suggested that this is no longer the case. In a study[11] undertaken between 1976 and 1978 of retailers attempting to sell their stores, it was discovered that approximately 18 per cent of the vendors contacted had failed to sell their business on a previous occasion either because nobody had been interested or the prospective purchaser had been unable to generate the necessary funding. For whatever reason, the trend is contrary to the belief that the ease of entry into retailing leads to higher birth rates in times of unemployment.[12] It results not only in the declining importance of the small store, but also in a situation where, quite frequently, elderly or failing traders are unable to release the capital tied up in their businesses.

While such conditions are characteristic of most small retail operations, not all small traders are unsuccessful and small-scale retailing like other small firms, provides 'a means of entry into business for new entrepreneurial talent and the seedbed from which new, large companies grow'.[13] Very little research has been undertaken to support or refute this statement but the experience of Sir John Cohen and the Tesco Empire lends credence to it, as do the apparently burgeoning small retail businesses being managed by Asian immigrants. However, the results of recent research seem to explode this myth, pointing out that among the Asian community small-scale retailing 'simply allows a small minority to exchange the role of marginal worker for that of marginal proprietor'[14] and enables the more successful to make 'short-term sacrifices in a foreign country in order to enjoy the spoils on return to the homeland'. Nevertheless, successful small retailers do exist, though very little is known about the conditions necessary for their survival nor about the characteristics of the successful entrepreneur. In contrast, considerably more is known about the problems facing the small trader and the measures which might be introduced to aid survival.

Table 9.2

Factors responsible for the demise of the small independent trader and policy implications[15]

Reasons for decline	Possible reactions
1. Broad economic and social change (inflation, recession, buying behaviour)	Nothing, except increased awareness of the changes
2. Competition from multiples and co-operatives	Form buying consortia. Compete by service not price. Seek effective locations. Market to specific consumer segments.
3. Increased operating costs (rates, electricity, etc.)	Better accounting to isolate cost items
4. Lack of capital for investment	
5. Availability of supplies of goods (price, quantity, delivery, etc.)	Form buying consortia. Co-operate with wholesalers.
6. Urban renewal	Explore retailer co-operative shopping centre development
7. Age of entrepreneur, (man approaching retirement)	
8. Poor locations	Attempt to relocate
9. Inflexible management attitudes	Be more willing to co-operate with other independents. Seek advice on store operation and management. Explore benefits of new technologies.

The problems of small retail businesses

According to some commentators, there is no one cause for the demise of the independent small trader, the reasons 'are multiple with a variety of factors interacting with each other'.[15] As Table 9.2 reveals, a variety of factors can certainly be identified and, at one level, this view is perfectly correct. For every store there is a whole set of factors operating which determine its viability. At another level, however, it is wrong and it is possible to view the demise of the small, independent retail business as the end-product of obsolescence. Indeed, each of the nine factors identified in Table 9.2 can be grouped into three categories of obsolescence.

Obsolescence of the trading environment (reasons 6 and 8 of Table 9.2)

In many localities, changes in the structure and distribution of the population have resulted in outlets being situated in locations which possess a population threshold barely, if at all, adequate to support a local store. This situation has been heightened by the fact that personal mobility levels have increased and, for the majority of consumers remaining in the area, it is possible to travel considerable distances to shop. In rural areas, the situation has resulted from continued migration from the countryside to the town, while in urban areas it is quite frequently a consequence of environmental renewal. While 'there is remarkably little evidence of the impact of urban redevelopment on retail structure',[16] it has been observed[17] that over the period 1961–71, for instance, about one million dwellings were demolished in Britain and the number of independent traders declined by about 55 411 — a loss of one shop for every 200 dwellings. Some, but by no means all, will have been demolished. Others will have closed because slum clearance programmes have deprived them of their catchments, while many will have been unable to obtain premises in new shopping developments. Although it is recognised in Britain that 'one of the most important objectives [of redevelopment schemes] will be to make fair and adequate provision for traders and other business interest',[18] there is little doubt that rarely is this objective achieved, a point recognised on both sides of the Atlantic.[19] Not only have many of these developments resulted in a reduced level of retail provision, but invariably, the units provided in such developments have been larger than those generally required by the small trader[20] and even when units of an appropriate size have been supplied, the rents and rates in such developments frequently have been prohibitively high for the small trader.[21]

Obsolescence of the retail form (reasons, 1, 2 and 5 of Table 9.2)

Increasingly the retail trades have recognised the benefits to be gained from economies of scale and invariably both businesses and stores have become larger. As a consequence, the retail trades are now highly concentrated[22] and as a result, manufacturers and producers have become 'very highly dependent on the supermarkets and chain stores'[23] which have been able to use their power to negotiate favourable terms and prices. With the abolition of Resale Price Maintenance in the early 1960s, these large firms have been able, in theory at least, to pass on to the consumer the benefits derived from such scale economies. In a period of marked inflation, many consumers have opted for price economy rather than personal service and convenience — the hallmarks of the independent small retail business.

By virtue of both its independence and its size, the small, private store has been unable to benefit from scale economies. In an attempt to introduce such measures and to reduce the buying advantage of the large companies, various contractual chains have emerged. These have ranged from informal local buying groups to the more formal, national voluntary wholesaling groups (such as Mace, Spar and VG in the food trades and the Numark Chemist Group in non-foods). These have met with only limited success, however. There are numerous reasons for this. First, many small traders are reluctant to become affiliated in this way because it means giving up some of their independence.[24] Second, even these larger groupings are unable to operate as effectively as the large firms because there are few economies of scale involved in distributing the products, owing to the size of their member stores.[25] Indeed, most of the major voluntary groups will not service the smallest businesses which have come to rely increasingly on cash and carry wholesaling.

Obsolescence of the managerial form (reasons 3, 4, 7 and 9 of Table 9.2)

Traditionally, small retail businesses are characterised by long working hours, low profit levels, the inability to attract and afford staff, family employment, persistent problems of capital availability, inefficient retailing methods, and so on. Especially in countries like Britain which lack any pre-entry training requirements, this is the manifestation of persistent economic under-performance and the lower productivity of small stores[26] which results from inefficient, unprofessional management. As outlined above, most of the new entrants to retailing have no knowledge of modern retail methods, nor of the methods of small business management. As a consequence they have to learn their trade by trial and error, and in the highly competitive market conditions which prevail, this can be costly and, quite frequently, fatal. Equally, many of the older traders have failed to change with the times and display not only the classic symptoms of management inflexibility, but also a lack of motivation. Perhaps most important of all, however, very few small traders, whether new or established, are aware of how to implement and interpret the necessary controls to facilitate sound management practice and prolonged business development. As a consequence, many small retail businesses require 'a hard daily cycle of work just to maintain the status quo; there is no sign of a path to expansion or improvement'.[27] While 'motivation, hard work, persistence and flexibility' are important pre-requisites for success in any small business,[28] in themselves they are not sufficient — the effort must be effective. All too frequently, however, the average small trader has little if any idea of where (or how) profits are being made or costs are being incurred. In many instances, therefore, effort is being misdirected and wasted.

By comparison, the most successful large retail businesses are increasingly aware of the benefits to be gained from sound, innovative management practice and in many countries the management gap between the large and the small retail business has widened considerably in recent years. If small-scale retailing is to survive, this gap will have to be narrowed somewhat and small retailers 'will require a vastly different and more flexible approach than has been manifest so far',[29] making use of the full management potential of micro technology.

The role of the small retail business

If, as the preceding discussion has emphasised, the small independent retail business is obsolete, such shops presumably have no part in a modern, efficient distribution system. Certainly this is true of the traditional inefficient small shop (and further closure of such business operations seems inevitable), but the efficient small store does fulfil, and will continue to fulfil, an important social and economic function in the modern distributive system.

In the USA, for instance, the retail system appears to be polarising with small convenience stores emerging to satisfy the need for local shops consequent upon the increasing scale of retail development and the virtual disappearance of the more traditional 'mom and pop' independent small stores. While such convenience stores are usually franchise operations belonging to a national or regional company, their role in the distributive system for the majority of consumers is for 'topping up', for use in 'emergencies' and for the purchase of perishables. For a minority of consumers (those unable or unwilling to travel long distances and/or to shop at the larger stores) they are used for the majority of their shopping needs. Essentially, however, the small shop fulfils a secondary role in a modern distributive system complementing rather than competing with the large retail business.[30]

This trend has been observed elsewhere in the Western world, most notably in Denmark,[31] France[32] and Sweden.[33] Indeed, one of America's largest and most successful convenience store chains (7-Eleven, operated by the Southland Corporation) has outlets in countries as far apart as Australia and Sweden, Britain and Japan. Thus it would appear that, even in the most concentrated and efficient of retail systems, there is a need for small, local stores — a need which can be met by the small, independent trader, but only if the business is efficiently organised and managed and matched to the function it is to perform in the distributive system.

In addition, it should be recognised that not all consumer segments are willing or able to shop at large stores. First, there are those households for whom the trend to mass merchandising is unacceptable. For these, the small, specialist store is important and there are signs, as Hall[34] has suggested, that with the growth of a more discriminating consumer society, this group is expanding.[35] Perhaps of even greater significance, however, are the needs and requirements of the underprivileged and deprived sectors of society. Inevitably, 'a market system steered by the free choice of consumers alone will tend to favour the bigger and stronger groups of consumers'.[36] With the decline in the number of small, local shops, it is the poor, the aged, the infirm and the immobile who are most disadvantaged.[37]

The small shop does not provide a social service only for the consumer minority, however. For all consumers it adds variety to the retail system — variety in both visual terms and in terms of both shopping locations and experiences. Moreover, in both urban and rural environments, the local small shop is frequently the focus of community life and point of contact, the shopkeeper acting as transmitter of information, confidant, social therapist and, frequently, a social welfare officer caring, particularly, for the well-being of the aged and infirm. In most rural areas there is no alternative to the small shop and its closure often leads to the break-up of the community and further rural-urban migration.

Assistance for the small retail trader

From the evidence available, therefore, a need for small, local stores appears to exist. However, it has to be recognised that this need will not be satisfied without greater efficiency on the part of the small trader. Clearly, there is much that individual retailers can do in this direction but it is unlikely that they can make significant progress without some form of government intervention or assistance, since they possess neither the expertise nor the resources necessary for change. Various forms of assistance are available to expedite this transformation process, and to facilitate analysis these will be examined as they relate to the problems with which the small business is faced.

The trading environment

In many inner city and rural areas where small stores are struggling for survival, measures are being introduced to stimulate population and industrial growth. Population redistribution merely to save the small store obviously is not a feasible policy option. One alternative strategy is to inform the existing population of the importance of the small shop and to encourage consumers to purchase more from their local independent small store. In Britain, such campaigns have been organised in recent years by both trade organisations and local community councils and have attempted to demonstrate to the consumer the advantages of using the local store. This has been achieved by: (i) comparing prices in a local shop with those in a neighbouring supermarket; and (ii) demonstrating the cost involved in using a private car for shopping purposes.

While the results of these campaigns look promising, they have not been monitored scientifically and no attention has been paid to the durability of their impact. In Norway, a similar national advertising campaign was conducted during the winter of 1976–7 by the Ministry of Commerce, and although relatively little is known about the success of the project, it would seem that such campaigns can do much to preserve the local shop, but that the effects on consumer behaviour are not permanent, the campaigns having to be repeated regularly if their impact is to be prolonged.[38] This might suggest a fundamental weakness of such campaigns. Consumers are being *advised* to use such stores rather than being *attracted* to them. A more effective and permanent strategy might be to encourage the retailers to market and promote their own businesses more effectively.[39] This sort of approach is being followed in Sweden and has been adopted in Britain by Mid-Wales Development; as part of its training and advisory service to village shops.

A further measure which can go some way towards offsetting the loss of trade resulting from inadequate population numbers is a subsidy or grant for running the business. In effect this is an income supplement given to shopkeepers in those areas where there is an identified need for a shop and where the catchment population is insufficient to support a viable entity. Such grants are available to village shops in Norway and Sweden, where they have proved to be both popular and successful, though unless carefully administered, they can protect inefficiency.

In several European countries, new types of 'department store' have been developed in which independent retailers work together in close co-operation and run their business within the same building.[40] In Britain, perhaps the most relevant example of such a development is 'The Village' at Corstorphine, Edinburgh. Formerly a two-storey, 18 000 sq. ft. retail furnishing store, the premises have been completely refurbished to provide 90 small low-cost shop units which are occupied by 56 different retail traders.[41]

The retail form

Since competition is regarded as one of the major factors responsible for the decline of the small shop, many would argue for legislation to curtail the power of the large retail company and to control competition. Several countries do possess legislation intended to protect the small trader against the bargaining power of the multiples[42] but in Britain it is generally believed that 'vigorous competition in the distributive trades and among their suppliers is the surest protection of the public interest'[43] and that government intervention is unwarranted. Certainly such legislation is unwieldy and difficult to enforce. Equally, it can protect inefficiency and preserve obsolete and unnecessary retail forms.

Rather than legislation to protect the small trader, perhaps government should intervene to help the small business compete more effectively and to trade more efficiently. There are several ways in which this can be achieved. As early as 1937, the point was made that while the small business has a chance of survival, 'his best chance is to become big'.[44] Very few small retail businesses have the resources to do this and, in Norway and Sweden, grants have been made available to village shops in an attempt to stimulate investment in the businesses and to promote their modernisation, expansion and greater efficiency in an attempt to improve their trading position. These grants, which are given only when certain stringent criteria relating to the size, location and function of the stores have been fulfilled, are for both major and minor modifications. The former include such items as conversion to self-service, provision of parking space, shop expansion, and so on, while the latter are intended mainly for the purchase of new equipment and fittings. The basis for the measures is the belief that modernisation will increase efficiency (and hence profitability), improve working conditions, increase the attractiveness of the businesses for consumers and potential entrepreneurs and increase customer loyalty. Similar schemes are in operation in other European countries (such as France and Germany) but while there is little doubt about the value of investment to business development, it must be recognised that a subsidised investment programme can have an adverse effect on the financial viability of a business and can be wasteful of scarce resources if not administered properly.

An alternative strategy propounded by Dawson[45] is to encourage 'small and local shops which are part of large company chain operations, corporate chains, consumer co-operatives and contractual chain groupings. Such a policy might involve not only land use planning policy initiatives, but also a national policy approach.' While co-operation among small traders is to be encouraged, a major problem with such a solution is that independent small businessmen are notoriously difficult to organise and equally reluctant to give up their independence.[46] Thus, in Japan, such efforts to promote co-operation have met with only limited success. Also, any development by a large commercial organisation (whether it be a multiple retail firm, a co-operative or a voluntary group) inevitably has profit maximisation as its primary objective. Under such circumstances, the areas where local shopping facilities are, perhaps, most needed (that is, the inner city and rural areas) seem unlikely to be served by such developments. Inevitably, the preferred locations will be the more prosperous urban and suburban communities where the population not only has a greater propensity to consume but also a higher level of personal mobility. Given the tendency for most major retailing companies to close their smaller, less profitable stores and the desire of the voluntary groups to service the larger orders, it seems inevitable that without some very radical government programme of intervention, local shopping will remain the province of the small independent retail business.

The management form

Not only do many small retail businesses lack the financial resources to expand but quite frequently also the management expertise and, especially where the proprietor is near, at or beyond the normal age of retirement, the motivation. In countries such as France and the Netherlands, therefore, financial assistance is given to enable and encourage elderly traders to retire.[47] Often such direct exit schemes are associated with schemes which attempt to deter marginal entrants and improve the efficiency and survival chances of those who do open shops. As Boer[48] observed in 1937: 'First, we must have measures to restrict those inefficient businesses which fall by the wayside from being replaced by others equally inefficient. Secondly, those remaining must be educated to greater efficiency in order adequately to serve the buying public.'

In Britain no such policies exist, though some of the voluntary groups do encourage new entrants to attend the pre-establishment courses which their training departments offer. Similarly, the voluntary groups run training courses for their established members and recently Mid-Wales Development has run a very successful training and advisory programme for village shopkeepers. The programme, which was designed by the author, was intended to help small traders become more efficient and profitable. Basically it was divided into three sections:

(i) A formal training programme, the purpose of which was to introduce the participants to basic elements of modern retail management and to encourage them to reappraise their own business operations. The course was divided into four modules (covering stock management, financial management, in-store management and customer management). Each module lasted for a day and an evening and was separated by a period of four to six weeks to allow for implementation.

(ii) A forum for discussion and group action. The participants were able to discuss both the course content (to ensure understanding) and common problems, trying to identify solutions, possibly utilising the resources of Mid Wales Development.

(iii) An advisory service consisting of on-site visits by a consultant to ensure that the techniques were properly understood and implemented and to advise on specific problems relating to the particular business.

While it is not possible to reproduce here the detailed results of the programme, it can be said that, as in similar schemes elsewhere,[49] the project was successful. In support of this, it is noticeable that, as a result of the programme, all of the participants are now trading more profitably and one business has been able to expand into new premises. Also, it is worth noting the views of a number of the participants:

[The course] has enabled me to survive a very bad period of

trading and I now feel more in control and I feel I have the ability to analyse trading results, enabling me to steer a course to better stability and profitability.

We believe that it is now true to say that we run the business and are aware of the likely results from any proposed action, which was certainly not true before we attended the course, whatever we may have thought to the contrary!

We certainly consider that the time spent on the course was probably one of the best investments that we ever made. It has more than paid for itself many times over! It is in our opinion a great pity that so many of the people who attended the initial meetings either thought they knew it all, or could not be bothered to try to improve the services they offer to their customers. Maybe this is the basic problem of the small shopkeeper.

These comments emphasise the point that many small retail traders are simply unaware of how to run their business efficiently and profitably, although most would not admit this to be the case, possibly not even realising their own deficiencies. If such businesses can survive, with sound management they can develop and prosper, even in areas where population thresholds are extremely low. Certainly this has been the conclusion reached from the experiment in Mid-Wales. However, there is little demand for such courses from within the trade and retailers are rarely prepared to pay the full commercial cost. This would suggest that if training programmes are to be effective, either there must be a formal training requirement or such programmes must be actively promoted and attractively packaged, probably involving some form of subsidy arrangement[50] and backed by a professional consultancy service.

Conclusion

From the evidence available, it would seem that even in the most concentrated distribution system there is a need for small, local stores. As well as fulfilling an important socioeconomic function in society, such stores complement the larger outlets in the retail system and protect the interests of the less mobile consumer segments. Ultimately, the new communications technology will revolutionise the whole of the retail trades and it could be that, by the turn of the century, the majority of all shopping will be done largely without stores. Such a development will obviously take time, however, and in the foreseeable future consumer needs are likely to remain relatively unchanged. Even when it does occur, it seems likely that there will be pockets of consumers (the deprived, disadvantaged and unwilling) who will be unable or reluctant to take advantage of this development. For these consumer segments some form of retail outlet will remain essential and for the purchase of everyday convenience items, the efficiently organised local small retail business would seem appropriate; it will satisfy the need for perishable commodities and emergency and forgotten items, as well as acting, possibly, as a dropping-off point for goods ordered from a supplier. In this latter context the Tesco experiment in Gateshead proves interesting.[51] The experiment operates from a local library but there is no reason why, especially in rural areas, the service could not be operated through the local store. Indeed, the local store could even become an outlet for library and other social services. In this era of scarce resources, such a multi-function arrangement seems sensible.

To survive, however, most existing small retail businesses need to become more efficient. In several countries (but particularly in Britain) the management gap between the small and the large business in the retail trades has become increasingly wide and it is now possible to argue that competition between the two sectors is unfair, not because of the bargaining power which the larger retail firms possess, but because of the differences in the levels of professionalism and managerial efficiency. In areas where the population threshold is simply too small to support a permanent store, it seems likely that without some form of financial support the store will close. However, it must be recognised that, providing they are run efficiently, small independent stores can survive in areas with very small population thresholds. This would suggest that if it is accepted that the small, independent retail business has a part to play in the retail system, some assistance is required, not as Dawson[52] has suggested, to preserve an inefficient and obsolete retail form, but to enable the small independent retail business to become a viable economic entity, capable of meeting the socioeconomic needs of the community it serves and fulfilling its role in a distribution system which is both efficient and equitable.

Notes

1. The Committee defined a small business in the retail trades as an outlet with an annual turnover of £200 000 or less. See H. Wilson,

Studies of Small Firms' Financing, Research Report no. 3, Cmnd. 4811, HMSO, 1979.

2. On average the small independent grocery store is open for approximately nine hours each day of the working week and almost half open for about five hours on a Sunday. See P. Bates, *The Independent Grocery Retailer: Characteristics and Problems — a Report of a Survey,* Research Report no. 23, Retail Outlets Research Unit, Manchester Business School, 1976.

3. J.A. Dawson and D.A. Kirby, *Small Scale Retailing in the U.K.* Saxon House, Farnborough, 1979.

4. K.B. Mayer and S. Goldstein, *The First Two Years: Problems of Small Firm Growth and Survival,* US Government Printing Office, Washington, 1961.

5. D.A. Kirby and D.C. Law, 'The Birth and Death of Small Retail Units in Britain: A Preliminary Study', *Retail and Distribution Management,* vol. 9, no. 1 (1981).

6. F. Bechhofer, B. Elliott, M. Rushforth and R. Bland, 'Small Shopkeepers: Matters of Money and meaning', *The Sociological Review,* vol. 22, no. 4 (1974).

7. D. Donleavy, 'Causes of bankruptcy in England' in A. Gibb and T. Webb, *Policy Issues in Small Business Research,* Saxon House, Farnborough, 1980.

8. W.A. Lewis, 'Competition in the Retail Trade', *Economica,* vol. XII, no. 4 (1945).

9. Bechhofer *et al.,* 'Small Shopkeepers'.

10. F. Bechhofer and B. Elliott, 'An Approach to a Study of Small Shopkeepers and the Class Structure', *European Journal of Sociology,* vol. 9 (1968).

11. D.A. Kirby, 'What happened to the local grocer?', *Retail and Distribution Management,* vol. 6, no. 5 (1978).

12. R. Lewis and A. Maude, *The English Middle Classes,* Penguin, Harmondsworth, 1953; E.D. McGarry, 'Retail Trade Mortality', *University of Buffalo, Bureau of Business and Social Research Studies in Business,* no. 4 (1930); and R.S. Spicer and A.E. Blake, *Marketing Survey of the United Kingdom,* Odhams Press, London, 1951.

13. J.E. Bolton, *Report of the Committee of Inquiry on Small Firms,* (Bolton Report), Cmnd. 4811, HMSO, London, 1971.

14. H. Aldrich, T.P. Jones and D. McEvoy, 'Ethnic Advantage and Minority Business Development' in R. Ward and R. Jenkins (eds), *Ethnic Communities in Business,* Cambridge University Press, 1984.

15. J.A. Dawson, 'Independent Retailing in Great Britain: Dinosaur or Chameleon?', *Retail and Distribution Management,* vol. 11, no. 3 (1983).

16. P.M. Shepherd and D. Thorpe, *'Urban Redevelopment and Change in Retail Structure, 1961–1971'*, Research Report no. 27, Retail Outlets Research Unit, Manchester Business School, 1977.

17. D. Thorpe, 'Retail Floorspace: Assessing the Need for Shops', *Retail and Distribution Management*, vol. 3, no. 6 (1975).

18. Ministry of Housing and Local Government, *Town Centres: Cost and Control of Redevelopment*, Planning Bulletin no. 3, HMSO, 1963.

19. D.J. Bennison and R.L. Davies, 'The impact of Town Centre Shopping Schemes in Britain: Their Impact on Traditional Retail Environments', *Progress in Planning*, vol. 14 (1980); and B. Zimmer, 'The Small Businessman and Relocation', in J.Q. Wilson, *Urban Renewal: The Record and the Controversy*, Michigan Press, Cambridge, Mass., 1966.

20. Centre for Advanced Land Use Studies, *Rent Assessment and Tenant Mix in Planned Shopping Centres*, College of Estate Management, Reading, 1975.

21. Dawson and Kirby, 'Small Scale Retailing in the U.K.'.

22. G.P. Akehurst, 'Concentrations in Retail Distribution: Measurement and Significance', *The Service Industries Journal*, vol. 3, no. 2 (1983); European Economic Community, *A Study of the Evolution of Concentration in the Food Distribution Industry for the United Kingdom*, Commission of the European Communities, Brussels–Luxembourg, 1977; K.A. Tucker, *Concentration and Costs in Retailing*, Saxon House, Farnborough, 1983.

23. R. Linda, *Methodology of Concentration Analysis Applied to the Study of Industries and Markets*, Commission of the European Communities, Brussels, 1976.

24. F. Livesey and E.A. Nagy, 'Independents versus Affiliation: What Factors Motivate Retailers?', *Retail and Distribution Management*, vol. 9, no. 3 (1981).

25. R.C. McConkey, 'The True Cost of Small Drops: Is it Realised by Suppliers', *Retail and Distribution Management*, vol. 3, no. 4 (1975); D. Thorpe, D.A. Kirby and C.H. Thompson, *Channels and Costs of Grocery Distribution*, Research Report no. 8, Retail Outlets Research Unit, Manchester Business School, 1973.

26. J.A. Dawson and D.A. Kirby, 'Shop Size and Productivity in the 1960s: Some Evidence from the 1971 Census of Distribution', *European Journal of Marketing*, vol. 11, no. 4 (1977).

27. P. Beresford, 'The Small Shopkeeper', *New Society*, 1 May 1969.

28. Mayer and Goldstein, 'The First Two Years'.

29. N.A.H. Stacey and A. Wilson, *The Changing Pattern of Distribution*, Pergamon Press, 1965.

30. D.A. Kirby, 'The Convenience Store Phenomenon — Implications

for Britain', in P. Jones and R. Oliphant (eds), *Local Shops: Problems and Prospects,* Unit for Retail Planning Information Ltd., Reading, 1976; D.A. Kirby, 'The Convenience Store Phenomenon: The Rebirth of America's Small Shop', *Retail and Distribution Management,* vol. 4, no. 3 (1976).

31. O. Kerndal-Hansen 'Retail Planning in Denmark' in R. Davies (ed.), *Retail Planning in the European Community,* Saxon House, Farnborough 1979.

32. B. Litke, 'Renaissance du magasin proximité', *Libre Service Actualité,* no. 600 (1976).

33. H.G. Lundberg, *Närköp: Local Shops,* Co-op document no. 5, K.F. International Department, Stockholm, 1978.

34. M. Hall, 'The Prospects for Small Shopkeepers', *Retail and Distribution Management,* vol. 1, no. 5 (1973).

35. F.E. Webster, *Social Aspects of Marketing,* Prentice-Hall, Englewood Cliffs, N.J., 1974.

36. K. Ekhaugen, 'Implications of the Movement towards Concentration', paper presented at the 22nd International Study Conference, at the Gottlieb Duttweiler Institut für wirtschaftliche und soziale Studien, Zurich.

37. L.F. Daws and A.J. Bruce, *Shopping in Watford,* Building Research Station, Garston, 1971.

38. D.A. Kirby, J.A. Olsen, P. Sjøholt and J. Stølen, *The Norwegian Aid Programme to Shops in Sparsely-Populated Areas,* Research Report no. 30, Norwegian Fund for Market and Distribution Research, Oslo, 1981.

39. D.A. Kirby, 'Promoting for Profit', *In Business,* no. 52; and 'Penetrating the Retail Market', *In Business,* no. 53 (1983).

40. Organisation for Economic Co-operation and Development, *The Distribution Sector: Evolution and Government Policies,* a report by the Industry Committee, Paris, 1973.

41. M.B. Leckstein, 'Retail Markets: The Re-use of Existing Buildings' in P.T.R.C., *Retail Planning and Development,* Proceedings of Seminar E, 1983.

42. A.R. Everton, *Price Discrimination: A Comparative Study in Legal Control,* MCB Monographs, 1976.

43. Monopolies and Mergers Commission, *Discounts to Retailers,* HMSO, 1981.

44. J.D. Phillips, 'Little Business in the American Economy', *Illinois Studies in Social Science,* vol. 1, no. 42 (1958).

45. J.A. Dawson, 'Planning for Local Shops', *The Planner,* vol. 69, no. 1 (1983).

46. F. Livesey and E.A. Nagy, 'Independents versus Affiliation: What

Factors Motivate Retailers?', *Retail and Distribution Management*, vol. 9, no. 3 (1981).

47. J.A. Dawson and D.A. Kirby, 'Problems and Policies Affecting the Small Shop', *International Journal of Physical Distribution*, vol. 7, no. 5 (1977).

48. A.E. Boer, 'Mortality Costs in Retail Trades', *Journal of Marketing*, vol. 2 (1937).

49. T. Krogeide and E. Røsrud, *Ny dag—nye muligheter: Rapporten om forsøksprogram for naerbutikker i Sogn og Fjordane*, Norges Kolonial-og Landhandel Forbund, Oslo, 1979.

50. D.A. Kirby, 'Training and Advisory Services for the Small Retail Business — The Case for Government Action' in J. Stanworth, A. Westrip, D. Watkins and J. Lewis (eds), *Perspectives on a Decade of Small Business Research*, Gower, Aldershot, 1982.

51. R.L. Davies, 'The Gateshead Shopping Experiment' in P.T.R.C. Retail Planning and Development, Proceedings of Seminar C, 1982.

52. Dawson, 'Planning for Local Shops'.

10 Worker Co-operatives: Factors Affecting their Success and Failure*

CHRIS CORNFORTH

The number of worker co-operatives in Western industrialised countries has grown rapidly in recent years. During a time of economic recession this growth has caused a growing interest as to the role that worker co-operatives might play within the economy. In the United Kingdom, for example, the number of worker co-operatives grew from approximately 30 in 1975 to approximately 500 in 1982, and that trend has continued since. In addition agencies have been established at national and local levels to promote the development of worker co-operatives. At the present time (1983) it is estimated that there are 40 local co-operative development agencies (CDAs) employing one or more development officers. This growth in development work has led to an increased concern with the questions of why co-operatives are established, how they perform and why they succeed or fail. This paper attempts to identify and describe the reasons why worker co-operatives succeed or fail as businesses based on a review of research in the UK. Given the shortage of systematic empirical research in this area the conclusions drawn should be regarded as working hypotheses to be further tested and elaborated. Indeed a major aim of the paper is to provide a framework and the stimulus for further research.

* From C. Cornforth, 'Some Factors Affecting the Success or Failure of Worker Co-operatives: A Review of Empirical Research in the United Kingdom', *Economic and Industrial Democracy*, Vol. 4, No. 2 (1983), pp. 163–90.

Exactly how the success or failure of worker co-operatives should be measured is a difficult and controversial question because of their mixture of commercial and social objectives and because of their unusual patterns of ownership and control (Thomas, 1982; Jones and Svejnar, 1982). In this paper the main criterion for success is taken to be survival. Where information is available the paper also examines the economic performance of worker co-operatives. No attempt has been made to analyse systematically the performance of worker co-operatives with regard to their democratic objectives, although some of the problems that co-operatives experience in this area have been summarised. In addition the paper does not attempt to examine the performance of co-operatives against the objectives which their members may have set themselves. The reader should bear in mind that the survival rate for new businesses is generally very poor, and that it is against this base line that overall survival rates for co-operatives should be judged.

Worker co-operatives have their origins in the late eighteenth and early nineteenth centuries, arising out of the struggles of working people to overcome the hardship and poverty they faced. They occurred along with numerous other self-help associations of working people aimed at improving their conditions. At times co-operatives sprang up in isolation as a response to local conditions, at other times they were promoted by leaders with a philosophy of co-operation as part of a co-operative movement (Thornley, 1981: p. 10).

During the latter part of the nineteenth century the idea of worker co-operation came under attack within the co-operative movement. Some argued that production should be carried out directly by the co-operative retail and wholesale societies, which were controlled by their consumer members. Others argued that production should be controlled by workers in those enterprises. A compromise between these competing theories of co-operation was suggested in the form of co-partnership co-operatives. These were productive organisations that had both workers and retail societies as members, both of whom were able to elect representatives to the board of the co-operative. Although many of the co-partnership co-operatives survived and prospered, the consumer movement began increasingly to set up its own productive organisation rather than support co-partnerships. The number of co-partnership co-operatives reached a peak of just over 100 in 1905 and then steadily declined.

This decline continued until the 1960s when new worker co-operatives began to be formed, but it was not until 1975 that there was major growth. The Industrial Common Ownership Movement

(ICOM), which is the major promotional body for worker co-operatives in the UK, claims that in 1975 there were only 30 co-operatives registered with its model rules, but that this number had increased to over 400 by May 1982 (ICOM, 1982). Wilson (1982: p. 55) has estimated that during 1976–81, 600 or more worker co-operatives may have existed, but that the total in existence at any one time was not more than 350. A directory by the national Co-operative Development Agency (CDA) recorded a total of approximately 300 worker co-operatives in 1980 (CDA, 1980). By 1982 this total had increased to approximately 480.

The vast majority of worker co-operatives are new businesses, and most are very small in terms of the number of workers employed. In Wilson's (1982: p. 66) survey of co-operatives the majority employed between one and ten workers. Typically, worker co-operatives are established in the service sector, particularly in retailing, catering and distributive trades or in craft related industries and light manu-facturing.

A typology of worker co-operatives

Research has shown that worker co-operatives do not form a homo-geneous group of organisations, but differ according to the objectives they pursue, organisational characteristics and their economic cir-cumstances (Jones, 1978; Paton, 1978b). Paton (1978b: p. 15) developed a typology based on the observation that the characteristics of new co-operatives were heavily influenced by the way in which they were formed and the objectives of their membership. It is an extension of this typology that is presented here.

(a) 'Endowed' co-operatives These are firms that have been 'given away' by their original owners to the employees. The motivation for this may vary from Christian socialist ideals to a pragmatic desire to keep the firm going in the absence of an heir. In most cases the shares of the co-operatives are held in trust for the work-force. These co-operatives are usually well established because they have arisen from a successful business, but may experience problems in developing genuine democratic control.

(b) 'Worker buyout' co-operatives The national Co-operative Development Agency (CDA) has had a number of enquiries from companies where the work-force is interested in buying out the original owners, and this represents another potential way in which a

co-operative might be formed. However, it was not possible to obtain hard evidence on the existence of any co-operatives of this type. In consequence they are mentioned for the sake of completeness, but not discussed further.

(c) 'Defensive' co-operatives These are co-operatives formed by employees in order to preserve jobs on the closure of a business. The co-operative is usually seen as a last resort to save jobs when other forms of action have failed. As the threatened closure is usually due to the failure of the business these co-operatives often inherit a difficult commercial situation. They also have the problem of developing a new structure in keeping with the provision for democratic control within a co-operative.

(d) 'Alternative' co-operatives These co-operatives have arisen out of the alternative movements of the 1960s and 1970s. Their members are usually middle-class, well educated and share a strong commitment to democratic ideals and producing for social needs rather than profit. At the present time they are the most numerous form of worker co-operative in the UK; common examples are wholefood shops, radical bookshops and printers. However, there are a growing number of more professionally orientated groups establishing for example, computer software businesses and language schools. Most of these co-operatives are less than ten years old, are small in size, and face many of the problems of new small businesses.

(e) 'Job creation' co-operatives In these times of high unemployment there are an increasing number of co-operatives being formed to create new jobs. In the past some were stimulated by the availability of money through government job creation schemes; more recently the establishment of co-operative development agencies has encouraged some unemployed people to start their own co-operatives. These co-operatives face the usual problems of any new businesses, for example, obtaining capital, acquiring expertise and developing markets. In addition they also have the problem of developing a system of democratic control of which the members are likely to have had very little experience.

Research on worker co-operatives formed during the nineteenth and early twentieth centuries

Jones examined the efficiency of these old producer co-operatives by examining the comparative performance of producer co-operatives with equivalent capitalist companies. He concluded:

> No comparative advantage was apparent. In general while labor productivity comparisons support the charge of alleged poor discipline in producer co-operatives, unit labour cost comparisons do not point firmly one way or the other and information on restrictive labor practices and strikes suggests better performance by producer co-operatives. Furthermore, there was no consistent relationship between these diverse indicators of labor efficiency and participation. (Jones, 1978: p. 156)

Jones' research has shown that some producer co-operatives can survive for long periods of time, and perform as well as similar private companies. He also showed that success was not necessarily achieved at the expense of degenerating into non-cooperative forms of business. Nevertheless, it is still true that many producer co-operatives did fail or degenerate.

As to the reasons for these failures, other researchers (for example Catherine Webb, 1928; Thornley, 1981) have in the main concurred with Beatrice Webb's (née Potter) early analysis (Potter, 1891). Four reasons for failure are given by Potter, Catherine Webb, and Thornley:

(a) Undercapitalisation   Many producer co-operatives had to rely on members' savings and the goodwill of the consumer co-operatives and trade unions for capital. In the event they were often under-capitalised and consequently vulnerable to the frequent fluctuations in market conditions (Thornley, 1981: p. 10). This was particularly true of co-operatives initiated by workers themselves, rather than by consumer co-operatives or through conversion from private ownership (Webb, 1928: p. 139).

(b) Lack of management and business skills   Many of the co-operatives were started by skilled craftsmen who were without experience of management, and consequently suffered from a lack of business and managerial skills (Thornley, 1981: p. 10).

(c) Lack of discipline   The practice of democratic control occasionally reduced discipline amongst the work-force. Catherine Webb (1928: p. 138) noted that: 'Discipline must be maintained in every organisation, and it has proved not easy to maintain discipline where every man has felt himself to be one of the owners of the place,

relieved (as he may have foolishly thought) from the obedience of a wage servant.'

(d) Poor relationships between management and workers Establishing a stable and satisfactory relationship between management and workers was sometimes difficult.

> The position of manager over men who, as shareholders, have the ultimate voice in the affairs of the society has not always been easy; and it is not always easy for working men to see the necessity for paying a manager liberally and securing a man of special ability for the work. (Webb, 1928: p. 138)

In addition Thornley suggests two more factors:

(e) A top-down approach to development. The ideals of worker co-operation were taken up by philanthropic members of the middle class anxious to alleviate the worst evils of industrialisation. These people formed the leadership of the movement and in their zeal attempted to establish worker co-operatives from above. These initiatives were often disastrous as the workers did not necessarily share the same commitments (Thornley, 1981: p. 11).

(f) Lack of political support. Thornley (1981: p. 26–8) concludes that a major weakness of the producer co-operative movement was its failure to gain the political backing of the labour movement. She argues that without this political support it did not gain the resources needed to grow and develop.

It is also important to ask why the later producer co-operatives fared better than those set up earlier in the century. This question has not been systematically researched, but a number of plausible explanations can be suggested:

1. Later co-operators learned from the experiences of earlier failures and were more cautious in their attempts to establish producer co-operatives.
2. Probably most importantly, many of the later producer co-operatives were co-partnerships and were established with the backing of the consumer movement. This eased the problems of under-capitalisation and establishing their market, as the consumer co-operatives bought shares in the co-partnership co-operatives and often provided a market for their goods.
3. Having external members on the board of co-partnership co-

operatives may have reduced or helped resolve any conflicts between management and workers that might have arisen.

Research on worker co-operatives formed since 1960

Wilson (1982) examines the problems faced by new co-operatives, and the impediments and constraints to their formation and growth, based on a survey of 72 worker co-operatives in the UK. As part of the survey he asked respondents to rank a set of ten problems in order of importance as they affected their co-operative. The aggregate rankings of problems for the sample is shown in Table 10.1

Table 10.1
Ranking of perceived problems facing co-operatives (1980)

Problems experienced on set-up	Current problems
1. Obtaining finance	1. Obtaining finance
2 Obtaining premises	2 Finding/keeping sales outlets
3 Finding/keeping appropriate skills	3 Finding/keeping appropriate skills
4 Finding/keeping sales outlets	4 Finding/keeping people willing to join the co-operative
5 Deciding on structure of co-operative	5 Decision-making
6 Obtaining equipment	6 Obtaining equipment
7 Obtaining supplies and materials	7 Obtaining premises
8 Finding product/service to provide	8 Deciding on structure of co-operative
9 Finding/keeping people willing to join the co-operative	9 Finding product/service to provide
	10 Obtaining supplies and materials

Source: Adapted from Wilson (1982: p. 72).

Based on these rankings and on the answers to additional questions Wilson concluded that co-operatives share the same main problems as other small businesses. He identified these problems as

the poor accessibility of finance, both for cash flow and for consolidation or expansion; the structure and incidence of taxation which hinders capital accumulation and restrains growth; the difficulties in acquiring adequate or suitable premises at the right price, and within the chosen set up location, or within reasonable reach of the potential labour price; and, more fundamental, the lack of the requisite skills, technical competence and abilities needed to establish the business, and administrate and negotiate both contracts and finance during formative years . . . the information advice gap, i.e. that new businesses simply are not aware of the extent of the infra-structure, advisory services and grant aid available (Wilson, 1982: p. 71).

Wilson also found that co-operatives face additional problems:

In combination with the above, co-operatives carry considerable added problems as they attempt, firstly, to introduce major innovations in organisational structure, working relationships and the internal decision-making process in an often sceptical, if not hostile, environment; or, alternatively, to maintain or create jobs in markets where conventional businesses have failed (Wilson, 1982: 71).

The results obtained by Wilson are broadly supported by Chaplin and Cowe (1977: p. 43) in a smaller but similar survey. However, obtaining finance was not seen as such an important current problem by these co-operatives. In addition there was a greater emphasis given to problems stemming from the co-operatives' structure and from inter-personal relationships.

Endowed co-operatives

There are at least six of these co-operatives in the UK, and there may be as many as ten. The largest and best known is Scott-Bader Commonwealth, a manufacturer of chemicals with about 350 employees. The second largest has about 200 employees: the rest are much smaller, all with less than 100 employees.

The main findings presented here are based on research in three of these co-operatives (Paton, 1978a, Thomas *et al.,* 1979, Paton and Lockett, 1982). All three were well established before they converted into co-operatives, all had experienced management and similar access to external sources of capital as other small businesses. Although the research has not examined economic performance in detail they all appear to perform well, and not to have suffered adverse effects from their conversion to co-operatives. To the author's knowledge there have been no failures of endowed co-operatives. This is probably because they have already survived the first years of business, which are the most risky, before becoming a co-operative.

Usually these co-operatives experience greater problems in developing effective systems of democratic control. Workers may find it difficult to adapt to their new role as members of the co-operative, particularly as the original owner often remains as manager. In practice workers often still find it difficult to exercise influence over decisions made in the co-operative (Paton, 1978a; Cornforth and Paton, 1981).

Defensive co-operatives

Current research suggests that between 30 and 40 of these co-operatives have been formed, and that the rate of formation has increased as unemployment rises. The best known are those set up with the assistance of the then Industry Minister, Tony Benn: Kirby Manufacturing and Engineering (KME), Triumph Meriden, and Scottish Daily News (Coates, 1976, Eccles, 1981), but there have been many similar less well-known defensive co-operatives.

These co-operatives are inevitably formed in situations of adversity. They are often faced with a very difficult commercial situation because the industry is declining, perhaps due to cheap foreign imports, or poor management, or because of a history of under-investment. Leadership for the co-operatives usually comes from the workers themselves or their local trade union leaders.

Lockett (1978) in his study of Fakenham Enterprises describes and analyses some of the typical problems that can beset a defensive co-operative. Fakenham Enterprises was set up after the workers occupied their factory when the parent company threatened its closure. It was a small production unit manufacturing footwear. The co-operative was established after loans and assistance from Scott Bader, a large common-ownership company. However, the declining and seasonal market for shoes made it difficult to establish a viable business. The co-operative tried to diversify but had little capital to invest in developing new products or to retrain staff. In addition the work-force had no experience of management and was dependent on outside assistance. The financial weaknesses of the co-operative and the members' lack of expertise meant that they were vulnerable to bids from outside to take them over. After recurrent crises many of the original co-operators left, and what remained of the co-operative was taken over by a private firm who had originally supplied the co-operative with work.

Although all of these co-operatives eventually failed as businesses it would be hard to call them failures given the circumstances of their formation. All were under-financed, and started in very difficult economic circumstances. Given this situation it is perhaps surprising that Fakenham, Meriden and KME survived so long.

Four recent examples from Scotland suggest more optimism for the possibility of establishing successful defensive co-operatives. In these cases the local CDA has helped groups of workers to save a potentially profitable part of a business on its closure. The CDA assisted by providing feasibility studies, interim managerial support and by assisting in arranging external loans (SCDC, 1982). These examples suggest that as long as the business is potentially profitable, the other problems faced by defensive co-operatives can be overcome with the right sort of external assistance.

Alternative co-operatives

At the present time, this group of co-operatives is by far the largest in terms of numbers of co-operatives, although there is some evidence to suggest that this situation is changing. There are probably between 300 and 400 alternative co-operatives in the UK.

Typically alternative co-operatives have a number of objectives which are different from those of conventional businesses (see, for example, Chedlow, 1978). Often these include:

1. producing for social need, rather than profit;
2. a belief in the importance of the product or service they are providing;
3. a firm commitment to democratic control and the avoidance of managerial hierarchies.

Given the lack of profit motivation it is inappropriate to judge the success of alternative co-operatives in purely economic terms. However, they do have to survive in a capitalist market and afford their members a living. Aston (1980) examined the returns of 69 alternative co-operatives at the Registrar of Friendly Societies. She analysed 91 annual returns covering the preceding three or four years. Treating each annual return as a separate observation, she used these data to examine the performance of the co-operatives. The data show a high standard deviation on all measures of performance. This suggests that the performance of alternative co-operatives varies quite widely whatever sector they are in.

Nevertheless, the figures do not give a favourable impression overall. Only some of what Aston has called 'the human capital intensive sector of co-operatives' (for example language schools) are paying what are normally accepted as decent wages. The profit and loss figures, combined with wage levels, suggest that only some of the human capital intensive co-operatives and possibly some of the printers and publishers would normally be viable businesses. The liquidity figures also suggest cash-flow problems for many co-operatives. Aston (1980: p. 21) concluded from this analysis that: 'Most of these "alternative" co-operatives appear to be surviving on a combination of zeal and help from social security.'

However, some caution is needed in interpreting these figures. It is likely that most of the co-operatives analysed were recently formed and would have had little time to become established as businesses. Given the frequent difficulty of obtaining external finance it is likely that some members of co-operatives were taking low wages in order to capitalise their businesses. Aston included loans by workers to their co-operatives under current liabilities in calculating liquidity, which makes these ratios look worse than they might otherwise be, as it is unlikely that the workers would withdraw their loans. The figures also do not take into account that some members might be only part-time in the co-operative; or that they might receive some payment in kind, for example food and accommodation.

Experience suggests a number of possible factors that might account for the financial performance of alternative co-operatives:

1. Many alternative co-operatives have chosen to operate in markets that are not very profitable, for example small shops selling wholefoods or radical books.
2. The people who establish alternative co-operatives often have not been trained in the business they are pursuing. In consequence the first years are used to train members on the job, which may lead to inefficiency.
3. Many co-operatives deliberately choose to use labour-intensive methods of working because of the importance attached to maintaining a social group or to preventing hierarchical relationships from developing.
4. The co-operators' belief in producing for need rather than profit is likely to mean profits and wages are kept deliberately low.

Aston's work did not examine the survival rate of alternative co-operatives, and there has not been detailed empirical work on this, but personal experience suggests that their rate of survival is good when compared with small businesses generally. This is probably due to the commitment of their members, and the importance they attach to the social goals of the co-operatives.

Job creation co-operatives

In recent years there has been an increasing emphasis on setting up new co-operatives with the objective of creating jobs. This has been an important factor in the funding of local co-operative development agencies. Job creation co-operatives have been set up in two distinctive ways:

1. By philanthropic individuals who have promoted the co-operative and then attracted people to work in them. These will be called 'paternalistic job creation' co-operatives.
2. By the potential work-force of the co-operatives. These will be called 'grass-roots job creation' co-operatives. These two forms of co-operative appear to have distinctive characteristics and will be regarded as sub-types.

As with alternative co-operatives both types of job creation co-operative face all the usual problems of setting up a new business: access to capital, acquiring expertise and developing markets. They also face the problem of developing an effective system of democratic control.

There have only been a small number of paternalistic co-operatives (probably less than 10) set up in the UK during the new wave of worker co-operatives. Case studies of three will be reviewed here (Tynan, 1980a, 1980b; and Rhoades, 1980). Two of these co-operatives failed. One was a small printing business where the promoter was heavily involved in financing and managing the co-operative. The second was established using government money as a training scheme for young unemployed people with the intention that it would eventually become a self-supporting co-operative. The third was a building co-operative which had ambitious aims for training young people. This has survived but in a modified form. It has adopted a much more conventional management structure, and lowered its targets for taking on a high proportion of apprentices for training.

A number of common factors emerged from these studies which offer an explanation for their failure or limited success:

1. In all cases the original promoters did not have a great deal of experience in the line of business pursued by the co-operatives. This probably led them to underestimate the difficulties of establishing a new business, and meant each co-operative suffered from a shortage of necessary management skills. In particular all three co-operatives paid insufficient attention to researching their market and analysing the feasibility of their plans. The training co-operative found it difficult to attract a competent manager at the wages it could pay.
2. At both the building and the training co-operative the problems of training an unskilled work-force reduced efficiency.

3.   In all cases there were problems in developing an effective democratic system of control. Many of the workers had little experience of co-operative democracy and were unsure of their role. This was additionally complicated by the fact that the initiative for the co-operatives came from the promoters rather than the work-force. In the case of the building and printing co-operatives, where the promoters were actively involved in management, this factor tended to reinforce traditional management–worker attitudes.

The contradiction of setting up a democratic organisation from above is probably the main barrier to setting up successful paternalistic co-operatives. Thornley (1981: p. 11) suggests that this has been the case historically.

During the late 1970s the availability of money through a government job creation programme led to some grass-roots job creation co-operatives. The Co-operatives Research Unit conducted research in one of these co-operatives, which eventually failed, and looked more briefly at one that was successful (Cornforth, 1981). Both employed between 20 and 30 people and manufactured garments. There were three main reasons why the first co-operative failed:

1.   The garment industry is a highly competitive and declining industry. The co-operative found it difficult to obtain sufficient business and was dependent on a few large customers.
2.   Some of the work-force were not properly trained. The original members of the co-operative had been trained in a related industry and had retrained themselves on the job. The pressure to meet orders meant that the co-operative found it difficult to invest in further training.
3.   The work-force of the co-operative lacked management expertise and failed to attract a manager with the necessary skills from outside. It is likely that potential managers thought that the job was very risky and that the wage available under the government funding was too low. In comparison, the co-operative that succeeded had a trained work-force and had persuaded an accountant from their previous firm, which had originally made them redundant, to be their manager.

Since 1980, although government funding has dried up, the availability of advice and assistance from local CDAs appears to have enabled a number of small grass-roots job creation co-operatives to be established successfully (see, for example, SCDC, 1982). As many CDAs expressly aim to promote co-operatives amongst the unemployed it is likely that their numbers will continue to grow.

192

Conclusions

The purpose of this paper has been to identify some of the factors affecting the success or failure of worker co-operatives. This was done both for co-operatives formed during the last century and beginning of this century, and for the recent wave of worker co-operatives established since the 1960s.

A number of factors have been blamed for the failure of many of the traditional producer co-operatives: under-capitalisation, lack of management and business skills amongst the members; the difficulties of introducing work-place democracy; the difficulties of imposing co-operative ideals from above and the problems of establishing a business in a declining industry or during economic recessions. It was suggested that some of the later co-partnership co-operatives were able to overcome these problems because their links with consumer co-operatives gave them better access to capital, a market for their products, and possibly helped reduce or resolve conflicts between workers and management.

The recent defensive and job creation co-operatives have often been set up with much the same motivations as the producer co-operatives of the last century. The analysis suggests that they frequently share the same problems. The defensive co-operatives examined were set up in difficult economic circumstances, they were under-capitalised and lacked, or failed to appreciate, the management skills needed to run the business. The 'paternalistic' job creation co-operatives demonstrated the problem of initiating democracy from above, and also showed a tendency to underestimate the commercial problems facing a new business and the skills needed to deal with them. Both the grass-roots job creation co-operatives studied were set up in a declining industry. The one that failed also suffered from a lack of management skills, and an under-trained work-force. In some defensive and job creation co-operatives the pursuit of social objectives, such as maintaining jobs or youth training, impeded their financial performance and possibly reduced their chances of survival. Nevertheless, despite these common problems experience over the last few years suggests that they can be overcome. A number of successful defensive and job creation co-operatives have been set up with the assistance of local CDAs. These agencies are often able to supply additional expertise and many facilitate the raising of external capital. A parallel might be drawn here with the external support that the successful co-partnership co-operatives received from the consumer co-operatives.

All the endowed co-operatives studied performed well financially and appeared not to suffer from a decline in efficiency after their conversion. This was probably due to the fact that they were all well-established businesses before they became co-operatives. They all experienced problems in achieving a system of democratic control which was satisfactory to both workers and management.

Alternative co-operatives were distinguished by their belief in producing for social need rather than profit and their commitment to direct democracy. In the absence of survey evidence it was suggested from personal experience that alternative co-operatives had a good survival rate compared with small businesses generally. This was attributed to the high commitment that members often have to the goals of their co-operative. In contrast survey data showed that the financial performance of many alternative co-operatives was poor. A number of factors were suggested to account for this: the commitment to producing for need rather than profit had led to their formation in less profitable sectors of the economy; the deliberate choice of more democratic but less efficient methods of working; an initial lack of commercial and productive skills. Given the wider social goals of alternative co-operatives and lack of profit motivation it is inadequate to judge their success solely in terms of either survival or financial performance.

Wilson's survey of perceived problems of worker co-operatives showed that they suffered from the typical problems of new businesses. The most important current problems were obtaining finance, obtaining and keeping sales outlets, and finding and keeping the appropriate skills to run the business. This general analysis reflected the common problems revealed in the analyses of case studies of defensive, job creation and alternative co-operatives.

References

Aston, B. (1980). *The New Workers' Co-operatives: A Survey,* University of Warwick: MA dissertation (unpublished).

Co-operatives Development Agency (1980 and 1982). *Co-ops: A Directory of Industrial and Service Co-operatives,* London: CDA, 20 Albert Embankment.

Coates, K. (ed.) (1976). *The New Worker Co-operatives,* Nottingham: Spokesman Books.

Chaplin, P. and R. Cowe (1977). 'A Survey of Contemporary British Worker Co-operatives', Manchester: Manchester Business School, Working Paper 36.

Chedlow, P. (1978). 'The Corporate Strategy of a Political Bean', Manchester: Business School, unpublished student report.

Cornforth, C. (1981). *The Garment Co-operative: An Experiment in Industrial Democracy and Business Creation,* Milton Keynes: Co-operatives Research Unit, Open University.

Cornforth, C. and R. Paton (1981). 'Participation and Power: The Case of the Jewellery Co-operative', paper presented to the First International Conference on Producer Co-operatives, Copenhagen, June.

Eccles, T. (1976). 'Kirby Manufacturing and Engineering' in K. Coates (ed.), *The New Worker Co-operatives,* Nottingham: Spokesman Books.

Eccles, T. (1981). *Under New Management,* London: Pan Books.

Industrial Common Ownership Movement (1982). ICOM Newsletter, The Corn Exchange, Leeds, May.

Jones, D. (1976). 'British Producer Co-operatives', in K. Coates (ed.), *The New Worker Co-operatives,* Nottingham: Spokesman Books.

Jones, D. (1978). 'Producer Co-operatives in Industrialised Western Economics', *Annals of Public and Co-operative Economy,* vol. 49, no. 2.

Jones, D. and J. Svejnar (1982). *Participatory and Self-Managed Firms,* Toronto: Lexington Books.

Lockett, M. (1978). *Fakenham Enterprises,* Milton Keynes: Co-operatives Research Unit, Open University.

Paton, R. (with M. Lockett) (1978a). *Fairblow Dynamics,* Milton Keynes: Co-operatives Research Unit, Open University.

Paton, R. (1978b). *Some Problems of Co-operative Organisation,* Milton Keynes: Co-operatives Research Unit, Open University.

Paton, R. and M. Lockett (1982). *The Jewellery Co-operative,* Milton Keynes: Co-operatives Research Unit, Open University.

Potter, B. (1891). *The Co-operative Movement in Great Britain,* London: George Allen and Unwin (republished 1930).

Rhoades, R. (1980). *Milkwood Co-operatives Ltd,* Milton Keynes: Co-operatives Research Unit, Open University.

Scottish Co-operatives Development Committee (SCDC) (1982). SCDC News, Glasgow: 100 Morrison Street, January.

Thomas, A. (1982). 'What is Meant by "Success" for Workers' Co-operatives?', Oxford: The Seventh Co-operative Seminar (available from the Plunkett Foundation, 31 St. Giles).

Thomas, A. *et al.* (1979). 'Final Report on Decision-making at NIC Ltd.', Milton Keynes: Co-operatives Research Unit, Open University (unpublished report).

Thornley, J. (1981). *Workers' Co-operatives: Jobs and Dreams,* London: Heinemann Educational Books.

Tynan, E. (1980a). *Sunderlandia,* Milton Keynes: Co-operatives Research Unit, Open University.

Tynan, E. (1980b). *Unit 58,* Milton Keynes: Co-operatives Research Unit, Open University.

Webb, C. (ed.) (1928). *Industrial Co-operation: The Story of a Peaceful Revolution,* Manchester: Co-operative Union (first published 1904).

Wilson, N. (1982). 'Economic Aspects of Worker Co-operatives in Britain: Recent Developments and Some Evidence', Proceedings of the Seventh Co-operative Seminar, The Plunkett Foundation for Co-operative Studies, 31 St. Giles, Oxford.

11 Ethnic Enterprise: The Popular Image

TREVOR JONES AND DAVID McEVOY

Despite the seemingly unheroic nature of his calling, the ethnic entrepreneur is in some danger of becoming a minor cult figure. The typical ethnic entrepreneur in present-day Britain is of course the Asian (Indian, Pakistani or Bangladeshi) shopkeeper, who far outnumbers other ethnic minority members in business and Asians in other forms of business. Until fairly recently, the Asian retailer was able to go unobtrusively about his affairs unremarked outside the inner city which is his principal sphere of operation. There have been, though, a few ominous signs that the outside world is beginning to consider him 'newsworthy' — with all the dangers of misrepresentation and stereotyping implied in that term. There has appeared a sporadic flow of newspaper features which, although sometimes acknowledging the grinding regime of bare survival endured by many Indian and Pakistani shopkeepers, nevertheless emerge under neon headings such as 'The Bazaar on the Corner' (Daily Telegraph Magazine) and 'From Street-corner Trader to Millionaire' (Smith, 1984), designed (almost literally) to add spice to plain unpalatable truth.

Whether stated or implied, the message is that black minorites can succeed economically within a fundamentally tolerant multi-racial society and that the British hosts themselves stand to gain from the presence of new dynamic entrepreneurs untainted by the national mood of decline (Forester, 1978). Recently this line of reasoning has been granted the royal seal of approval: 'There is little doubt in my mind that the Asian community in this country frequently sets an outstanding example of what hard work, close family ties, service to the customer and reliability can, in fact, achieve' (HRH, the Prince of Wales, reported in *The Times*, 20 November 1981).

This image of immigrants to Britain as active and indeed successful businessmen is far from being confined to entrepreneurs from the Indian subcontinent. In recent years, small entrepreneurs of Chinese, Cypriot, Italian and other overseas origins have established a conspicuous presence in many inner urban areas, particularly in trades such as catering, retailing and various service activities. Predating any of these by centuries, however, are the Jews, the classic ethnic trading group, so closely associated in the non-Jewish mind with trade and finance that business acumen is frequently seen as an integral part of the 'Jewish personality'. All this is part of a traditional tendency on the part of majority group members to label certain ethnic minorities in terms of their occupational specialisation, real or alleged. In the most recent phase of popular folklore, the established ethnic stock figures — Goldstein the jeweller, Cameron the doctor, Luigi the ice-cream vendor, Evans the rugby master — have been joined by a newcomer, Patel the grocer.

Do these cardboard cut-out figures have a basis in reality or should they merely be regarded as candidates for a new multi-cultural version of the 'Happy Families' card game? On the face of it, there is good reason for popular labelling. Historical precedent abounds in favour of the notion that *ethnicity* — that cultural distinctiveness which characterises groups of immigrant origin — is linked with occupational specialisations such as petty commerce and finance. In the literature of race relations, the term 'middleman minority' (Bonacich, 1973) has been coined to denote any *émigré* group which derives a large part of its livelihood from entrepreneurial activities, from selling goods and services to the host population of its country of adoption. Bonacich and Modell (1980: pp. 269–71) list no fewer than 65 instances of 'groups treated as middleman minorities by several authors of comparative studies'. Outstandingly, these include Jews in nine countries or continents, overseas Chinese in seven separate locations, Lebanese, Syrians, Greeks, Armenians and, most significantly for the present argument, Indo-Pakistanis in no less than eleven locations. In addition to the well-known East African connection, Indian trading communities are active in several regions of the old British Empire, from the Caribbean to Burma (see especially Tinker, 1976). It seems that, whatever their original backgrounds, members of certain nationalities become imbued with the spirit of capitalism as soon as they set foot outside their native lands.

Comparative studies of ethnic middlemen

In our search for the link between ethnicity and enterprise, we must turn first to the USA, where the commercial prowess of groups such as Chinese, Japanese, Jews and Greeks is long established and well recognised. Here, the most influential students of the question (Light, 1972, 1980; Bonacich, 1973; Bonacich and Modell, 1980) are unanimous in dismissing any crude assertion that certain nationalities are culturally (still less genetically) better endowed for enterprise than others, or more 'naturally' predisposed towards self-employment in small business. Primary emphasis is laid on the interaction between migrant group and receiving society; and on the circumstances common (though in varying degree) to all migrants irrespective of origin. In essence, their interpretation rests on two universal propositions about migrant-host relationships:

1. ethnic enterprise results from the *exclusiveness* of the migrant group *vis-à-vis* the receiving society;
2. ethnic enterprise is reinforced by the migrant group's *exclusion* from full participation in the receiving society.

Exclusiveness

Whether one is English, Albanian or Mongolian, the very act of transferring to a new society with alien customs and incomprehensible language is in itself likely to heighten awareness of one's own cultural or national identity. The classic response is to seek out the society of fellow *émigrés* and to forge close bonds with those of similar nationality, language and, in certain circumstances, religion. Such ethnic communities are invariably distinguished by close ties of loyalty among members and by the tenacious persistence of customs imported from the homeland.

The key point to grasp here is that this ethnic solidarity provides a vital business resource. For the minority businessman, his ethnic brotherhood represents a potential source of capital, with borrowing and lending based on the mutual trust of fellow group members (see especially Light, 1972, 1980); of customer loyalty, with buyers patronising firms run by their own group members in preference to others (Hannerz, 1974); and even of cheap labour, in the many cases where the migrant community is comprised largely of extended family networks (Aldrich, Jones and McEvoy, 1984). As in the cases of the American Jews (Light, 1972; Rosentraub and Taebel, 1980), the Californian Chinese (Light, 1972) and Japanese (Bonacich and Modell, 1980) and more latterly the Koreans (Light, 1980), this mobilisation of the group's assets in favour of its own entrepreneurs can give ethnic firms a competitive advantage over their non-ethnic rivals and often enable the former to oust the latter from certain branches of the economy. Ethnic minority business development may therefore be viewed as a particularly successful form of collective self-help (Cummings, 1980).

As well as identifying with their expatriate community, migrants also cling to the country of origin, maintaining contacts with family and friends left behind and cherishing the belief that one day they themselves will return permanently to the homeland. Even where the hope of return is mere illusion (Cater, 1984), this 'sojourner' mentality is clearly consistent with entrepreneurial behaviour and supportive of entrepreneurial goals. As Bonacich (1973) notes, it provides sufficient motivation for the self-employed proprietor to subject himself and his family to gruelling hard work and self-denial — present gratification traded off against future prosperity to be enjoyed in the homeland. One of the principal ways in which ethnic minority businesses enjoy a competitive edge over their non-ethnic rivals is in the matter of hours worked, where the ethnic trader tends to be far more willing to seek custom at evenings, weekends and holidays (Aldrich, Jones and McEvoy, 1984).

Exclusion

Just as migrants perceive the receiving society as alien, so they themselves are regarded as alien by that society. Throughout modern history, the common thread running through migrant–host relationships is one of exclusion of the former by the latter.

Whichever case we focus on — the Irish in nineteenth-century Britain (Miles, 1982), Orientals in California (Light, 1972), 'New Commonwealth' migrants in Britain (Sivanandan, 1976), or 'guest-workers' in the EEC (Castles and Kosack, 1973), we find a grudging tolerance of the migrants' economic role as cheap labour coupled with a marked reluctance to accept their presence as full human beings. This is evident despite the liberal use of euphemisms such as 'guest' and 'host' to which the literature of ethnic relations is prone.

Somewhat paradoxically at first sight, this climate of hostility is a major stimulus to ethnic enterprise. As Bonacich and Modell (1980: p. 12) explain:

Societal hostility promotes small business since it restricts the minority in what it can do. Minority members face discrimination as employees and so tend to strike out on their own and become self-employed. Their precarious social status acts as a motivation for them to succeed in business.

Furthermore, societal hostility frequently excludes minority members from social recognition and political power and the closure of these spheres of activity further ensures that business success is the only real avenue open to ethnic talent and energy.

In summary, ethnic enterprise is generated by the interaction of the minority's own exclusiveness and its exclusion by the majority group (Aldrich, Cater, Jones and McEvoy, 1981). While it is correct to emphasise various attributes internal to the ethnic group — solidarity, loyalty, trust and the collective willingness of group members to mobilise resources for its businessmen — it is also vital to recognise that ethnic enterprise is *reactive* in nature (Light, 1980), a response to the group's structural position in its adopted society. Put baldly, societal hostility is the stick and self-enrichment the carrot which propels the ethnic mule in the direction of business proprietorship.

Application to recent migrant groups in the UK

How does this logic apply to the most recently arrived ethnic/racial minorities in the UK? In applying theory to practice, we need to enquire not only about the genesis of ethnic minority business in the UK but also into its impact on:

a. Ethnic businessmen themselves — do they perform more success-fully than their English counterparts? What kinds of reward do they derive for their efforts?
b. The ethnic communities as a whole, notably the non-entrepre-neurs who considerably outnumber the entrepreneurs.
c. The surrounding British society, particularly the inner city areas which, it is often claimed, are enjoying a rejuvenation inspired by the newcomers.

For convenience, we define two principal sets of ethnic minorities — Asians and Afro-Caribbeans — examining the entrepreneurial achievements of each in turn.

The Asians

One of the first specialised and empirically based studies of Asian business in Britain was conducted in 1975 by Aldrich (1980), who interviewed Asian and white shopkeepers in Wandsworth. His results, which revealed Asian firms to be in many cases commercially marginal and to enjoy few decisive competitive advantages over non-Asians, ran counter to popular folklore and to much existing research and journalism. Hitherto, the question of business and self-employment had not been approached as a specialism but as one of several elements in the more general study of the Asian condition. In many ways, these early works (Hiro, 1971; Dahya, 1974) reproduced the 'common-sense' intuitive view of a community aloof, acquisitive and businesslike, the latest heirs to the Jewish mantle (Patterson, 1969). Culturally sealed off from the external world and internally welded into a quasi-masonic brotherhood, Asian society provided the aspiring capitalist with a ready source of loyal customers, willing workers and trusting investors. Asian capitalism, in short, possessed all the hallmarks of proposition 1 (above).

Of these early works, Lyon's paper on Gujarati social organisation is the most persuasive. Gujarati Hindus are now one of the major Asian minorities in Britain but, long before arriving in large numbers in this country, they had gained renown as a trading group, both in India itself and in East Africa, where they comprise the largest of the Asian minorities (Lyon, 1973). Prior to the anti-Asian purges in Kenya and Uganda, they owned many of East Africa's largest private firms. This success was based upon the exclusiveness of the group, its fraternal transactions whereby each Gujarati firm gives preference to other Gujaratis in the matter of buying, selling, lending and borrowing. According to Lyon (1973), this ethnic vertical integration is international, with fraternal contacts criss-crossing between India, the UK and several African countries.

Although Gujaratis appear as the archetypal Asian middleman, overseas Indians in general had acquired a justifiable reputation for high business achievement. Hence, by the early 1970s when the proliferation of Asian shopkeepers and traders began to impinge on the national consciousness, it was logical to assume that Britain was to become yet another geographical extension of the Asian capitalist empire. This assumption was further reinforced by the refugee influx from East Africa. As a counter to the ensuing political hysteria, official sources busied themselves with propagating an exaggerated picture of the newcomers as middle class in attainment and aspiration, whose industriousness, thrift and ambition could bring nothing but material gain to their new country (for a critique of this view see Kuepper *et al.*, 1975; Ward, 1973). In fairness, it should be acknowledged that this attempt to substitute a new Hindu Spirit of Capitalism for the old Protestant Ethic was largely benevolent in intent: it was designed to defuse racial tensions and in any case it contained a serious truth in that many of the newcomers did bring with them the tools of the aspiring entrepreneur — educational qualifications, practical experience in family firms (Ward, 1973) and, despite Amin, considerable financial assets (Aldrich, Jones and McEvoy, 1984). Intellectually, however, the effect of all this was to elevate the Asian-as-entrepreneur image from the realms of speculative folklore to a status close to academic respectability.

From the moment that the conventional wisdom became subject to serious academic scrutiny, it was exposed as at best an oversimplification and at worst a misrepresentation. Aldrich's pilot project in Wandsworth became the precursor of a far more comprehensive 1978 survey of 580 shopkeepers (approximately half Asian and half non-Asian), divided in roughly equal proportions between the three urban areas of Bradford, Ealing and Leicester (McEvoy *et al.*, 1979). This was supplemented by abbreviated follow-up interview surveys in 1980 and 1982, together with a full enumeration of Asian shops in Bradford in 1978. The findings may be summarised as follows. (See also Cater and Jones, 1978; Aldrich, Cater, Jones and McEvoy, 1981; Jones, 1981–2; Aldrich, Jones and McEvoy, 1984.)

Employment and self-employment The Bradford shop enumeration exercise revealed that, despite an impressively large absolute number of Asian outlets (over 500 or one-quarter of the city's total), this represented self-employment for at most 5 per cent of the city's economically active Asians. Asians in Bradford are therefore not a middleman group in the Bonacich sense. By no stretch of the imagination can they be said to have developed an occupational specialisation.

Nationally, too, it is difficult to see Asians as an exclusively commercial caste: their concentration in particular urban areas (Jones, 1983–4) ensures that wherever they are numerous, they outnumber the retail opportunities. Only Asians who have moved away from the ethnic cluster can find self-employment without having to out-manoeuvre numerous co-ethnics.

Family Background Our 1978 interview survey produced some evidence to support the common view that Asian retailers in Britain possess a background particularly suitable for business (Table 11.1). Almost half the Asian respondents had a self-employed father, compared with less than 30 per cent of whites; more Asians than whites owned another business; and more Asians than whites had relatives owning shops. Asian shopkeepers had had a slightly longer education than whites and far more of them had obtained a degree. (The degree figures reflect a similar pattern in the employed population as a whole (Employment Gazette, 1983).) The very low level of business inheritance among the Asian shopkeepers can be seen as a consequence of immigration, as can the lower proportion of Asians previously self-employed.

Table 11.1
Personal background of Asian and White shopkeepers

	Asians	Whites
Percentage whose father was self-employed	49	28
Percentage self-employed in previous job	14	16
Percentage currently owning another business	21	18
Average years of education	10.2	9.7
Percentage with degree	20	3
Percentage who inherited business	2	8
Percentage with relatives owning shops	44	40

Sources of Capital The figures on assistance received by shopkeepers from family and friends (Table 11.2) also give sustenance to the notion of the Asian community as a supportive mechanism for enterprises. Asians have more than twice the number of relatives in their employ than white retailers. The figures suggest that this additional family labour comes from the Asian extended family, rather than a sub-stantially greater commitment from wives and children. Significantly, Asians are also able to obtain more unpaid assistance, whether from family or friends, than their white competitors.

Table 11.2
Shopkeepers: assistance from family and friends

	Asians	Whites
Averge number of relatives employed	1.35	0.61
Percent married	92	81
Percentage of married owners with spouse working in business	55	54
Percentage of married owners with children working in business	22	25
Average number of unpaid employees	0.82	0.23
Percentage raising capital through family	27	14
Percentage raising capital through friends	30	6
Average percentage of capital obtained from family	7	6
Average percentage of capital obtained from friends	7	2

Family support for Asian business extends to the provision of capital almost twice as often as is the case with white businesses. Perhaps surprisingly, friends provide capital even more often than family for Asians; white businesses obtain such assistance with only a fifth of the frequency of Asians. The idea of the Asian network of kinship and acquaintance as an easily tapped source of venture capital is, however, an exaggeration. The amounts involved are clearly small, as they are for whites, and may often be symbols of support rather than forms of substantial assistance.

Competitive Behaviour   Popular stereotypes of Asian shops are certainly supported when simple forms of competitive behaviour are examined (Table 11.3). Asians open more hours a day and more days a week; on Sunday, Asians are over three times more likely to be open than whites. The Asian shopkeeper also works somewhat longer hours personally than his white counterpart, though the latter is hardly relaxing with a 57 hour working week.

Table 11.3
Competitive behaviour

	Asians	Whites
Days open per week	6.2	5.6
Hours open per day	10.1	8.9
Percentage open Sundays	52	17
Percentage in co-operative buying organisation	14	13
Percentage making deliveries	36	44
Hours worked per week	61	57
Percentage selling on credit	37	38

With less basic forms of competition the Asian advantage is less marked or non-existent. There is little difference between the two groups in terms of credit provision or in membership of buying organisations. Whites offer a delivery service more frequently. If the Asian community is truly a fountain of business talent, it is strange that its competitive zeal emerges only in a willingness to ensure the tedium of being 'open all hours'.

Performance   Doubts as to the superiority of Asian businessmen emerge very clearly in some of our measures of success (Table 11.4). More whites than Asians claimed to have made a profit in the year preceding our main interview; and more expected a profit in the following year. Half the whites, but only a quarter of the Asians, said that they had been able to accumulate savings from the business. It is true that more Asians than whites own the freehold of their business premises, this is at least partially accounted for by the fact that more Asians 'live in', in contrast to a white preponderance of owner occupation other than over the shop. Our measure of turnover suggests an Asian advantage, as does the difference in the numbers hoping that their children will ultimately take over the business.

Table 11.4
Measures of success

	Asians	Whites
Percentage making profit in previous year	72	82
Percentage expecting profit in subsequent year	70	78
Percentage with savings from business	25	50
Percentage owning premises freehold	65	45
Percentage living in business premises	47	32
Percentage living in own house elsewhere	48	55
Percentage grossing £750 a week or more	41	29
Percentage wanting children to take over business	44	26
Percentage surviving 1978–80	84	67
Percentage of replacement business Asian 1978–80	94	52
Percentage surviving 1980–2	70	76
Percentage of replacement business Asian 1980–2	91	39

Survival The first of our call-back surveys in 1980 appeared to confirm the view that, despite all the reservations entered above, the Asian businessman ultimately survives and prospers. Eighty-four per cent of our 1978 Asian businesses were still operating in 1980, compared with only 67 per cent of white concerns. However, between 1980 and 1982, the relative advantage was reversed; the Asian survival rate fell below that of whites, whose rates of persistence increased. The really important features of these figures, though, is not the relative advantage of one group or another, but the truly appalling rate of failure for all. Only four years after our initial survey, only 59 per cent of Asian respondents were still trading at the same site, and only 55 per cent of whites. The indications were that only about one-fifth of these disappearances represented relocation in different premises; the vast majority were business failures (McEvoy and Aldrich, 1984).

We believe that it is a mistake to see the proliferation of Asian enterprises as a sure sign of a particular talent to prosper. Rather is it a reaction to a position of structural disadvantage in the labour market. Mass immigration was a response to Britain's former labour shortage and Asians usually took the jobs whites did not want. So, too, Asian businesses often occupy residual niches in the economy abandoned by whites, accepting whatever limited opportunities are available rather than competitively ousting white rivals. This is dramatically illustrated by the last two rows of Table 11.4. A substantial proportion of previously white-owned shops changing hands between 1978 and 1982 were taken over by Asians, but very few formerly Asian shops were acquired by whites. It appears that once the white economy dispenses with a business opportunity, it is unlikely to want its return (Aldrich and McEvoy, 1984).

A further indication of the difficulties faced by Asian shopkeepers lies in the ethnic character of their customers. Our Asian sample said that 64 per cent of their customers were themselves Asian, while whites claimed 70 per cent white custom, despite location in the same areas. Many Asian retailers are thus disproportionately dependent on the minority population with its linked disadvantages of low income, high unemployment and high dependency ratios (Employment Gazette, 1983). We are not arguing that all Asian businesses must fail. We are denying, however, that individual stories of sometimes spectacular success are representative of universal prosperity among Asian shopkeepers. The burdensome hours, high levels of family assistance and other manifestations of commitment so frequently noted are as likely to be indicators of a vain struggle for survival as the basis of ultimate success. The belief that, 'Asians have found, with astonishing ease, yawning gaps in the British economy where it looks almost laughably easy to make money' (Smith, 1984), must be recognised as stereotypical fantasy rather than sober fact.

Afro-Caribbeans

'It would be a mistake to place too much reliance on a great increase in employment and capital growth in black businesses' (Brooks, 1983–4: p. 42). If Asian business is growth without development, then West Indian and African business each represent an acute case of arrested development. In its disproportionately low levels of business owner-ship and its confinement within a narrow range of specialisms, Britain's Afro-Caribbean population exhibits striking parallels with the black population of North America, whose inability or unwilling-ness to participate economically as owners and managers has been lamented by a succession of commentators from Booker T. Washing-ton (1907) onwards. Here we note the existence of minority groups whose occupational stereotype is an extremely negative one, the symmetrical inverse of the Jewish–Indian–Chinese model. The relative absence of enterprise among Afro-Americans and West Indians in

Britain tends to be rationalised in terms of the absence of those group traits — exclusiveness, solidarity, mutual trust — which have promoted and supported Indian and Chinese business. In turn, this lack of a strong ethnic identity may be put down to the cultural genocide which resulted from transportation and slavery.

Whatever the historical explanation, there can be no doubt that blacks in Britain have made a minimal impact as business operators. As the *Guardian* (3 August 1982) asks: 'How come there are so few Black businessmen?' Just as business underdevelopment has been seen as an obstacle to black American self-advancement (Cross, 1969), so too in Britain it is put forward as a possible cause of economic deprivation and social maladjustment. The same *Guardian* article invokes the Scarman Report to raise the possibility that street violence itself is a symptom of black non-participation in business: 'the encouragement of black people to secure a real stake in their own community through business and the professions is of great importance if further social stability is to be secured' (Scarman, 1981).

On reflection, it is conceivable that Scarman has confused cause and effect. In the absence of convincing evidence to the contrary, we are entitled to speculate that black alienation from capitalism *causes* their non-participation rather than results from it (Tabb, 1970).

Whatever the merits or flaws of the above argument, it is not a prominent issue on the agenda of Britain's top-level decision-makers. The official wisdom is well expressed by the Home Affairs Committee on Racial Disadvantage (1981), which considers it to be 'in the interests of the whole community that obstacles to the full participation by members of any minority group in the creation and running of small businesses should be removed' (para. 216, cited in Brooks, 1983–4).

By and large it is fair to say that most of the recent spate of fact-finding studies of black enterprise are inclined to treat this reasoning with extreme caution and scepticism (Phillips, 1978; Kazuka, 1980; Ward and Reeves, 1980; Wilson, 1983; Brooks, 1983–4; Sawyerr, 1983–4). This is hardly surprising in view of the empirical evidence assembled by these writers, which shows West Indian and African business to be suffering from many of the same structural disabilities as Asians and possibly in an even more acute form. Apart from the fact that these groups have achieved a much lower level of self-employment than Asians (Ward and Reeves, 1980), the comparatively few entrepreneurs who do exist seem even more negatively motivated (Brooks, 1983–4) and even more trapped within localised minority markets. Against this, West Indians are found to be rather less dependent upon retailing and more diversified into artisanal activities such as motor repair (Ward and Reeves, 1980; Brooks, 1983–4). Furthermore, Afro-Caribbeans as compared to Asians seem more optimistic about future prospects (Brooks, 1983–4).

On the question of the role of official policy for black business development, the key point is made by Ward and Reeves (1980; para 5.2):

> The measures we put forward . . . are not designed to encourage more West Indians to consider going into business. They are intended to improve the prospects of those already in business . . . It would in our view be irresponsible to encourage others to go into business without considering whether their interests (or those of their ethnic community) are best served by setting up on their own or by gaining access to other types of employment.

Ward and Reeves recognise that many sectors of the economy are already swamped by a mass of struggling small firms, many of which are destined to die in infancy; and that policy should be directed at improving the quality rather than the quantity of minority enterprise. This reasoning has been followed by Brooks in his review of local authority action in Lambeth; and by Sawyerr in his advocacy of a 'total resources' approach by central government. Together with Ward and Reeves, these authors are implicitly concerned to strengthen the existing black economy by injecting into it capital, information and above all management skills in far larger doses than are currently available (see Table 11.5).

Structural constraints on minority business

> Once no individual could direct the market, but now the small man feels, often correctly, that it is fixed against him (Mills, 1956: p. 30).

As we have seen, conventional wisdom as pronounced by Scarman and the Home Office is rooted in the assumption that minority business is good and more minority business is better. Ward and Reeves's critique of this assumption is no mere isolated insight but is fully supported — indeed superseded — by historical experience in several areas outside Britain. In the USA, for example, federal government policy for black business development has been attacked both from inside and outside the black community. Among other grounds for complaint, it is argued that (a) minority business growth is of benefit only to the few who can

Table 11.5

Summary of black business proposals submitted by several authors

	Central government	Local government	Private companies	Educational institutions
	Grants, loans and guarantees to black business.	Loans for start-ups. Information on available small business aid.	Conscious investment in black firms.	Business education geared to small and black consultancy services
Capital	Information/publicity on available small business aid.		Banks more sensitive to black needs and potential.	
	Establish and subsidise management and advisory service.	Establish/administer black business advisory service	Lend management and technical assistance to black firms	
Management training and guidance	Locate small firms centres and local enterprise centres in			

Premises	premises in black areas.		Actively seek black suppliers	Research into black business
	Racially sensitive planning policies			
Other	Gather more information on black business.			
	Identify black enterprises as special needs category.			
	Encourage/support black co-ops and training workshops.			

211

participate as owners; (b) it is a means of obtaining cheap products at the expense of black labour, thereby intensifying an already unacceptable process of racial exploitation; (c) it is ultimately dependent upon the large white-owned corporate sector, the source of capital, materials and markets; (d) it merely confirms the imprisonment of blacks in the lowest and most marginal recesses of the economy (Bonney, 1975; Tabb, 1970). These allegations raise enormous questions about the role of the entire small business economy and the place of ethnic groups within it.

Under the influence of the pervasive ethnic stereotypes current in Western culture, it is all too easy to indulge in clichéd fantasies about rags-to-riches immigrants, Stepney to Hendon in three generations. Yet sober reflection on the historical experience of ethnic middleman groups suggests that small business has played — and can play — only a relatively minor part in economic development, barring exceptional circumstances. As Table 11.6 shows, high levels of specialisation in small business ownership tend to be attained by (a) very small minorities in (b) youthful fast-growth economies, neither of which conditions pertains for Asians and West Indians in the large conurbations of present-day Britain. There have also been major opportunities for minority traders in colonial societies, as in the case of East African Indians, whose success rested on their performing tasks which whites would not and Africans could not (or were not allowed to) do (Tinker, 1976; Mangat, 1976).

It would be naive in the extreme to expect Asians to reproduce this role in Britain, where no such ethnic monopoly exists (Aldrich, Jones and McEvoy, 1984).

Even where, as in the above instances, ethnic minorities have emerged as fully-fledged business specialists it is debatable whether in itself this has been responsible for their socioeconomic advancement. While there is no doubt that American Jews and Orientals, for example, have shown both a high propensity for self-employment and a high degree of economic advancement (see Cummings, 1980 and Lieberson, 1980 for an assessment of their current socioeconomic status profiles) there is room for argument about the precise connection between these two traits. In addition to enterprise, many Jews and Orientals have advanced by using the American education system as a gateway to professional and white collar employment: as Bonney (1975: p. 80) remarks, 'even among the Jews where it [enterprise] is of the greatest importance, other channels of employment have greater importance in absolute terms'.

At the most, enterprise seems essentially to have been a transitional stage in group evolution, a short ladder giving access to longer ladders.

Table 11.6
Three *émigré* trading groups compared

	Japanese in pre-war California	Asians in colonial East Africa	Asians in present-day Britain
Demographic position	*Very small minority*, less than 3 per cent of state population	*Very small minority*, never greater than 0.3 per cent of the population of any of the three countries	*Comparatively large minority* in the larger cities, e.g. 30 per cent of Bradford, (inner city)
Entrepreneurial Specialisation	*Intense* — 36% self-employed and 44% in urban small business in Los Angeles (1941) Sales predominantly to the general (non-ethnic) market	*Intense* — e.g. owning over 80% of enterprises in Uganda (1966)	*Slight* — self-employment rate approximately on a par with general population. Sales predominantly to ethnic market
Socioeconomic status	*High and Improving* — majority of pre-war immigrants classed as proprietors, managers and professionals. Even higher professional proportion among the second generation	*Very high relative to indigenous population* — almost complete absence of unskilled manual occupations	*Low* — semi-skilled and unskilled employment the leading occupations
Opportunity Structure			
Primary determinants	Rapid economic growth shortage of established entrepeneurs	Commercialisation of subsistence economy. Virtual absence of indigenous competitors	Slow or non-existent economic and populative growth. Surfeit of established small businesses. Dominance of corporate level
Functional role	Cater to needs of expanding consumer market	Link indigenous economy with world economy	Cater to residual markets

Bonney (1975: p. 79) refers to 'the importance of this small business sector . . . in establishing the financial and cultural supporting environment for the mobility of subsequent generations through other channels'. In other words, petty capitalism breeds among its members an ethos of ambition, deferred gratification and high aspiration; and provides just sufficient finance to buy the requisite education qualifications. Comparative studies ranging from the Japanese of California (Bonacich and Modell, 1980), through the Asians of the three-cities survey (Aldrich, Jones and McEvoy, 1984) to the small shopkeepers of Edinburgh (Bechhofer et al., 1974) yield a wealth of evidence for the generalisation that independent family businesses provide their offspring with a springboard to higher things. Evidently there is an important subsection of the small business fraternity (both ethnic and non-ethnic) whose ambitions for their children go far beyond the inheritance of the family firm.

In moving from the world of petty trading (grocer's daughter turned industrial chemist!) to the professions, the offspring of the petty bourgeoisie undertake a profound shift from one level of the capitalist economy to another qualitatively distinct plane. Mobility and self-enrichment are contingent upon escape from the structurally disadvantaged backwaters of the economy and upon entry into the mainstream. In arguing thus, we follow Galbraith's (1971) analysis of the mature capitalist economy as essentially dualistic in structure, comprised of two components identified as *an 'upper' corporate level,* variously referred to as the 'industrial state' (Galbraith, 1971), the 'centre economy' (Averitt, 1968), 'monopoly capital' (Baran and Sweezey, 1968) or the 'primary labour market' (Wilson and Portes, 1980); and *a 'lower' small-firm level* referred to as 'petty capital', 'peripheral economy', 'secondary labour market', and so on. It is this lower level upon which ethnic minority firms characteristically reside.

Despite over a century of increasing scale and centralisation progressing to the point where 'monopolistic tendencies . . . are no longer a statistical anomaly but constitute perhaps *the* defining feature of advanced capitalism' (Wilson and Portes, 1980: p. 297), the small business sector lives on (Aldrich, Jones and McEvoy, 1984; Boissevain, 1984). This is because, to paraphrase the infamous lager advertisement, it reaches the parts which the corporate level cannot reach — i.e. markets which fail to provide a rational return for large-scale, profit-seeking capital. In the retail industry, for example, the large centralised organisation is unable to attend to day-to-day shopping needs, especially those of the poor and immobile in areas such as the inner city. It is these areas which provide a niche —

precarious and dwindling but still large in absolute terms — for the survival of small family shops.

There is then a rationale for the survival of the lower level but it is a negative rationale of dependency and disadvantage. As Wilson and Portes (1980: p. 297) observe, the small firm operates largely on terms laid down by the corporate level of industrial and finance capital, which effectively determines its costs of materials, capital and renting premises; and the size and quality of markets open to it. It seems that 'independence', that cherished pillar of the small shopkeeper's creed, is something of an illusion for practical purposes (see, for example, Bechhofer *et al.*, 1974). Moreover, as a direct consequence of its subordinate economic role, petty capitalism is a conspicuously underrewarded activity, a fact made painfully obvious by studies such as that of Bechhofer *et al.* (1974) whose British shopkeeper sample was subject to an annual failure rate of 20 per cent, an average 10½ hour working day yielding hourly incomes below those of manual workers and working conditions described by the authors as 'oppressive'. Leaving aside the question of 'psychic rewards' accruing from 'independence' (Jones, 1981–2; Brooks, 1983–4), it seems that the corporate economy offers better material prospects to most of its wage workers than the small firm economy offers to many of its capitalists.

Conclusion

A full blown policy prescription is beyond the brief of this essay. Nevertheless we can hardly conclude without drawing attention to some of the more obvious policy implications raised by the foregoing discussion. On the positive side, the study of ethnic business reminds us that grass-roots neighbourhood communities are considerable repositories of creative energy and talent. Regrettably — and this is the very crux — these assets tend to be stifled or squandered, a wastage which will continue as long as policy-makers remain wedded to one of the two standard approaches of private enterprise or welfare bureaucracy. There is a clear need to experiment with alternative strategies which break away from such fixed conventions. One possible model might be the Neighbourhood Development Corporations now operating in several American inner city areas with high proportions of ethnic and racial minorities. Here the emphasis is placed on the local community as a *collective manager* and the object of the exercise is the use of local unemployed labour in producers' co-operatives and in housing and environmental improvement projects (Cummings, 1980). Whatever mechanisms may be adopted to stimulate ethnic enterprise, the objective should be maximum community participation rather than the creation of more and more sub-viable businesses.

References

Aldrich, H.E. (1980). 'Asian Shopkeepers as a Middleman Minority: A Study of Small Businesses in Wandsworth' in A. Evans and D. Eversley (eds), *The Inner City: Employment and Industry,* London, Heinemann.

Aldrich, H.E., Cater, J.C., Jones, T.P. and McEvoy, D. (1981). 'Business Development and Self-Segregation: Asian Enterprise in Three British Cities' in C. Peach, V. Robinson and S. Smith (eds), *Ethnic Segregation in Cities,* London, Croom Helm.

Aldrich, H.E., Cater, J.C., Jones, T.P. and McEvoy, D. (1983). 'From Periphery to Peripheral: The South Asian Petite Bourgeoisie in England' in I.H. Simpson and R. Simpson (eds), *Research in the Sociology of Work,* vol. 2, Greenwich, Connecticut, JAI Press.

Aldrich, H.E., Jones, T.P. and McEvoy, D. (1984). 'Ethnic Advantage and Minority Business Development' in R. Ward and R. Jenkins (eds), *Ethnic Communities in Business,* Cambridge, Cambridge University Press.

Aldrich, H.E. and McEvoy, D. (1984). 'Residential Succession and Inter-Ethnic Competition for Business Sites', paper presented to American Sociological Association, San Antonio, Texas.

Averitt, R.T. (1968). *The Dual Economy: The Dynamics of American Industry Structure,* New York, Norton.

Baran, P. and Sweezey, P. (1968). *Monopoly Capital: An Essay on the American Economic and Social Order,* London, Pelican.

Bechhofer, E., Elliott, B., Rushforth, M. and Bland, R. (1974). 'The Petit Bourgeois in the Class Structure' in F. Parkin, *The Social Analysis of Class Structure,* London, Tavistock.

Boissevain, J. (1984). 'Small Entrepreneurs in Contemporary Europe' in R. Ward and R. Jenkins (eds), *Ethnic Communities in Business,* Cambridge, Cambridge University Press.

Bonacich, E. (1973). 'A Theory of Middleman Minorities', *American Sociological Review,* vol. 38, p. 583–94.

Bonacich, E. and Modell, J. (1980). *The Economic Basis of Ethnic Solidarity: Small Businesses in the Japanese American Community,* Berkeley, University of California Press.

Bonney, N. (1975). 'Black Capitalism and the Development of the Ghetto in the USA', *New Community,* vol. 4, pp. 1–10.

Brooks, A. (1983–4). 'Black Business in Lambeth: Obstacles to Expansion', *New Community,* vol. 11, pp. 42–54.

Castles, S. and Kosack, G. (1973). *Immigrant Workers and the Class Structure in Western Europe,* London, Oxford University Press.

Cater, J.C. (1984). 'Acquiring Premises: A Case Study of Asians in Bradford', in R. Ward and R. Jenkins (eds), *Ethnic Communities in Business: Strategies for Economic Survival,* Cambridge, Cambridge University Press.

Cater, J.C. and Jones, T.P. (1978). 'Asians in Bradford', *New Society,* 13 April, 81–82.

Cater, J.C. and Jones, T.P. (forthcoming). *Social Geography: Contemporary Issues,* London, Arnold.

Crace, J. (1978). 'The Bazaar on the Corner', *Sunday Telegraph Magazine,* 26 November, pp. 82–99.

Cross, M. (1982). 'The Manufacture of Marginality' in E. Cashmore and B. Troynes, *Black Youth in Crisis,* London, George Allen & Unwin.

Cross, T. (1969). *Black Capitalism,* New York, Athenaeum.

Cummings, S. (1980). 'Collectivism: the Unique Legacy of Immigrant Economic Development', in S. Cummings (ed.), *Self-Help in Urban America,* Port Washington, Kennikat Press.

Dahya, B. (1974). 'The Nature of Pakistani Ethnicity in Industrial Cities in England' in A. Cohen (ed.), *Urban Ethnicity,* London, Tavistock.

Employment Gazette, (1983). 'Ethnic Origins and Economic Status', *Employment Gazette,* vol. 91, pp. 424–30.

Forester, T. (1978). 'Asians in Business', *New Society,* 23 February, pp. 420–421.

Galbraith, J.K. (1971). *The New Industrial State,* New York, Mentor.

Hannerz, U. (1974). 'Ethnicity and Opportunity in Urban America' in A. Cohen (ed.), *Urban Ethnicity,* London, Tavistock.

Hiro, D. (1971). *Black British, White British,* London, Eyre and Spottiswoode.

Home Affairs Committee of the House of Commons (1981). Fifth Report, *Racial Disadvantage,* vol. 1, London, HMSO.

Jones, T.P. (1981–82). 'Small Business Development and the Asian Community in Britain', *New Community,* vol. 9, pp. 467–77.

Jones, T.P. (1983–4). 'Residential Segregation and Ethnic Autonomy', *New Community,* vol. 11, pp. 10–22.

Kazuka, M. (1980). 'Why so few Black Businessmen?', Report on the Hackney Ethnic Minority Business Project, London Borough of Hackney.

Kuepper, W.G., Lackey, G.L. and Swinerton, E.N. (1975). *Uganda Asians in Britain,* London, Croom Helm.

Lieberson, S. (1980). *A Piece of the Pie: Black and White Immigrants since 1880,* Berkeley, University of California Press.

Light, I. (1972). *Ethnic Enterprise in America: Business and Welfare among Chinese, Japanese and Blacks,* Berkeley, University of California Press.

Light, I. (1980). 'Asian Enterprise in America' in S. Cummings (ed.), *Self-Help in Urban America,* Port Washington, Kennikat Press.

Lyon, M.H. (1973). 'Ethnicity in Britain: the Gujarati Tradition', *New Community,* vol. 2, pp. 1–11.

Mangat, J.S. (1976). 'The Immigrant Communities (2): the Asians' in D.A. Low and A. Smith (eds), *History of East Africa,* vol. 3, Oxford, Clarendon.

McEvoy, D. and Aldrich, H.E. (1984). 'Survival Rates of Inner City Retailers', paper presented to the Institute of British Geographers, University of Durham.

McEvoy, D., Aldrich, H.E., Cater, J.C. and Jones, T.P. (1979). *Retail and Service Business and the Immigrant Community,* Final Report, to Social Science Research Council, HR 5520.

Miles, R. (1982). *Racism and Migrant Labour,* London, Routledge and Kegan Paul.

Mills, C.W. (1956). *White Collar: The American Middle Classes,* New York, Oxford University Press.

Patterson, S. (1969). *Immigration and Race Relations in Britain, 1960–67,* London, Oxford University Press.

Phillips, M. (1978). 'West Indian Businessmen', *New Society,* 815, 354–6.

Rosentraub, M.S. and Taebel, D. (1980). 'Jewish Enterprise in Transition' in S. Cummings (ed.), *Self-Help in Urban America,* Port Washington, Kennikat Press.

Sawyerr, A. (1983–4). 'Black-Controlled Business in Britain', *New Community,* vol. 11, pp. 55–62.

Scarman, Lord Justice (1981). *The Brixton Disorders, 10–12 April 1981,* Cmnd 8427, London, HMSO.

Sivanandan, A. (1976). *Race, Class and the State: The Black Experience in Britain,* Race and Class Pamphlet no. 1, London.

Smith, G. (1984). 'The Patels of Britain: From Street-Corner Trader to Millionaire', *Sunday Times,* 20 February, pp. 33–34.

Tabb, W.K. (1970). *The Political Economy of the Black Ghetto,* New York, Norton.

Tabb, W.K. (1979). 'What Happened to Black Economic Development?', *Review of Black Political Economy,* vol. 9, pp. 392–415.

Tinker, H. (1976). *Separate and Unequal: India and Indians in the British Commonwealth 1920–1950*, London, Hurst.

Ward, R. (1973). 'What Future for the Uganda Asians?', *New Community*, vol. 2, pp. 372–8.

Ward, R. and Reeves, F. (1980). *West Indians in Business in Britain*, memorandum submitted to the Home Affairs Committee Race Relations and Immigration Sub-Committee, Session 1980–1, London, House of Commons, 15 December.

Washington, B.T. (1907). *The Negro in Business*, Boston, Hertal Jenkins (reprinted 1970, New York, Johnson Reprint Corporation).

Wilson, K.I. and Portes, A. (1980). 'Immigrant Enclaves: An Analysis of the Labor Market Experiences of Cubans in Miami', *American Journal of Sociology*, vol. 86, pp. 295–319.

Wilson, P.E.B. (1983). *Black Business Enterprise in Britain*, London, Runnymede Trust.

12 The Female Entrepreneur: Her Background and Determinants of Business Choice — Some British Data*

JEAN M. WATKINS AND DAVID S. WATKINS

Prior work on female entrepreneurship

The recognition by academic students of entrepreneurship that around half the human race is composed of women, but that few businesses are female-led, was a long time in coming. The first serious call for research on this topic was contained in the 1973 edition of the Centre for Venture Management (CVM) *Bibliography on the Entrepreneur and New Enterprise Formation* in which Schreier and Komives argued that: 'particular attention should be brought to the female entrepreneur, the emerging role of women in business, the need for research on the subject of women entrepreneurs and, most importantly, the need for more women to become entrepreneurs'.[1] Shortly thereafter research in which the female-led business was the unit of analysis began to appear in the American literature.[2]

More recently this work has become explicitly comparative, with the reference frames taking several forms, such as female minority versus non-minority businesses[3] and female entrepreneurs versus female executives,[4] as well as the expected comparison between the characteristics and problems of females versus males in an entrepreneurial role.[5]

---

* From the *International Small Business Journal*, vol. 2, no. 4, (Summer 1984).

Outside the USA such literature hardly exists. Whereas classic elements of the American entrepreneurship/small business literature have usually given a breakdown of the sample by gender (even if the female representation is extremely low), British equivalents such as the Bolton Report[6] or Boswell[7] have not done so. It is not simply that gender has been consciously discounted as an explanatory variable, it has not been discussed at all. As a result, when reviewing a decade of development in the entrepreneurship/small business research field in the UK, it was necessary to commission a special paper highlighting the lack of interest in female entrepreneurship in Britain.[8]

Some preliminary findings

The present paper discusses some initial results from a UK study of female entrepreneurship. It is concerned primarily with the influences leading women to adopt an entrepreneurial career — family history, educational background, previous employment history and the extent of previous entrepreneurial endeavour. Here the key question is the extent to which such preparation has been well suited to the economic and social role adopted by this group of women.

The core data relate to a group of 58 women running between them 49 businesses. In terms of legal form these comprise sole proprietorships, partnerships, limited liability companies and one seven-member co-operative. This data set was collected through a series of personal depth interviews with each woman utilising a semi-structured interview schedule. The sample was not a random one in a formal sense since the universe of British female-led businesses could not be defined. Nor was there available any readily-definable group of women's businesses of known bias from which a sample could be randomly drawn. Instead, a short-period, network-activation approach was adopted on a national geographic basis.

From the resulting list, very small-scale retail businesses were deliberately excluded and the rest of the firms then contacted on a sequential basis. Included in the procedure was a cull of some 20 firms selected at random by postcode from the files of an important small-firm representative body. Any bias in this element of the sample would be to smaller-scale economic activity. This was a deliberate attempt to mitigate any unconscious bias towards 'high-potential' ventures implicit in activating other elements in the professional network. The authors recognised the limitations of this (and alternative) sampling procedures, but were confident that the choice of businesses — which ranged in age from more than 12 years to less than one year and in size from turnover in excess of £10 million to less than £4000 — would give a sufficiently wide range of experience to indicate both interesting policy questions and hypotheses for more detailed research at a later date. In this context one should note that a *wholly* representative sample would be of little interest as it would be biased unmercifully to the 'corner shop' level of operation. Statistical series giving a breakdown of business *activity* in the UK on a male/female basis are flimsy in the extreme. A surrogate is the comparison between male and female self-employed as shown in Table 12.1. This demonstrates clearly the extreme bias of female self-employment to services of all kinds and (retail) distribution in particular.

Table 12.1
Distribution by industry of UK male and female self-employment
(1975)

	Men (%)	Women (%)
Manufacturing	6.9	5.2
Agriculture, forestry and fishing	13.9	8.4
Miscellaneous services	14.5	33.6
Professional and scientific services	11.5	10.0
Insurance, banking and financial services	2.6	3.8
Distributive trades	19.6	38.0
Transport and communications	5.2	0.5
Construction	25.8	0.5

Source: Adapted from *Department of Employment Gazette,* June 1975.

The secondary data set, which forms the basis of certain comparisons in the present paper, relates to a similar number ($N = 43$) of male-led businesses. The basic male/female comparison was the obvious one, but beyond that it is by no means clear on what basis a comparative male sample should be structured. In our own study it would have been quite feasible, using the good offices of the representative body mentioned above, to construct a male-led sample in which each female business was matched for nature, size and age of business and the entrepreneurs matched for, say, age. However, this rigorous approach would have forced us to beg a number of the more interesting questions which are unanswered in the UK context. For example, it would have precluded any discussion of male-led versus female-led business stereotypicality; nor would it have enabled us to address the question of whether the normal age of entry into entrepreneurship is different for men and women.

It was finally decided to select a quasi-random male sample on a similar basis to the female-led business sample; thus 43 male entrepreneurs on whom we had some relevant file data from previous studies (and who had been introduced to us over a period via the same professional network) formed the basis of the comparative sample.

Family influences on the female entrepreneur

The general entrepreneurial literature suggests that a high percentage of (male) entrepreneurs had fathers who were also entrepreneurs or otherwise self-employed.[9] It has come to be accepted that this paternal link provides the most credible role model for filial entrepreneurial endeavour in later life. To what extent, then, does an entrepreneurial father perform a similar role for the future female entrepreneur? And what maternal roles might also influence the entrepreneurial decision positively?

A minimum of 37 per cent of the female entrepreneurs had fathers who had run a business of their own or were otherwise self-employed. (A further 10 per cent had fathers whose occupations were directly related to business activity but were *probably* not self-employed). This is an extremely high figure when compared to the general incidence of self-employment in the male labour force (relatively stable at around 9 per cent).

Of the mothers of the women in our sample, 16 per cent also had direct own-business experience either on a completely independent basis or as a partner in a wider family-run firm. This compares with an average rate of female self-employment of around 4 per cent.[10]

Thus a female entrepreneur is some four times more likely to have been subject to the influence of an entrepreneurial parent (father *and/or* mother) than a member of the general population. These figures certainly support the view that an entrepreneurial father is as critical an element in the socialising influences on the female entrepreneur as on her male counterpart. The small numbers involved do not permit us to form a view on the *relative* importance of a male versus a female entrepreneurial role model. However, the figures do demonstrate that a maternal role model can have at least as great an influence as a paternal one; furthermore, since the number of women in self-employment seems to be increasing in the UK (in absolute terms if not in direct proportion to the growth in supply of female labour to the overall labour market), the availability of such models in the future, and hence their *relative* importance, is likely to increase.

Another particularly relevant aspect of family background and circumstances is the marital status of the women at the time of the entrepreneurial event. Here the sample group showed considerable differences from the male control group (see Table 12.2). Less than half of the women were currently married or had the equivalent of a stable marriage relationship. In contrast, more than 90 per cent of the men were part of a stable marriage relationship in which the woman played a traditional family role and/or was a supportive element in the business venture. There was no indication that the husbands of the female entrepreneurs were similarly prepared to adopt a supportive homemaker role, and in those few cases where the husband (or former husband) was involved with the business it was usually in an *ad hoc,* peripheral, 'expert' role rather than a supportive, subservient one.

Table 12.2
Marital status of entrepreneurs at point of business entry

	Men (%)	Women (%)
Married (or equivalent)	48	91
Widowed	4	0
Divorced/separated	29	0
Single	19	9
	100	100

There were strong indications, not only among our sample group but also from the experience of women undertaking entrepreneurship training courses,[11] that the business initiation process places far greater strains on the personal relationship if the woman takes the entrepreneurial role. The man often feels threatened by the greater potential for economic success shown by his wife and can be deliberately obstructive. However, the reverse causality has also been observed: namely, entry into entrepreneurship as a route to building the economic independence that will *enable* the woman to break an unsatisfactory personal relationship.[12]

The most extreme case within the sample itself was the sole co-operatively organised business. This was founded as much to meet feminist-social objectives as economic ones. All members of the co-operative were divorced and most were heads of single-parent families in an isolated rural area. The business was both a symbol of their independence and one of the few routes open to its achievement. This was a rare case where the business was organised and managed around the personal constraints of the owner-managers rather than vice versa. However, similar feminist overtones could be discerned to a greater or lesser degree in a number of the other businesses which otherwise had traditional economic values predominating.

The role of the marriage partner as a stabilising factor in male-led businesses, but not generally in female-led businesses, may go some way towards explaining the very different distribution of age-at-foundation data for the male and female groups.

American research has suggested that the age of (male) entrepreneurs at the point of business formation lies in the range 25 to 40.[13] Liles[14] describes this as the 'free choice period' in that experience, self-confidence and a financial base have been developed, but social and business prestige and family and business responsibilities have not developed to the point where they are significant constraints to entrepreneurial risk. In a European context, where advancement may be as much dependent on age as ability and the accumulation of capital from income is more difficult, this analysis has always appeared suspect. Thus the average age of our male control group (median 39 years; mean 39.2) was no surprise. However, the distribution of the women entrepreneurs' ages was quite different. First, it was bimodal. Second, the average age of the prime mode (median 32 years; mean 32.7) was significantly lower than the more evenly distributed male sample (see Figure 12.1). Possible reasons for this are raised in the discussion.

Table 12.3
Business operation areas: female versus male entrepreneurs

Business area	Women's businesses (%) N = 49	Men's businesses (%) N = 43
Distribution	12	2
Catering	6	0
Other consumer services	14	2
Industrial/Commercial Services	29	21
(All Services)	(61)	(25)
Manufacturing/Remanufacturing	31	67
Construction	0	2
Transportation	2	2
Primary Extraction	0	2
Agribusiness	6	2
	100	100

Educational background

19 per cent of the women were educated only to 'O' level or below (16 years), 10 per cent to 'A' level (18 years) and 26 per cent to first degree

Figure 12.1

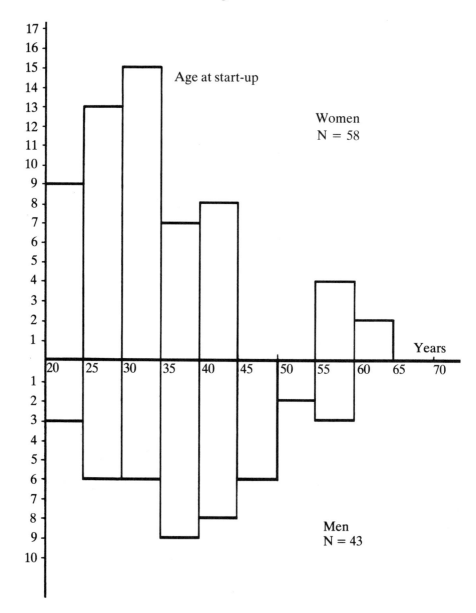

level or equivalent. In addition, 19 per cent had qualifications in commercial subjects at a sub-degree level (secretarial courses or the equivalent) and 26 per cent had professional qualifications.

Almost nothing that had been studied in the education system *per se* was perceived as relevant to the choice of business eventually founded and operated (as listed in Table 12.3). In only two cases was the 'highest level' (that is, degree course) educational content relevant to the business eventually pursued. It emerged clearly in discussion that this was a result of pressure to pursue non-practical, liberal arts subjects while at school (and hence at university) because 'nice' girls did not indulge in practicalities.

In complete contrast, 80 per cent of the *professional* qualifications obtained had been of some direct relevance to the business career pursued, as had some 55 per cent of the commercial qualifications. However, despite the high frequencies the perceived *impact* — except in a handful of cases — was very low.

Table 12.4
Educational level of female and male entrepreneurs

Level	Women (%)	Men (%)
'O' level or equivalent	19	23
'A' level or equivalent	10	2
Degree or equivalent	26	22
'Secretarial' type qualifications (sub-degree commercial)	19	2
Recognised professional qualifications	26	52

It is interesting to compare this with the numbers of men for whom educational or professional experience was directly relevant. The overall educational level of the male control group was very similar to that of the women (see Table 12.4). However, as one might expect, almost no men had taken so-called 'commercial' subjects on leaving school. Instead, twice as many (52 per cent as opposed to 26 per cent) had taken recognised professional qualifications. Moreover, in 88 per cent of cases the educational or professional qualification was also of relevance to either the specific business venture undertaken or to business in general.

Thus the process of education and professionalisation can for many members of the male sample be seen as a steady progression culminating eventually in the formation of a specific business venture well suited to that individual's interests and skills (albeit the entrepreneurial event may well have been *triggered* by some other displacement). In contrast, the female entrepreneurs were basing their businesses on a more restricted experience base acquired *after* the cessation of a largely irrelevant educational process (which had in many cases also disbarred them from easy entry into those higher-level professional qualifications related to business).

Work experience

It has been recognised both that prior attempts to create a business constitute good learning which increases the chances of future success[15] and that patterns of repeated entrepreneurship may themselves form a distinct career path or paths.[16] Nevertheless, it is surprising to note that only 60 per cent of our sample were in their first business. One woman was in her fourth (successful) business and several others had had the experience of running more than one successful venture (often in parallel). No case of previous outright failure was reported, although there had been a number of conscious decisions made to discontinue marginal or unprofitable businesses. Interestingly, although the creation of successively more complex ventures did not appear to be a conscious strategy of the women interviewed, the subsequent ventures were normally both larger and more sophisticated businesses than the earlier ones (usually a progression from simple retailing to more complex services or to manufacturing as well as trading).

Among the male sample there had been somewhat fewer prior attempts to initiate a business (48 per cent reported such attempts). This difference was not significant taken in isolation, but it should be remembered that the male sample was significantly older than the female one.

For those women not entering their current venture as part of an already established pattern of entrepreneurial activity, the nature of their immediate prior employment can be seen as crucial. There is considerable evidence that different kinds of employment situation 'incubate' new ventures at different rates.[17] Do women's patterns of employment then lead them to work in more or less productive incubators than men? Even when one includes women who moved directly from a previous own venture to a current one, managerial responsibility was rare. Only 24 per cent of the group could previously be termed 'managers' (in the male sample this figure was 72 per cent). Moreover, the previous work experience was related to the venture formed in only 40 per cent of the cases studied (in the male sample, 84 per cent).

When one considers both direct experience of a related business *and* managerial responsibility together, the picture is even more sharply defined. Only 5 per cent of men entered a venture of which they had no direct prior experience without any managerial experience in a different business context. Fully 50 per cent of the women did so. For the male sample, the normal route into entrepreneurship was to replicate a business of which the man had good prior knowledge, in both technical and managerial terms, as an employee of someone else; for the female sample this was almost unknown.

Discussion

It seems clear from the results presented that the background and experience of women entrepreneurs prior to the entrepreneurial event differs substantially from that of male entrepreneurs. This severely constrains the business-choice decision and may force women into stereotypically 'female' businesses where the prior existence of other successful female-led businesses reassures potential financiers, customers and suppliers.

Our male control group fits the traditional displacement model of entrepreneurial activity perfectly. The male entrepreneurs acquired technical and business-related educational and professional qualifications and moved on steadily through an employment-based career structure which gave them the experience of managing a business or business-unit which they could comprehend technically. Redundancy, policy differences or changed personal circumstances then precipitated these men into *an essentially similar occupation* on an independent basis. The basic change, and hence the motivation required, was quite small.

For the women studied the situation was quite different. Little or nothing in their educational and professional backgrounds had prepared most of the women interviewed for running an independent business. Moreover, women in general require a much greater stimulus even to push for self-advancement, let alone push *themselves* into an independent business venture.[18] Thus, whereas the occupational choice for the men was logical and, in its context, the pursuit of that activity on an independent basis not an illogical decision, for many of the women the decision to enter entrepreneurship was determined not by logic but by a strong motivation to autonomy and achievement — which had been frustrated by the individual's prior training and background. In many cases the timing of the decision was 'illogical' (that is, too early for relevant experience and capital to have been accumulated or as an antidote to impending retirement). In many cases, too, the choice of business *appears* illogical simply because no logical alternative existed which would fulfil the women's overriding motivational requirements. This may force female entrepreneurs to seek out business areas where technical and financial entry barriers are low and where the managerial requirements are not *immediately* central to success or failure. Thus the choice of business can be seen in terms of high motivation to immediate independence tempered by economic rationality, rather than a conscious desire to operate 'female-type' businesses.

The implication of this is that only through fundamental changes in the nature of the education offered to girls will female entrepreneurs be able to play a full and active role in entrepreneurial activity. However, in the shorter term some increase in female entrepreneurial activity could probably be stimulated through carefully structured post-experience training programmes.[19]

Acknowledgement

The MBS study of female entrepreneurship was made possible by the generosity of the Small Business Unit of Shell U.K. Oil. This paper was first presented to the Babson Entrepreneurship Conference, Babson College, Wellesley, Mass. in Spring 1983.

References

1. J. Schreier and J. Komives, *The Entrepreneur and New Enterprise Formation: A Resource Guide,* Centre for Venture Management, Milwaukee, Wn., 1973.

2. For example, J. Schreier, *The Female Entrepreneur: A Pilot Study,* Centre for Venture Management, Milwaukee, Wn., 1975; E.B. Schwartz, 'Entrepreneurship: The New Female Frontier', *Journal of Contemporary Business,* vol. 5 (Winter 1976), pp. 47–76; R. Hisrich and M. O'Brien, 'The Woman Entrepreneur From a Business and Sociological Perspective' in K. Vesper (ed.), *Frontiers of Entrepreneurship Research,* Babson College, Wellesley, Mass., 1981.

3. J. De Carlo and P. Lyons, 'A Comparison of Selected Personal Characteristics of Minority and Non-Minority Female Entrepreneurs', *Journal of Small Business Management* (December 1979), p. 22.

4. D. Sexton and C. Kent, 'Female Executives and Entrepreneurs: A Preliminary Comparison' in K. Vesper (ed.) *Frontiers of Entrepreneurship Research.*

5. For example, N. Smith, G. McGain and A. Warren, 'Women Entrepreneurs Really Are Different' in K. Vesper (ed.) *Frontiers of Entrepreneurship Research,* Babson College, Wellesley, Mass., 1982.

6. J.E. Bolton, *Report of the Committee of Inquiry on Small Firms,* (Bolton Report), Cmnd. 4811, HMSO, London, 1971.

7. J. Boswell, *The Rise and Decline of Small Firms,* Allen and Unwin, London, 1973.

8. J. Watkins, 'The Female Entrepreneur — American Experience and Its Implications for the U.K.' in J. Stanworth *et al.* (eds), *Perspectives on a Decade of Small Business Research,* Gower Publishing Co., Aldershot, 1982. This situation has since begun to change. For example, see R. Goffee and R. Scase, 'Business Ownership and Women's Subordination: A Preliminary Study of Female Proprietors', *Sociological Review,* vol. 31 (November 1983).

9. *Inter alia,* O. Collins and D. Moore, *The Organisation Makers,* Meredith, New York, 1970; A. Shapero, *An Action Program for Entrepreneurship,* Multi-Disciplinary Research, Austin, Tx., 1971.

10. *Royal Commission on the Distribution of Income and Wealth, Report No. 8. (Fifth Report on the Standing Reference),* Cmnd. 7679, HMSO, London, 1979, Table 2.11.

11. Such as those described by Jackson (Chapter 10) and by Morris and Watkins (Chapter 7) in T. Webb *et al.* (eds), *Small Business Research: the Development of Entrepreneurs,* Gower Publishing Company, Aldershot, 1982.

12. Genuine partnerships — real 'family' businesses in which complementary but equal role differentiation is evident — were excluded from both samples. For an interesting recent discussion of such firms see J. Hayes 'Family and Business: Inside the Small Hotel' in D. Watkins *et al.* (eds), *Stimulating Small Firms,* Gower Publishing Company, Aldershot, 1982.

13. See, for example, A. Cooper, 'Technological Entrepreneurship: What Do We Know?', *R & D Management,* vol. 3 (February 1973).

14. P. Liles, *New Business Ventures and the Entrepreneur,* R.D. Irwin, Homewood, Ill., 1974.

15. Compare, for example, L. Lamont, 'What Entrepreneurs Learn from Experience', *Journal of Small Business Management* (July 1972); A. Cooper, *The Founding of Technologically-Based Firms,* Centre for Venture Management, Milwaukee, Wn., 1971; J. Morris and D. Watkins, 'U.K. Government Support for Entrepreneurship Training and Development' in T. Webb *et al., Small Business Research.*

16. See R. Ronstadt, 'Does Entrepreneurial Career Path Really Matter?' in K. Vesper (ed.), *Frontiers of Entrepreneurship Research,* Babson College, Wellesley, Mass., 1982.

17. A. Cooper, *The Founding of Technologically-Based Firms.*

18. For example, Hofstede (1978: 'Cultural Determinants of Individualism and Masculinity in Organisations', Brussels. European Institute for Advanced Studies in Management Working paper 78–4) has argued that men and women value important elements in their work quite differently across a range of cultures. Men in employment value factors such as advancement, earnings, innovativeness and the contribution they can make to their organisations, whereas women employees place most value on a friendly atmosphere, position security, physical environment and co-operation with others. Cited by I. Cunningham, 'Management Development and Women', *Management Education and Development,* vol. 12, no. 1 (1981).

19. See J. Watkins and D. Watkins, 'Training Needs and the Female Entrepreneur', paper presented at UK Small Business Management Teachers Association (UKSBMTA) Annual Research Conference, Durham University, 1983, for a discussion of the criteria for the design of such programmes.

13 The Franchised Small Enterprise: Formal and Operational Dimensions of Independence*

JOHN STANWORTH, JAMES CURRAN AND JENSINE HOUGH

Policy-makers, bankers and academics attempting to aid the small business sector frequently encounter difficulties in clarifying the status of the franchised business. Since franchising constitutes a rapidly expanding form of business activity in our modern economy, it is worthwhile examining the key issue which, at least in some minds, separates the franchised business from the conventional independent small business — that of independence. Should the franchised small business be regarded as a genuine small business, albeit with its own distinctive characteristics, or should it be seen as little more than a branch outlet of some larger enterprise?

Independence from external control has been widely regarded as a fundamental characteristic separating entrepreneurial small business activity from what might be termed the corporate activity of the larger enterprise (Bolton 1971: p. 1). However, as the Bolton Committee pointed out, even the independence of the conventional small business is always less than total and often difficult to assess accurately in practice. A small enterprise, whatever its form, is part of a wider

* From: J. Lewis, J. Stanworth and A. Gibb (eds), *Success and Failure in Small Business*, Gower Publishing, 1984, pp. 157–77. The authors would like to acknowledge the financial support provided by the Social Science Research Council, now the Economic and Social Research Council, (Ref. HR 7310/1) for the fieldwork stages of the research on which this paper is based.

network of economic interaction summed up in the economist's notion of 'the market' and, arguably, it is from this source that the main limitations on independence are derived.

Perspectives on franchisee independence

The problems of assessing the independence of the franchised small business are even more difficult to resolve than those connected with the conventional small business. Mainly, the additional problems arise because of the close links between the franchised small business and another, usually bigger, firm (the franchisor) with whom it operates. A good deal of the literature on franchising treats it simply as a marketing strategy, largely avoiding any consideration of the independence of the franchised business, but this is to ignore one of the most important aspects of this increasingly significant form of business activity.

A franchise may be defined as comprising a contractual relationship between a franchisee (usually taking the form of a small business) and a franchisor (usually a larger business) in which the former agrees to produce or market a product or service in accordance with an overall 'blueprint' devised by the franchisor. The relationship is a continuing one with the franchisor providing general advice and support, research and development, marketing and advertising services. In return, the franchisee pays a royalty, normally based on the level of turnover and/or a mark-up on supplies purchased from the franchisor. The franchisee provides the capital for the outlet and is legally independent of the franchisor.

At one extreme, the franchised small business may be viewed as an emerging form of independent small business in advanced industrial societies whose distinguishing characteristic is its overt and close association with another, usually larger, enterprise. This association, however, might be seen as being little different, except in degree and the explicit form it takes, to that now found between many small businesses and other firms with whom they do business. In an increasingly interdependent economy, such a close association may simply be a reflection of the fact that 'no firm is an island entire of itself' in a modern economy.

At the opposite extreme, it has been argued that the franchised enterprise is, in reality, a *managed* outlet in the larger marketing pattern of another truly independent business — that of the franchisor (Rubin, 1978: p. 225). This distribution strategy has certain advantages for the larger enterprise, but the fact that the manager of the outlet has a capital stake in the business dressed up in the language of entrepreneurship is no reason to confuse a franchise with a genuinely independent small business. The language of independence and entrepreneurship, it might be argued, is being used to tempt people into buying a franchise since it exploits the cultural approval given to economic independence in our society and, thereafter, the illusion of independence is maintained because it continues to serve both party's interests. This is not to say that the arrangement cannot be highly beneficial to both but illusion should not be substituted for reality in a rigorous analysis of the status of the franchised outlet.

The extent of franchising in Britain is not precisely known but it has been widely present in some industries for several decades. In petrol retailing, for example, the operation of independently owned petrol stations in association with one or other of the major oil companies has been common for a long time. (The Institute of Petroleum (1983) has estimated that there are around 13 000 outlets operating on this basis.) But it has been over the last decade that franchising in Britain has expanded most rapidly. Many of the major operations in franchising are now household names, such as Wimpy with over 400 outlets in the United Kingdom, and Kentucky Fried Chicken with almost 350 outlets. All told, it has been estimated that there are now 80 000 businesses running on a franchised basis in Britain (Curran and Stanworth 1982).

Two main reasons can be suggested for this recent rapid emergence of the franchised small enterprise in Britain. First is the shift towards a greater emphasis on tertiary activities in the economy with a corresponding decline in primary and secondary activities. Franchising is especially suited to service and people-intensive economic activities. Commonly, tertiary activities require a large number of geographically dispersed small outlets servicing local markets and it is this characteristic which links with the second reason for the expansion in franchising. Economic concentration in Britain, as in most advanced industrial societies (although more so in this country) (Prais 1976), has produced an industrial structure which, in many ways, is ill-suited to the shift towards tertiary activities.

Second, running a large number of dispersed outlets from a central head office produces diseconomies of scale which may more than outweigh any economies of scale resulting from large size. The main diseconomies here are motivational and manifest themselves at the outlet level. Economic success depends crucially on effectively serving the customer but the personnel who deal directly with customers are often poorly rewarded and poorly motivated. The size and turnover of the outlet also rarely permits the employment of highly paid or motivated supervisory personnel. Converting the outlet into the owner-operated form is a partial solution to these problems.

The best-known franchised businesses in Britain usually started in the franchised form with the originator of the franchise package choosing this business form for a further advantage — the ability to expand rapidly to achieve nationwide coverage with the minimum of capital since the bulk of the latter is provided by franchisees.[1] But recently some major companies, not previously involved in franchising, have started to adopt the franchised form for some of their operations.

A major difference between franchisor–franchisee relations and relations between the conventional small business and large companies who are its customers or suppliers, is that the franchisor has a powerful vested interest in the survival and success of franchisees. The franchisor's own success is often wholly bound up in his franchisee's success; failure of the latter will often lead to failure of the franchisor. Even where the franchise is only part of a company's activities, any widespread failure of franchisees will be damaging to the company's reputation.

The overall argument advanced in this paper is that the dichotomy between the conventionally independent small enterprise and the franchised small enterprise is essentially a false one when viewed on many of the accepted criteria of independence. Certainly many conventional small enterprises are more independent than the typical franchised outlet but the difference is a relative one. A goodly proportion of nominally independent conventional small businesses may, in practice, enjoy no greater degree of real independence than many franchised enterprises.

In other words, rather than a dichotomy, we suggest a continuum of degrees of independence with various kinds of small enterprise being located on different points of the continuum. A priori, we need not assume that franchised small businesses are necessarily always located at the least independent end of the continuum. Support for these propositions requires an empirical examination of the independence of the small franchised enterprise. This examination further necessitates a close observation of what may be termed the formal and operational dimensions of independence.

Franchise research sample

Research data were collected from franchisors and franchisees in four leading franchise operations in Britain over the period 1980–2. These operations were a mobile car tuning franchise with 118 franchisees; a high-speed printing franchise with 96 franchisees; a central-heating installation franchise with 47 franchisees and a vehicle rust-proofing franchise with 93 franchisees.

Franchisor executives and a core sample of 80 franchisees, drawn proportionately from the four operations, were interviewed using a semi-structured interview schedule. All interviews were tape-recorded and some franchisor respondents were interviewed more than once; franchisee interviews (usually carried out at the franchisee's place of business) typically lasted 1½ hours.

The remaining potential sample of 274 franchisees were surveyed by mail using a simplified version of the schedule devised for the core sample face-to-face franchisee interviews. The response rates were 100 per cent for franchisor respondents, 91 per cent for the core sample franchisees and 49 per cent for the mail survey franchisees. Overall, 61 per cent of all franchisees in the four operations co-operated in either face-to-face interviews or replied fully to the mail survey questionnaire.

In addition, one or other of the researchers attended a number of franchisor–franchisee conferences, and conferences directed at potential franchisees. Informal interviews were also conducted with members of franchisor–franchisee committees and with representatives of the industry's trade association. Documentary data was collected on franchising both for the four operations studied and for other franchises in the United Kingdom. Many of the research strategies were based upon the experience and findings of a previous study of British franchising (Stanworth 1977).

Formal independence

Data on the formal level of independence were obtained through a close analysis of the contracts issued by franchisors together with further clarification on the duration and renewal criteria of contracts, areas of possible negotiation and the extent of intra-franchise variations. Both franchisors and franchisees were questioned on aspects of their contractual relations including their views on the strictness with which contracts were enforced and the extent to which the contract occupied a central place in their day-to-day relations.

The franchise contract is very comprehensive in the close specification of the business relationship between franchisee and franchisor. Looked at from a non-legal point of view (which is as it appears to most franchisees) it seems to be clear-cut, comprehensive and long.

The contract for one well-known franchise, for example, runs to 30 pages. In terms of franchisee independence some of the provisions seem closely to circumscribe his freedom of action as a businessman.

One contract, for example, stipulates that the franchisee

> will conduct his franchised . . . business in all respects as shall be *laid down by the Company from time to time in the Manual or otherwise.* The Franchisee will keep the copy of the Manual in his possession up to date with all variations thereto which the Company may make.[2]

This form of contract has been extensively criticised in the American literature (Hunt 1972: p. 36) since it involves, in effect, the franchisee's commitment to an open-ended agreement: 'Since the provision of the operating manual can be changed at the prerogative of the franchisor, the franchisees find themselves in the tenuous position of being bound to a contract that can be modified *unilaterally* by the franchisor' (Hunt, 1972: p. 36–7, emphasis in original). Contracts are also explicit in relation to restrictions on the franchisee's right to dispose of his franchised business. Sometimes the franchisor claims the right of first refusal to purchase and written permission must be obtained before the outlet can be sold to another person. The franchisor also often insists on being informed of all the confidential details of any transaction — value of the premises, and so on — intended to result in the sale of the outlet. In two of the franchises under study, the franchisor was entitled to demand a percentage of the sale price when the franchise changed hands although in one of these the franchisor claimed that this clause had never been exercised.

Of course, obligations are imposed on the franchisor also. But, given that the contract is drawn up by the franchisor's legal advisers, it is rather less constraining for the franchisor. Hunt (1972: p. 37) has drawn a distinction between *contracts of adhesion* and *contracts of negotiation.* A contract of adhesion is more akin to an insurance policy than a contract in the ordinary sense of the latter term. That is, rather than being the end result of a process of bargaining between the parties, it is offered by one of the parties (the franchisor) on a take-it-or-leave-it basis. The fact that franchisors claim that they are very reluctant to vary their standard contract to suit individual franchisees underlines the restrictive character of the contract.[3]

On the other hand, in the present study, franchisors admitted that they sometimes did vary certain aspects of the contract for a new franchisee particularly with regard to size of territory and, to a lesser extent, by modifying requirements on minimum capital required or other starting costs. These findings were generally confirmed by franchisee respondents. Thus, one-fith of the franchisees interviewed face-to-face[4] claimed that they renegotiated the territory they were originally offered. But none of these variations would be termed major and most franchisors claimed to enforce the contract 'strictly' or 'fairly strictly'.

Over time, contracts were judged by franchisees to have become more comprehensively prescriptive and more strictly enforced, and all franchisors reported some enforcement problems. Franchisors also claimed that they would be very reluctant to agree to a non-standard contract when contracts came up for renewal. Yet there were also indications that franchisors tried to tread lightly concerning contracts. For instance, no franchisor reported frequent mention of the contract in their relations with franchisees, and over 80 per cent of the core sample franchisees claimed that their franchisor never mentioned the contract in everyday relations.

Other franchisee responses on questions about the contract suggested some ambiguity in their views. For example, only just over half of all franchisees believed that the contract favoured the franchisor whilst almost 40 per cent stated that they thought it was about neutral between the two parties. Only six per cent, on the other hand, were convinced that the contract was weighted in favour of franchisees. Despite these findings, almost 60 per cent of franchisees stated that there was no section of the contract they felt should be altered.

The beginnings of a divergence in the views of franchisors and franchisees were indicated by the finding that, although most franchisor respondents believed that they strictly enforced the contract, franchisees — those over whom the contract was allegedly being enforced — did not accept this view. Less than a quarter of franchisees reported feeling that the contract was 'very strictly' or 'fairly strictly' enforced.

In other words, at the formal level, relations between the franchisor and franchisee might be described as implicity exploitative since the contract is drawn up on a virtually non-negotiable basis by the franchisor and imposed on the franchisee on a take-it-or-leave-it basis. But the findings also hint strongly that considering franchisor–franchisee relations solely at the formal level may be misleading. There is clearly ambiguity in the perceptions of the two parties about how the contract governs their relations and on the connections between the contract as a prescription for actual or desirable patterns of franchisor–franchisee relations, and what actually happens. For instance, findings from both franchisors and franchisees suggest that the contract, although central in a formal sense to their relations, is not permitted a similarly explicit position in their day-to-day relations. For example, franchisors not infrequently have to pursue franchisees for their monthly statements or royalty payments. But this rarely involves an explicit reference to the franchisee's contractual obligations. Instead, the appeal is usually framed in terms of the need for administrative efficiency and couched in the form of informal, personal pleas for co-operation from the franchisee.

Operational independence

The above discussion suggests that there is what might be termed an operational realm in franchisor–franchisee relations which is not necessarily encompassed or revealed by an analysis of the contractual or formal level of relations, however detailed. It may be suggested that this is no less than might be expected given that no contract can fully define everyday relations and, more important, a contract of adhesion essentially embodies one party's view of how it would *like* relations to be patterned. In practice, all kinds of other influences will push and pull relations into other patterns.

Recognition of the above begins with perceptions of operational autonomy. Franchisors and franchisees were asked in detail about who they felt were responsible for certain key aspects of the outlet's operations. As Table 13.1 indicates, franchisors and franchisees were in broad agreement on the division of responsibilities on six key aspects of outlet decision-making. Franchisors claimed responsibility for control over the product mix and pricing while franchisees claimed control over hours of opening, employment of personnel, book-keeping and quality standards.

However, these findings cannot be accepted as a firm consensus on the division of operational decision-making in the running of the outlet. As the percentages alongside franchisees' and franchisors' views indicate, there were sizeable minorities holding contrary views on some of these aspects and especially on quality control and product mix changes. Thus, almost 20 per cent of franchisees felt that they had equal say in product mix additions, deletions or alterations and, somewhat surprisingly, a further 26 per cent believed they had most influence.

Another aspect of the franchisee's operational freedom is measured by day-to-day contact with the franchisor. Almost 35 per cent of franchisees reported contact with their franchisor as occurring at least once a week. For the remaining franchisees for whom information is available, the typical frequency of contact with their franchisor was

Table 13.1
Franchisor and franchisee views on operational aspects of the franchised outlet

	Franchisors' view (N = 15)	Percentage agreeing with view	Franchisees' view (N = 215)	Percentage agreeing with view
Additions/deletions to the product/service	Mainly or totally the decision of the franchisor	93.3	Mainly or totally the decision of the franchisor	55.3
Responsibility for pricing	Mainly or totally the decision of the franchisor	80.0	Mainly or totally the decision of the franchisor	62.8
Hours of operation	Mainly or totally the decision of the franchisee	66.6*	Mainly or totally the decision of the franchisee	78.1
Employment of staff/staff wage levels	Mainly or totally the decision of the franchisee	60.0/93.3	Mainly or totally the decision of the franchisee	93.5/88.4
Quality of service to the customer	Mainly or totally the decision of the franchisee	46.7	Mainly or totally the decision of the franchisee	74.4
Book-keeping	Mainly or totally the decision of the franchisee	73.3	Mainly or totally the decision of the franchisee	85.1
Local advertising	Mainly or totally the decision of the franchisee	33.3**	Mainly or totally the decision of the franchisee	91.6

* One franchisor claimed total responsibility for hours of operation which were precisely defined in the franchisor–franchisee contract.
** Eight of the 15 franchisors claimed that responsibility for local advertising was equally distributed between franchisor and franchisee.
(Because the number of franchisor respondents is low, no statistical importance can be attached to the percentage figures given; rather, the figures are presented more for their qualitative importance.)

once a month. Among the face-to-face core sample respondents, three-quarters reported that they, rather than the franchisor, initiated these contacts in the majority of instances. Their replies indicated that they were generally using the franchisor as a resource in these contacts, that is, seeking solutions to technical and other operating problems. In other words, a high proportion of franchisor–franchisee contacts are initiated by franchisees rather than by franchisors positively supervising franchisees.[5]

Franchisees reported a relatively low level of franchisor representative visits to their outlets. Less than 10 per cent were visited more frequently than once a fortnight, and 18 per cent claimed they were *never* visited. The typical reported frequency was monthly or bi-monthly.[6] These figures hardly token close supervision by franchisors and correlate well with franchisees' declared preferences on the frequency of franchisor visits. They also correlate with the replies of franchisee respondents in the face-to-face interviews of whom almost two-thirds felt that the level of assistance from their franchisor was about right.

This did not mean that franchisees were uncritical of franchisors on the quality of assistance provided. Among those franchisees who had been operating their franchise for over a year, 17 per cent rated the assistance provided as 'poor' or 'very poor' while a further 34 per cent rated it as only 'adequate'. However, these findings have to be balanced against the almost 50 per cent who rated franchisor assistance as 'good' or 'very good'. Over time the level of approval tended to rise since these franchisees were more satisfied now than with the level provided in their first six months of operation.

Assistance is not the same as supervision and franchisees in the face-to-face interviews were asked whether they would prefer more or less supervision from their franchisor. Only 5 per cent felt they were over-supervised while over 80 per cent felt the level was about right. Indeed, 12 per cent would have liked more supervision than they were currently receiving. Keeping in mind the adage that it is impossible to please all the people all the time, it does seem from these findings and those in the preceding paragraphs, that franchisors have achieved a reasonable compromise between being perceived as providing too little assistance and over-supervising. Given that three of the franchisors have around 100 outlets this might be accepted as constituting a high level of effective franchisee management by franchisors.

Franchisors did report problems in maintaining what they regarded as a satisfactory level of control over franchisees. Franchisor respondents in two of the franchises mentioned problems in getting franchisees to make proper and full financial returns on time and these problems tended to be greater with longer-established franchisees. Marketing was also a problem because all franchisors put great emphasis on this aspect but often felt that franchisees were very deficient in marketing skills. All the franchisors had instituted methods of detecting evasion in the form of incorrect financial information or franchisees purchasing supplies from non-approved sources. Finally, since maintaining the franchise's national image is crucial to its success, quality control at the outlet is a permanent problem — a single franchisee's failure here could do enormous damage to the franchise's reputation.

Commenting on the disadvantages of franchising from their point of view, franchisors conceded that the franchise relationship inevitably meant a loss of control compared to the conventionally managed outlet. It required a more persuasive style of management since franchisors were well aware that attempts to control franchisees too closely were likely to be counter-productive. (This did not, of course, prevent them from exerting very close control over particular franchisees from time to time, even to the point of terminating the contract if necessary, but this was relatively rare).

Indications of tension in the operational realm from the franchisees' viewpoint are perhaps most clearly exemplified in the formation of franchisee associations. The latter take two forms. The first is an organisation set up by the franchisor for an exchange of views between franchisees and between franchisor and franchisees, over which the franchisor exerts sufficient control to ensure the association's activities broadly serve his interests. The second is an independent association freely founded and controlled by franchisees with the aim of increasing their bargaining power in relation to the franchisor and to act as a vehicle for exchanging ideas and information among franchisees. The first variety is often established to prevent the emergence of the second. Some franchisors freely admit that the completely independent franchise association is, from their viewpoint, too similar to a trade union, undermining franchisor authority and power.

Latent forces pushing franchisees into an independent association to protect their interests in relations with the franchisor are widely recognised on both sides of the industry. A minority of franchisor respondents saw the emergence of such associations as inevitable. Only one of the franchises actually had an independent association at the time the research was being conducted but almost 40 per cent of all franchisees in the study thought franchisees should have a national association. However, in relation to their own franchise, franchisees were very much less enthusiastic and even sceptical of what such an association might achieve.

Vickers (1981), in research forming part of the present project, studied franchisor–franchisee joint committees and independent franchisee associations in four franchise companies including two from among the four franchises whose findings are reported in this paper. The response of the one franchisor in the present sample whose franchisees had formed an independent association (to which over 90 per cent of the franchisees belonged) was entirely predictable. He considered it 'unnecessary' and claimed that it caused 'hindrance and delays' in dealing with franchisees. Franchisee members, on the other hand, plainly saw the association's main aim as serving their interests particularly with regard to the standard contract which the franchisor had unilaterally changed to be more restrictive from the franchisees' viewpoint.

Some franchisees believed the effect of the association had been to achieve a more favourable contract than would otherwise have been the case. Some also believed that the subsequent restoration of a more amicable relationship between franchisees and franchisor was helped by the activities of the association. The franchisor may well have adapted his behaviour at the operational level to take into account the threat posed by the franchisees' association but this is, of course, not easy to demonstrate. It does show, however, how occurrences at the operational level may 'feed back' to the formal level.

The independent franchise association is a latent influence in the other three franchises in the study in the sense that, although there is none currently in existence, it is always possible for the franchisor to provoke its emergence. It might also be brought into existence by other influences. For example, if the market for the franchise's product or service becomes very uncertain, franchisees might band together to seek a common solution or to put pressure on the franchisor to provide more help. Franchisors, on the whole, prefer such associations not to appear and, at the operational level, we might expect their decisions and behaviour in relation to franchisees to be tailored accordingly.

At the operational level, therefore, it can be seen that franchisee independence is clearly manifest. In several significant areas of decision-making both franchisors and franchisees accept that the latter has overall responsibility. Franchisors might claim that, by virtue of the authority derived from the contract which forms the basis of the formal level of relations, these franchisee prerogatives are strictly limited. On the other hand, franchisees are the only decision-makers who, in practice, could effectively make many of the decisions. Indeed, it might be doubted whether franchisors would ever *want* to make some of these decisions even if they claimed the ultimate right to do so. For instance, one of the attractions of franchising for franchisors is *not* having to worry about personnel problems at the outlet level.

In other areas the franchisor's exercise of control is likely to be too remote or too late. Quality control over service to the customer at second hand, for example, is unlikely to be fully effective or when exercised is often an indication that things have already gone wrong. Typically control is through the visits of the franchisors's field officers but 'dummy' consumers may also be used or an open invitation may be made to dissatisfied customers on promotional literature or invoices to contact the franchisor's head office. However, as reported earlier, franchisor field representative visits may be infrequent and responding to consumer complaints means acting after the quality lapse has occurred.

More subtly, relations between franchisors and franchisees which relate to the latter's independence are also influenced by other latent factors. Franchisors need the goodwill of franchisees and attempts to over-supervise or to impose new contractual obligations against the will of franchisees quickly exhaust this goodwill. This may even promote a franchisees' association thus increasing franchisee bargaining influence. Franchisors can cope with such an association but they would prefer not to have to. There is also the threat of seeking external help to which franchisees could resort. For instance, politicians and the mass media offer further resources for franchisees. This is no idle threat for an industry which has shown itself to be very sensitive indeed to its public image, as the British Franchise Association's activities make abundantly clear.

Conclusions

The issue of franchisee autonomy, whether the franchised small business can realistically be seen as a genuinely independent small business, has been the central issue addressed by this paper and we have sought to demonstrate that the issue is by no means easy to settle. In pursuing our analysis, we have distinguished between the formal and operational levels of independence on the grounds that the two levels should analytically and empirically be separated since franchisee autonomy at one level may vary independently of the other.

At the formal level the franchisor–franchisee contract, which constitutes the basis of this level, is clearly weighted in favour of the franchisor. This is recognised by both parties and largely accepted as a fact of life by franchisees. However, at this level one key point running contrary to the overall weighting should be remembered. This is that, legally, the franchised outlet as a business belongs to the franchisee. This is important because the law, with its rather literal approach to social and economic reality, may, from time to time, give this point overall importance, countering the normal balance of power at the formal level.

It is the above point which explains the way in which in the United States, for example, state and federal law have often come down on the side of the less powerful franchisee (Nevin *et al.* 1980). As a legally independent enterprise, the franchised outlet may be treated as the equivalent of the conventional enterprise for interpreting conventions on 'fair' business practices, which has frequently meant bolstering franchisee autonomy. In Britain franchisors appear nervous of this being repeated here.

The operational level is both more complex and more variable than the formal level. The data demonstrated that, at the everyday level, operational autonomy is much more evenly spread between franchisors and franchisees than is suggested by consideration of the formal level alone. More importantly, there were indications that the formal level does not explicitly intrude on the operational level to any very marked degree except perhaps at times of crisis. There are clear limits to the control franchisors can exercise physically or normatively at the operational level. In some instances, such as personnel issues in the individual franchised outlet, the franchisor would not wish to be greatly involved anyway but in others, such as hours of opening, the franchisor often finds it convenient not to be restrictive since over-supervision may produce negative results.

Compared to the conventionally independent small business, the franchised small enterprise is less independent at both the formal and operational levels. But this distinction is a relative one. In practice, in a successful franchise, it might be argued that differences between a franchisee and a conventionally independent small business owner, particularly where the latter is operating in a highly competitive market, are not large. The emphasis here must be on the operational level for this is the reality of small business ownership. To be totally independent in a formal sense but slowly going bankrupt as the market turns to other suppliers or products may be small comfort. To be a franchisee running a business based on somebody else's idea and methods, which produces a high return on capital invested, involves infrequent visits and supervision from the franchisor or his representative but offers back-up in a crisis, may be a more than fair exchange for nominal total independence.

The franchise relationship remains potentially exploitative but recognition of this potential should not draw attention away from either the fact that, in practice, exploitation by franchisors is not typical (or likely to be successful except in the short term) or the realities of small business ownership generally. In a semi-monopolistic economy, dominated by very large enterprises often operating on a multinational basis, the conventional small enterprise exists in a hostile economic environment and, while it shows remarkable powers of survival, its situation should not be seen in terms of any ideological notions of 'total independence'. The study of the franchised small business and the extent of its autonomy remind us of this truth about the small business more generally in our society. The policy-maker, banker or academic seeking to aid the small enterprise also needs to keep these points firmly in mind.

Notes

1. Rubin (1978: p. 225) has argued that the widely accepted view that franchisee-provided capital enables franchisors to expand rapidly is fallacious in the light of modern capital theory. But his grounds for rejecting the view involve making several important and untested assumptions about franchisee and franchisor reasoning and behaviour which might appear to some to be highly questionable.

2. This is taken from the contract of one of the franchise operations investigated in the present study. The emphasis has been added.

3. Commenting on an earlier version of this paper, the managing director of one of the franchises under study wrote: 'We are the vendor and the shape of the product is primarily our responsibility . . . at no time do we enter into a social contract with our franchisee . . . the contract between franchisor and franchisee is essentially a business arrangement for the benefit of both with the advantages slanted toward the initiator'; and 'the contract in a franchise should never be the result of bargaining between franchisor and franchisee, as the franchisee is supposed to be buying a uniform arrangement which puts him on the same base as any other franchisee within a tried and tested business format'. (Letter to one of the researchers, 5 October 1982).

4. The question was not put to the mail survey respondents. Unless otherwise stated, if the findings refer only to the core sample franchisees it may be taken that the question was not put to all franchisees in the study. The reason for this practice was that, as is well known, mail questionnaires suffer high levels of non-response if they are over long, and are unsuitable for questions where there is likely to be any marked ambiguity in the question itself for respondents or in

interpreting their replies, since clarification cannot be sought as in face-to-face interviews.

5. Of course, franchisors inevitably use these contacts to monitor franchisee performance but nevertheless they remain franchisee-initiated.

6. Some franchisees were relatively newly established when interviewed and the level of contact with the franchisor would be higher in these instances. They have not, however, been excluded from these figures though their exclusion would tend to strengthen the point made in this paragraph. When franchisees were asked when the last visit from a franchisor representative had occurred, the replies indicated a slightly higher frequency of visits but almost two-thirds still stated that it was over a month since the last visit.

References

Bolton, J.E. (1971). *Report of the Committee of Inquiry on Small Firms*, Cmnd. 4811, London: HMSO.

Curran, J. and Stanworth, J. (1982). 'Bolton Ten Years On: A Research Inventory and Critical Review' in J. Stanworth *et al.* (eds), *Perspectives on a Decade of Small Business Research, Bolton Ten Years On*, Aldershot, Gower Press, pp. 3–27.

Hunt, S.D. (1972). 'The Socioeconomic Consequences of the Franchise System of Distribution', *Journal of Marketing*, vol. 36, pp. 32–8.

Institute of Petroleum. (1983). *Petroleum Retail Outlet Survey*, London.

Nevin, J.R., Hunt, B.D. and Ruekert, R.W. (1980). 'The Impact of Fair Practice Laws on a Franchise Channel of Distribution', *MSU Business Topics*, vol. 28, pp. 27–37.

Prais, S.J. (1976). *The Evolution of Giant Firms in Britain*, Cambridge University Press.

Rubin, P. (1978). 'The Theory of the Firm and the Structure of the Franchise Contract', *Journal of Law and Economics*, vol. 21, pp. 223–233.

Stanworth, J. (1977). *A Study of Franchising in Britain*, Report to the SSRC, London.

Vickers, A. (1981). *Franchisor–Franchisee Relations*, Polytechnic of Central London Small Business Unit, London.